Additional Praise for *The Pride of the Yankees*

"When it comes to the confluence of sports, business, and culture, nobody hits and fields like Richard Sandomir, an all-star, maybe even an Iron Horse."

—**Robert Lipsyte, author of *An Accidental Sportswriter***

"Think you know all there is to know about Lou Gehrig and the movie that so movingly tells his tragic story? Think again. In this fascinating new book, the great Richard Sandomir takes us inside the making of *The Pride of the Yankees* while also delivering rich new detail about Gehrig's short life. It's a cliché to say 'this book is a home run,' but it's true."

—**Christine Brennan, *USA Today* sports columnist**

THE PRIDE OF THE YANKEES

Lou Gehrig, Gary Cooper, and the MAKING of A CLASSIC

RICHARD SANDOMIR

hachette
BOOKS

NEW YORK   BOSTON

First Edition: June 2017

Hachette Books
Hachette Book Group
1290 Avenue of the Americas
New York, NY 10104
hachettebookgroup.com
twitter.com/hachettebooks

Hachette Books is a division of Hachette Book Group, Inc.
The Hachette Books name and logo are trademarks of Hachette Book
Group, Inc.

The publisher is not responsible for websites (or their content) that are not
owned by the publisher.

The Hachette Speakers Bureau provides a wide range of authors for
speaking events. To find out more, go to www.hachettespeakersbureau.com
or call (866) 376-6591.

Excerpted quotes from *The Pride of the Yankees* copyright © 1942 by Jo
Swerling, Herman J. Mankiewicz, and Paul Gallico.

Library of Congress Cataloging-in-Publication Data has been applied for.

ISBNs: 978-0-316-35505-6 (hardcover), 978-0-316-35516-2 (ebook)

Printed in the United States of America

LSC-C

10 9 8 7 6 5 4 3 2 1

To Griffin, my beautiful love

Contents

THE PRIDE OF THE YANKEES

Foreword

"Of all the great and glamorous athletes, the gigantic and sometimes screwy sports figures of the Dizzy Decade who clattered across the sports stage with fuss and fume and fury, and the thunder and lightning of their compelling personalities, Lou Gehrig, the ball player, was probably the simplest, the most retiring, the most sensitive and honest."

—Paul Gallico, sports columnist
and first screenwriter of
The Pride of the Yankees

The Pride of the Yankees—the story of a simple, sensitive, brilliant, and honest athlete—was the first great sports film. A big-budget movie in 1942, the first full year of America's involvement in World War II, it brought us Gary Cooper as Gehrig: a near-perfect marriage of a modest, heroic subject and an actor who specialized in modest, heroic characters. *Pride* helped define Cooper's career, but more crucially, his performance is critical to defining Gehrig's legacy as a man of integrity who somehow tells a stadium full of fans that he is "the luckiest man on the face of the earth" despite having a disease, amyotrophic lateral sclerosis (ALS), that had just ended his career and would end his life two years later.

Seventy-five years have not diminished *Pride's* powerful evocation of a man struck down in his midthirties, who was loved deeply by an intimidating immigrant mother; his adoring wife, Eleanor; his teammate Bill Dickey; and his manager, Joe McCarthy. He was an ordinary man who did extraordinary things in ballparks until ALS stopped him.

Pride would only hint at the seriousness of the disease, but its telling intimations of his mortality (a sudden stabbing pain in his shoulder, the loss of dexterity that rendered him unable to tie his bow tie) suggest the terrible reality.

As his life ebbed, Lou Gehrig needed friends to distract him, to cheer him up, to let him talk about anything but amyotrophic lateral sclerosis. One of the regulars was John Kieran, a friend and sports columnist for the *New York Times*. Kieran maintained a positive tone during visits to Lou at his house in Riverdale, in the Bronx, in mid-March 1939, ignoring the clear signs of Lou's decline—his weight loss, his faltering voice, his inability to move from his chair on his own—in his columns.

So Kieran relied on what Lou wanted to discuss. Baseball, football, and swimming. Facing Grover Cleveland Alexander in the 1928 World Series. The Yankees' plan to move second baseman Joe Gordon to first base.

"He can't miss!" Gehrig said. "Just give him a little time to practice and he'll be a whiz at first base. Maybe he'll make the Yankees forget Lou Gehrig."

Hardly. No one has forgotten him in the seventy-six years since his death.

He batted .340 over 17 seasons, with 493 home runs.

He drove in more than 170 runs three times, including 185 in 1931.

He *averaged* 40 doubles and 12 triples a season.

No one was calculating OPS in his day, but his career on-base and slugging percentage of 1.080 ranks third in history, behind Babe Ruth and Ted Williams.

And, despite myriad broken bones and maladies, he played in 2,130 consecutive games—from the first in 1925 to his last in 1939.

He was an exemplary player, second to Ruth.

And an exemplary man, far better than Ruth.

His humanity emanates in so much that was written and said about him as he radiated joy—and somehow gratitude—while ALS was killing him.

In one of his columns, Kieran described a visit by Gehrig's doctor, Caldwell B. Esselstyn (whose son developed a heart-healthy vegan diet that President Bill Clinton followed to great success). The doctor had been a guard on the Yale football team twenty years earlier. If patient and doctor discussed anything medical, Kieran did not record it. But that is no surprise. There was no effective treatment for ALS, then or now. Lou's medical team was probably telling his wife, Eleanor, just to keep Lou comfortable. And this visit was evidence of that: The friendly family doctor, a big man who loved sports almost as much as Gehrig, was there to keep up Lou's spirits.

One of the subjects that day was swimming.

"I was telling Lou about the new breast stroke—sure, it's the 'butterfly stroke'—because it was all new to me," Esselstyn said. Lou wanted to learn more about it from Yale swim coach Bob Kiphuth.

"Doc has told me all about him," Lou said, sounding enthused.

"His teams won more than a hundred and fifty straight meets and his swimmers set hundreds of records."

Four days later, Kieran arrived again at 5204 Delafield Avenue while Lou was listening to a spring training game. Kieran spotted a first baseman's glove on a shelf—which let Lou spin a story and allude to his diminished health.

"It's the last glove I used," Gehrig said as Kieran examined it. "Jimmie Foxx gave it to me. For years I used the smallest glove of any first baseman I know. But toward the last, when I couldn't bend over so well, I was having trouble getting in the low throws and short hops. Jimmie suggested that I try a bigger glove. He gave me one. That's it." The conversation turned to a picture of Lou rounding third base in the 1928 World Series. Lou laughed, but Kieran did not understand. Nothing appeared to be funny in the shot. So Lou explained.

The picture showed him getting revenge against Cardinals right-hander Grover Cleveland Alexander, who had beaten the Yankees twice in the World Series, and saved a third game two years earlier. With Ruth and Cedric Durst on base in the first inning of Game 2 of the 1928 Fall Classic, Gehrig whacked a three-run homer.

"There was Alex, thinking he'd have us feeding out of his hand, as usual," Gehrig said. "Well, with two on in the very first inning he threw me one—the first ball—right where I liked it and I smacked it away up in the right-field bleachers. Man, oh, man! You should have heard what he called me as I ran around the bases. That's why he's looking at me in the picture. He's pouring it on—and I'm laughing. In fact, I'm still laughing."

This was Gehrig distilled to his essence—a man talking animatedly but unable to do much more than toss nuts through the window of his house at his favorite pheasant. By now, he probably knew he was dying, or that the disease was not slowing its course. But if Kieran's accounts of Lou's strong spirits were true, then some combination of faith and optimism, friendship and Eleanor's care had to be preventing him from despair. The public could not see him this way. Fans knew he was a decent man and understood that he was sick, but few could possibly know that ALS was a death sentence and that Lou would be gone very soon.

They witnessed, heard, or read about his humble farewell speech on July 4, 1939, between games of a doubleheader. It was his baseball funeral, a gathering unlike any in baseball history, with teammates, past and present, surrounding him on the infield at Yankee Stadium and 62,000 nearly filling the Coliseum-like arena unsure what to make of this suddenly thinner, weaker Iron Horse before them.

He shook and wobbled. Some wondered if he would fall in the heat.

But when he spoke, he declared he was the "luckiest man on the face of the earth" because of the blessings of his teammates, his managers, his wife, his parents, his mother-in-law, team president Edward G. Barrow, and even the New York Giants. His disease? A "bad break."

He concluded that he had "an awful lot to live for."

But not for long.

His life pivoted at this point. No longer a ballplayer, he was a victim, soon to be baseball's version of a martyr. And if he wasn't thankful for the dubious gift of an awful disease, he was grateful for what he had left.

Tragedy had made Lou Gehrig film-worthy.

And *The Pride of the Yankees* was born.

The movie became essential to Gehrig's afterlife.

It pushed Ruth—the megastar—to the role of a supporting player.

It starred Cooper, who specialized in playing men of quiet dignity.

And it gave perpetual life to Gehrig's "luckiest man" speech, the most important ever delivered by an athlete and one of the most memorable by an American in any profession. It deified Gehrig, not just on that hot summer's day, but for what has passed for all time. Cooper not only re-created the speech but recast it in the image of all the characters of quiet dignity that had built his reputation.

All these decades later, Cooper has *been* the dying Gehrig, standing in baggy, billowing pinstripes, speaking into a bank of microphones and declaring that he was not just a lucky man but "the luckiest man on the face of the earth."

For the past seventy-five years, Gehrig's legacy became inseparable from *The Pride of the Yankees*, which was not a baseball film but a Gary Cooper movie, much as *Sergeant York, High Noon,* and *Meet John Doe* were.

Gehrig's speech is more familiar to fans through *Pride* than through the few bits of surviving newsreel. His life, however fictionalized to suit the conventions of a Hollywood romance, is better known through *Pride,* as is his marriage to Eleanor, filtered through Cooper's and Teresa Wright's portrayals of well-matched sweethearts.

Cooper became Gehrig. Gehrig slipped into Cooper's lanky body. He animated the static, limited archive of Gehrig imagery that showed him healthy—slashing a double, flashing his dimples with that warm smile, embracing a cloche-wearing Eleanor.

Cooper disappeared into Gehrig's character as he did Sergeant Alvin C. York, Marshal Will Kane, and Long John Willoughby. But Cooper approached the Gehrig role with some trepidation. He did not know how to play baseball, his lithe build was very different from Lou's thickly muscled physique, and portraying someone so real to so many people presented a steep challenge. He met it, of course, and became Gehrig's cinematic, pinstriped doppelgänger. No actor has ever embodied a real-life athlete as Cooper did with Gehrig.

Pride's depiction of Gehrig has reinforced his place in the Yankee pantheon. Dying so young prevented him from attending events after his retirement, as nearly every great Yankee did, at Old-Timers' Days, and celebrations in their honor, since World War II. Before dying in 1948, Ruth made two storied performances at Yankee Stadium, the House that Ruth Built, one of them while croaking out a message in a voice struggling to be heard against advancing cancer, and the second, in pinstripes, his body more clearly ravaged, famously leaning on a bat.

Other Yankee stars endured as icons for decades after their playing days ended, bringing a *Field of Dreams*–like atmosphere at the stadium. With repeated appearances into the 1990s, some in uniform, many more in a sober business suit, Joe DiMaggio nurtured his title (announced at his insistence) as the "greatest living ballplayer." Yogi Berra became a cuddly catcher-philosopher before our eyes with each trot onto the field, building his immense late-in-life popularity by facing down owner George Steinbrenner for being cruelly fired as manager sixteen games into the 1985 season. A more recent crop of retirees like Derek Jeter and Mariano Rivera receive the adulation and riches that modern free agency and a powerful media confer and have decades of worship ahead with each return to the stadium.

Gehrig's death deprived fans of seeing him age into an old-timer, watching him unveil his centerfield monument or becoming an elder riding a golf cart to join other old-timers along the first base line.

But *Pride* perpetuates Gehrig's image as a reserved, selfless son, husband, and teammate; he is preserved in cinematic amber, demonstrating his integrity again and again. Cooper could not make us remember Gehrig's particular muscularity, but he still reminds us of his character's humility. No film has influenced an athlete's image more than *Pride*.

Pride also set the bar for portrayals of inspirational athletes by Hollywood studios. Characters played by Sylvester Stallone (*Rocky*), Robert Redford (Roy Hobbs in *The Natural*), Hilary Swank (Maggie Fitzgerald in *Million Dollar Baby*), and Kevin Costner (Crash Davis in *Bull Durham*) advanced Cooper's model for integrity, all in different ways, much as Gregory Peck's Atticus Finch in *To Kill a Mockingbird* is the template for high-minded, courageous morality in law.

Pride's long tail of influence led to other unintended achievements: It gave early recognition to ALS, a devastating, incurable disease that was mysterious until it came for Gehrig, and became known as "Lou Gehrig's disease" by 1940.

And Cooper's delivery of the "luckiest man" speech became the measuring stick that all retiring athletes are judged by.

None have equaled him.

Its greatest achievement was to establish a formidable, continuing physical legacy for Gehrig, almost like an annuity that renews itself with each showing. The actual speech is an elusive document. Only bits of newsreel from it exist. It was not transcribed as a presidential address would be. No copies of what he read aloud appear to exist—if they ever did. But the speech exists in *Pride*, shorter and different from the original, but re-created so well that it has become the de facto version. And the life of Lou and Eleanor, as depicted in *Pride*, is how we continue to view a couple who had only six years together before ALS came for him.

"To this day," said Yankees historian Marty Appel, "we see *Pride of the Yankees* as an accurate portrayal of Lou Gehrig."

A Brilliant Career, a Tragic Death

1

O n a late March day in 1939, Tommy Henrich played first base for the Yankees in a spring training game against their Kansas City farm club. Ordinarily, Henrich's position in a meaningless exhibition would not make news. On that day in Haines City, Florida, though, Henrich's unexpected shift from outfield to first base caused a stir: He was replacing Lou Gehrig, whose lackluster, even embarrassing, spring training was worrying teammates and the Yankee brass. He had cooled off considerably in 1938. At thirty-five, he might simply have been shedding his greatness.

The thought of Gehrig nearing the end—of his career, not his life—was difficult to accept. He had been there every day since 1925. He was adored. He was heroic. Anything worse than an athlete nearing his natural end was unfathomable.

It was impossible not to notice the sharp diminution in Lou's skills. Team president Edward Barrow was concerned, saying he wished "the old guy" had played against Kansas City. Manager Joe

McCarthy said he was resting Gehrig. Emotional when Lou was the subject, McCarthy was a fierce protector and unlikely to tell reporters the full truth. Lou, however, looked like a different man from the one who showed up at spring training the year before or the one who had played in 1938, when he was good (.295 batting average, 29 homers, 114 runs batted in, especially after a dreadful April) but not as routinely extraordinary as in the past.

James Kahn of the New York Sun detected that something was wrong with Lou during a long slump during the '38 season: "I have seen him hit a ball perfectly, swing on it as hard as he can, meet it squarely—and drive a soft looping fly over the infield. In other words, for some reason that I do not know, his old power isn't there. He isn't popping the ball into the air or hitting it into the dirt or striking out. He is meeting the ball, time after time, and it isn't going anywhere."

Once the spring training of '39 was in full swing, nearly every reporter admitted to seeing what Kahn had seen—and had the guts to say it in print.

"His throwing has been open to question," the New York Times's James Dawson reported, "he has not fielded balls like the old Gehrig, he has not been even a reminder of the Gehrig he was. He has committed five errors in ten games. In thirty-eight trips to the plate, he has connected for five hits, all of them singles."

Something had caused this steep decline. No one knew what; Lou did not learn the diagnosis for another three months, when he went to the Mayo Clinic.

Gayle Talbot of the Associated Press wrote that Gehrig "has slowed up dreadfully and has been brooding for a month over his inability to hit." Talbot's AP colleague Dillon Graham described him with delicacy: "not so pert."

Jimmy Wood of the *Brooklyn Daily Eagle* said that Gehrig's failure to end his consecutive games streak was behind his poor play. And George Kirksey, of the United Press, quoted a pitcher who said Lou had lost his batting eye: "Gehrig bends over backward and away from the plate on pitches that are right over."

Still, Lou had enough goodwill in the press corps that some were willing to give him the benefit of the doubt. Kieran, for one, refused to make a panicky judgment and cited three minor signs of a change in him: He was thinner (but a "very husky citizen just the same"), his hair was graying, and his step had slowed. He let Lou explain himself (saying he had skipped the Haines City exhibition game the year before and had missed others in previous springs—no big deal). Gehrig joked that the press was casting him in a movie called *Buried Alive*.

"Yes, sir," he said, "the pallbearers have me dead and buried. Do I look it?"

On the contrary, Kieran wrote.

Kieran was an intellectual in the midst of a long run as a panelist on the NBC Radio quiz show *Information, Please!* And in this column, he cited Oliver Wendell Holmes's poem "The Wonderful One-Hoss Shay" to deflect other reporters' Gehrig prophecies about a "sudden plunge from his old heights." Lou, he wrote, was not like the poem's titular horse-drawn carriage, which falls apart "all at once and nothing first, just as bubbles do when they burst." He was correct; Lou was falling apart gradually and inexorably, as ALS takes its victims.

The column was a brief in defense of Lou—an influential friend's plea to stop the drumbeat of grim predictions, most of them right, of Gehrig's demise.

"Lou's request," he wrote, "is for the volunteer pallbearers to stand away from the Iron Horse's head. He thinks he can pull his own weight and maybe a little bit more."

It would have been convenient to blame his decline on aging limbs and less supple muscles and the toll of playing in 2,122 games, to that point with injuries and broken bones. His wife, Eleanor, had witnessed a litany of woes that suggested something much more dire: Lou could get inexplicably drowsy; he stumbled over curbs like a "punch-drunk fighter"; he flopped around while ice skating at PlayLand Ice Casino. She remembered, too, a vomiting fit between games of a doubleheader accompanied by a 104-degree fever that a doctor diagnosed as a gall bladder condition.

"Lou had a greenish color," she reported. Another doctor told him to avoid butter, fried foods, and bread. Another diagnosis suggested he was low on calcium.

His local doctors—none of them yet neurologists, who likely would have understood the signs of ALS—were failing him as surely as his body was.

Lou was understandably confused: How could someone with so much power and coordination—who could hit whistling line drives like no one else, who fielded his position brilliantly, and who, since Ruth's departure from the Yankees in early 1935, was the team's undisputed leader—lose his skills so rapidly?

His teammates saw it. Joe DiMaggio watched him whiff at nineteen consecutive batting practice pitches that he would normally destroy. "He didn't have a shred of his former power or his timing," he wrote in his autobiography. Johnny Sturm, a minor leaguer at St. Petersburg that spring, recalled that Gehrig told him, "I can't do it no more." In German, Gehrig told Sturm that he felt *schlect*, or terrible.

There was little question of Lou making the 1939 roster. Barrow and McCarthy could only hope that Gehrig would recover his form and give the Yankees a season like 1938.

"McCarthy will keep him in there," Talbot wrote, "as long as the club is in the race, though he doesn't hit over .250 and fields only the balls that are hit right down his gullet... They have in Joe Gordon a great second baseman, a kid who can go so far to his left and come up with the ball that few spectators will ever realize he's helping Gehrig with his chores."

But that was wishful thinking. His stumbles were only too noticeable.

The Yankees headed north from Florida—at a stop in Norfolk, Lou's two homers brought fleeting encouragement that he was renascent—and played the Dodgers in an exhibition game at Ebbets Field. Frank Graham of the New York *Sun* recalled a few years later in his biography of Gehrig that McCarthy sidestepped reporters' questions about Lou's condition. He would not concede anything definitive but guided reporters to the all-too-obvious before them.

"Watch Lou," he told the press as fielding practice began.

"Lou looked very bad," Graham wrote, continuing:

"He would go down for a ground ball hit straight at him, and the ball would go through him. Or he would come up with the ball and throw it to second or third base and then start for first base to take a return throw but he would be woefully slow. Back of first base some fans jeered at him. 'Why don't you give yourself up?' one of them yelled. 'What do you want McCarthy to do, burn that uniform off you?'"

Lou played as awfully as he felt, as the season began. *Schlect,* indeed.

He played eight games starting April 2. His streak was up to 2,130 games.

In 28 at-bats, he had no home runs. Just 4 singles, and 1 run batted in, collected in a game where he had 2 hits but exhibited further proof that his athletic death was moving rapidly closer.

On April 25 against the Philadelphia A's at Yankee Stadium, he singled DiMaggio to second. In the fifth, his weak dribbler to A's first baseman Nick Etten scored Henrich. And in the eighth, a weak fly ball—a Texas Leaguer—gave him his second hit of the day. Then, as he tried to turn it into a double—an instinct, perhaps, or a vain attempt to prove that his skills weren't gone—he was tagged out standing up at second base. *Times* writer Arthur J. Daley dropped a disquieting note late in his story that Yankee reserve second baseman Bill Knickerbocker "saved Gehrig from an error in the fourth when he fielded a ball that had caromed off Lou's glove, Ruffing making the putout at first."

Lou knew it was over. On an off day before the Yankees traveled to Detroit, he came home to Larchmont. Eleanor wrote that she saw a man "troubled, even shocked" by the stinging remark of a teammate—so simple and hurtful.

"He's through," he heard the teammate say.

Lou was hurt by whispers that had grown louder about his failures at bat and in the field. He knew he wasn't giving the team what he used to. Eleanor reminded her devastated husband that "he'd always said he would step down" if he felt he could no longer help the team. Her devotion was to her husband, not his team, although he had, since they wed in 1933, balanced his loyalties to both. Eleanor saw more than a Yankee: She saw the man she loved.

"I told him the heartbreaking words," she said. "Maybe that time's come.'"

That moment came the next morning in the lobby of the Book-Cadillac Hotel in Detroit. Gehrig saw McCarthy at the cigar counter and they rode the elevator to the manager's room. He told McCarthy he was benching himself.

"I'll let him take a rest," McCarthy told reporters before the game, "and then when he is feeling better, I'll put him back in to see how he goes. Meantime, I will give Babe Dahlgren every opportunity to win a regular job."

That afternoon, when Lou brought the lineup card to the umpires at home plate, Tigers announcer Ty Tyson told the crowd that the consecutive games streak was now over. "Give a good ballplayer a good—" Tyson said, but fans cut him off with rousing cheers. Lou tipped his cap and walked to the bench, his head bowed.

The *Detroit Free Press*'s coverage of Gehrig's decision included two large pictures, one of Lou sitting on the Yankee bench, another of Dahlgren at first. Over the images, the headline read: "DETROIT, JINX CITY, IS PLACE WHERE HIS LONG STRING IS ENDED." A caption explained that he had, over the years, been sick or injured during games at Briggs Stadium but always managed to keep his streak going.

Now it was over, and he poured out his feelings to Eleanor in a letter written on Book-Cadillac's hotel stationery, with its tiny corporate crest above its name.

Taking himself out of the lineup, he wrote, "was inevitable, although I dreaded the day, and my thoughts were with you constantly—How would this affect you and I—that was the big question and the most important thing underlying everything. I broke just before the game because of thoughts of you—not because I didn't know you are the bravest kind of partner but because my inferiority grabbed me and made me wonder and ponder if I could possibly prove myself worthy."

He still had hope, but it was tempered.

"As for me," he added, "the road may come to a dead end here, but why should it?—Seems like our backs are to the wall now, but there usually comes a way out—where, and what, I know not, but who can tell that it might not lead right out to greater things—Time will tell—"

━━━━━━

Nothing could stop ALS. Incurable then. Incurable now.

A month later, Lou was still with the team, slipping into his uniform at home and on the road, still the team captain. On June 1, a team secret became public knowledge. The Yankees were in Cleveland for a three-game series with the Indians with a six-and-a-half-game lead in the American League. Johnny Schulte, a journeyman catcher serving McCarthy as a coach, was speaking to a Knights of Columbus group and blurted out that Lou was headed for an examination at the Mayo Clinic.

"Lou is a sick man," he said. "Sometime in the next few days he's going to Rochester to find out what it is that's been sapping his strength. We hope it's nothing serious, though it doesn't look good now," he said.

Lou denied it as a rumor. A few days later, though, he confessed it was true, and he said that he lied because he hadn't told Eleanor about his plans. Given their relationship, and Eleanor's strong personality, not telling her of his pending Mayo visit sounded unlikely and even rash. What he said also contradicts Eleanor's written account in her memoir, *My Luke and I*, that it was her idea for him to go to Mayo, and that she called the clinic from the 21 Club to schedule the appointment. She had waited until after the Yankees finished their game in Chicago the following week to call Lou, who quickly agreed to fly to Rochester, Minnesota, the next day. Her version might be entirely true, but her tendency to put herself at the center of a critical event like this makes Lou look almost like a passive player.

Lou's remarks suggested how worried he was by the early signs of the disease that he preferred not to divulge—typically, they are muscle cramps, twitching, weak limbs, and clumsy hands—and how much denial he was in.

"I'm not sick," he told reporters. Almost certainly lying, he added:

I feel fine. Never better in my life. But there must be something wrong. A ballplayer of my age and physique doesn't lose his ability as suddenly as I did. There must be a reason for it . . . the way the news broke and the way it has been built up, everybody thinks I'm falling apart, and I'm not. I haven't an ache or a pain. I simply want to find out why I lost my ability to play ball so suddenly.

Finally, he went to the Mayo Clinic, where he was examined and tested over a week. The staff didn't need much time to determine that he had ALS. Although Lou told the first physician to examine him, Dr. Harold Habein, that his only problem was that his left hand felt a "bit clumsy," as soon as Gehrig removed his clothes, Habein knew what was wrong.

"There was some wasting of the muscles of his left hand as well as the right," Habein wrote in his unpublished memoir. "But the most serious observation was the telltale twitchings or fibrillary tremors of numerous muscle groups. I was shocked because I knew what these signs meant—amyotrophic lateral sclerosis. My mother had died of the disease a few years before."

The clinic did not want to rush the diagnosis or keep Eleanor in the dark.

"We think it's serious," Dr. Charles Mayo warned her by telephone.

She and Lou had discussed what would happen at the end of his career—that he had to make the decision, probably by age thirty-five or thirty-six, rather than be released for poor play. He had already taken action to remove himself from the lineup with a vague hope that he might, somehow, return, if he regained full health. Now, six weeks after his last game, ALS was taking the bat out of his hand.

"I waited and worried and prayed back home," Eleanor wrote.

Dr. Henry W. Woltman, the clinic's head of neurology, continued the examination with a series of questions. He also tested the reflexes in Lou's knees, ankles, and elbows with a Trömner hammer, a simple tool that had telling results.

Dr. Habein's early, informed guess was almost certainly accurate.

The doctors told Lou the ALS diagnosis first, then followed with a call to Eleanor, to whom they further elaborated that Lou had perhaps two and a half years to live. Eleanor said that she extracted a promise that the clinic would give Lou a sunnier version of their report, one that would give him a little hope and not put a time limit on his life. Lou seized on the possibility that he might not be an invalid, which acted as a coping mechanism as he cycled through treatments that ultimately did not help. But if his doctors at the Mayo Clinic, with its great reputation, told him something less than the truth, they would likely have been compromising their professionalism. Eleanor's insistence that she got the doctors to, in effect, lie to Lou suggests her need to be the heroine of the story.

"There is a fifty-fifty chance of keeping me as I am," he wrote to Eleanor from Rochester, perhaps overstating his chances for his wife's sake. "I may need a cane in ten or fifteen years...They seem to think I'll get along all right if I can reconcile myself to this condition which I have done but only after they assured me there is no danger of transmission or that I will not become mentally unbalanced and thereby become a burden on your hands for life."

He added: "I adore you, sweetheart."

Lou was back at Yankee Stadium two days later for the announcement, made by Barrow, that he had ALS. His teammates cheered his arrival in the clubhouse "and then the rafters rocked with the acclaim he received from his fellows," the *Times* wrote. As he put on his pinstripes, he talked to reporters eager to understand his reaction to the news.

"You have to take the bitter with the sweet," he said. "If it's my finish as a player, I'll have to take it. But I'm going to give it a fight."

In the dugout, he sat on the steps and told his teammates about the diagnosis and testing at Mayo. The photograph of the group shows catcher Bill Dickey, Lou's closest friend, looking devastated.

One reporter labeled the ALS diagnosis "a death warrant in his pocket."

Lou remained with the team for the rest of the season and joined his teammates for the World Series in Cincinnati. His condition was worsening. He was losing weight and losing his balance as he was walking.

Bill Corum of the New York *Journal-American* spotted Gehrig at the Netherland Plaza Hotel before Game 3. He decided to follow him and wrote:

He didn't know I was behind him and I saw him edging over to put his hand against the wall as he came to the first step. So there were tears in my eyes as I turned into the coffee shop and ordered a drink I did not want.

Sue Goodwin, of the *Cincinnati Enquirer*, a rare female sportswriter in the era, interviewed Gehrig before one of the games at Crosley Field. Then, almost serendipitously, she found herself speaking to one of Lou's doctors.

"What do you say, Doctor?" she asked the physician.

"Nothing," he told her. "It's just a matter of time."

Standing beside them, McCarthy's wife, Elizabeth, sobbed.

Lou's need to earn a living (Barrow offered him nothing in the front office after his 1939 contract, which paid him $35,000, expired) led to an unexpected lifeline from an admiring Mayor Fiorello H. LaGuardia. He asked that Lou join the New York City parole board as a commissioner. The salary would be $5,700, but he would have to move within the city's geographical limits. He and Eleanor quickly left Larchmont for Riverdale, one of the northernmost burgs in the five boroughs of New York City, to comply with the residency rule. He began work soon after the Yankees swept the Reds in the Series.

For more than a year, he tried to help prisoners and parolees. He felt he had something to offer, even without experience in penology. Eleanor drove him to his office on Centre Street, or to meet prisoners at Rikers Island or the Tombs.

"He'd see them all—rapists, hookers, pimps, addicts," Eleanor wrote. "It was quite a shock to his noble and somewhat innocent soul but he took it."

One day, the future middleweight boxing champion Rocky Graziano came before him. In his autobiography, Graziano said he watched as Gehrig entered the hearing room on crutches, his face creased with pain. Gehrig asked him to stand and told him: "I've been over your record, and it's pretty bad. You've caused a lot of grief." They spoke, and Gehrig ordered him returned to Rikers Island for violating his parole. Graziano cursed Gehrig and was led away by guards but would years later praise Gehrig for a tough decision that eventually benefitted him.

Lou's body was wasting away. It became increasingly difficult for him to do his job. Eleanor had to help him sign his name and light a cigarette. She knew he could not continue much longer and briefed LaGuardia about his condition and prognosis. Lou followed with a letter, written two months before his death, seeking a six-month leave of absence. Gehrig wrote that his doctors assured him there was an "excellent chance for me to affect [sic] a turn in the right direction," and added, "It is my sincere wish that Our Lord will look with favor and start me in the right direction so that I may again come down and take up my work where I left off."

There would be no favorable turns for Lou, only the further descent into paralysis that is characteristic of ALS. In his final stages, he was confined to the first floor of his house, at the mercy of Eleanor; her mother, Nell Twitchell; and two servants. Eleanor kept up a steady flow of visitors to buoy Lou's spirits, but he invariably lifted theirs with his tenacious belief that he would recover some of his lost mobility. While Lou might have been shielded by Eleanor from his prognosis, he surely knew, at least, that there was no grand future awaiting him. He might even have sensed his doom. Even as he told a friend he had a fifty-fifty chance of regaining enough strength to return to work, he said, "I'm beginning to wonder."

In his final months, there remained unsettled business with his mother, Christina, an imperious German immigrant whose excessive doting on her only surviving child kept her from accepting Eleanor; Lou and Eleanor had arranged their quickie wedding in 1933 without Mom to avoid further friction with her.

One day, Eleanor recalled that Nell was cooking peas for Lou when Mom Gehrig declared that they were no good for her boy because they lacked the vitamins that beans did. Already unwelcome in her son's home, she told Nell that if Eleanor "hadn't come into his life, all this wouldn't have happened, it was all her fault."

Nell amplified the scene, remembering that Christina raged bitterly, shouting: "If Louie had stayed with me, this never would have happened!"

Eleanor's subsequent eruption at Mom Gehrig must have been something to behold. "Your face will be awful red someday if it is ever proved that Lou's disease is inherited," she recalled telling her. "You're going to end up a very lonely old woman. You've lost your son's love and now you've lost mine."

In her recollection, Nell added more to what Eleanor told Christina by further quoting an angry remark to her mother-in-law:

"You and your cooking. Look at Pop—he is epileptic. Look at yourself—you have high blood pressure and heart trouble. And that boy upstairs is sick. Now look at me—look at Nell—look at Bud [Eleanor's brother]. We are so healthy. Maybe some day when the cause of this disease is known, it might be you who will blush."

Hearing the story, Eleanor said, Gehrig banished his mother.

The relationship between Eleanor and her mother-in-law was fractious and the stories she told are bitter, and perhaps exaggerated; they would play a major role in how Mom Gehrig was painted in *The Pride of the Yankees*, for which Eleanor spoke extensively with screenwriter Paul Gallico. The truth is that Eleanor adored Lou and that for six years, they had a marriage of joy and discovery; he gave her stability and unswerving love, and she lent him sophistication and an adult love to complement or counter his mother's. After the ALS diagnosis, though, their marriage gradually turned into a caregiving arrangement with no possibility of the patient recovering.

"Maybe if, one day, he had pulled up a little and he got a little hope out of it, it mightn't have been so hard for him," she confessed to the *Sporting News*. "But he never gained, just died away by inches, every day a little bit more, and if you saw him at the end of a week you couldn't remember what he had looked like at the beginning of the week." She added: "Every once in a while, when a new symptom came on, when another part of him fell still on him and became dead, he'd break down somewhat and shake his head and say he didn't think he was going to come out of this thing so well or say he wasn't sure he was going to lick it."

In his final weeks, Lou's breathing slowed "like a great clock winding down," Eleanor wrote. About a week before his death when Dickey and Tommy Heinrich called before the Yankees left on a six-city, fifteen-game road trip, Lou assured them, "I'm sure going to beat this. I hope the boys have a good trip."

A few days later, a Saturday, Barrow visited. Barrow kissed Lou on the head and told him: "Keep your chin up, old boy." Still alert, Lou responded, "Never mind me, boss. You keep those Yankees up there. I'm going to lick this thing."

Early on June 2, Gehrig looked up from his bed at Eleanor, Nell, and a doctor and said, "My three pals." At that stage of his illness, his voice likely would have been barely audible, so it is possible he whispered or mouthed the words. Soon after, Lou slipped into a coma, and "everything was still," Eleanor wrote.

"The most beatified expression instantly spread over Lou's face, and I knew the precise moment he had gone. His expression of peace was beyond description. A thing of ecstatic beauty, and seeing it we were awestricken and even reassured. We didn't cry. We seemed stronger, and not one of us left that room without feeling: There *is* a better place than this. Whatever it is, no tears, no tyrant."

As she wrote her autobiography thirty-five years later, she pondered three questions: Did she have an answer to "two years of ruin" after six years of "towering joy"? Did she waver between bitterness and anger, or was she simply filled with anguish? Would she trade her life with Lou for "lesser joy and lesser tragedy"?

To the final question, she responded: "Not ever."

News of Lou's death was page one news, above the fold, in the *New York Times*, next to a report of the retirement of Supreme Court Justice Charles Evans Hughes and to the left of the day's top news about a meeting in the Alps between Hitler and Mussolini. The *Times*'s headline told the story in four decks:

GEHRIG, IRON MAN OF BASEBALL,
DIES AT THE AGE OF 37
Rare Disease Forced Famous Batter to Retire in 1939—
Played 2,130 Games in Row

SET MANY HITTING MARKS

Native of New York, He Became Star of Yankees—and Idol of Fans Throughout the Nation

In Bensonhurst, Brooklyn, ten-year-old Larry Merchant came home from school to see his mother, Anne, weeping. The Merchants were Yankee fans who had just moved from the South Bronx, near Yankee Stadium. Larry and his father, Emanuel, whose favorite player was Babe Ruth, regularly attended Yankee games.

His mother loved a certain muscular first baseman with dimples. "She told me that Lou Gehrig had died," said Merchant, who would become one of the nation's leading sports columnists two decades later. "And it struck me: I didn't know until that moment that he was so important to her."

In faraway Nebraska, the *Lincoln Star*'s headline used a cliché to convey the gravity of Lou's death: "DEATH CALLS STRIKE 3 . . . ON LOU GEHRIG."

In western Pennsylvania, which is Cleveland Indians country, the *News-Herald* in Franklin offered a lesson in local priorities. Under a banner headline across seven columns about Indians pitcher Bob Feller's victory over the Yankees that moved the Tribe into first place was the less prominent and somewhat curious one that heralded Lou's death and could have been written by his mother:

Lou Gehrig, Good Boy of Baseball, Is Dead.

The afternoon after his death, his body was put on view in Manhattan at the Church of the Divine Paternity on 76th Street and Central Park West. Lou was dressed in a dark, pinstriped suit.

Among those who filed past him were forlorn members of the baseball team at Commerce High School, Lou's alma mater, all carrying their gloves. Firefighter Patrick McDonald delayed the start of his vacation to take a final look at his favorite ballplayer. When he left, he said Lou's face showed no sign of his fatal illness. Instead, it bore the hint of a smile.

At some point before or after the viewing, Lou's body rested on the funeral director's couch at the church—a solitary image. A widely circulated photograph showed him, behind two ornate, open gates and beneath stained glass windows, alone. "Baseball Idol in Death," read one caption for a private, if not intrusive shot.

In his office that day, Barrow told reporters how much Lou's body had deteriorated. He had lost sixty pounds, Barrow said. His hair had gone white at the temples. He needed help to eat. "He went to sleep about noon yesterday still thinking he would get well," he said, "and he just didn't wake up."

Lou's body was moved later that afternoon to Christ Episcopal Church, near his home in Riverdale, for a second viewing that extended into the evening, and for the next day's funeral. Thousands stood on line to pay their respects to Gehrig in a church that Eleanor could see from the windows of her home on Delafield Avenue. Babe Ruth arrived with umpire Bill Klem. As Ruth looked at his teammate and sometime friend in an open casket, flowers surrounding it, he wept so hard he had to be led by an attendant into an adjoining room. This was yet another ending for the Babe: in 1934, the Yankees released him; in 1939, owner Jacob Ruppert, who had acquired him from Boston, died. Now Lou.

When the Babe left the church, "he brushed unsmiling through a hundred fans who had trooped with him to the door of the church," Gayle Talbot reported.

The doors to the church closed at ten p.m. "and the lights behind the stained glass windows went out one by one, until only one remained," William Dickinson of the United Press wrote. "A half moon was luminous in a hazy sky and the hum of cars along the parkway sounded louder now. The little groups of Lou Gehrig's fans lingered a few moments more, and dwindled away."

Rain came down steadily the next morning for the funeral. Hundreds of people stood outside as the service began at ten o'clock. About a hundred people were inside, about half the church's capacity. The Reverend Gerald V. Barry led the honorary pallbearers, among them McCarthy; Dickey; tap dancer Bill "Bojangles" Robinson; Andy Coakley, the baseball coach at Columbia during Lou's years on the team; Lou's physician, Dr. Caldwell Esselstyn; and Lou's fellow parole commissioners.

Eleanor followed, with her brother, Frank Twitchell, Jr., and their mother, Nell. They sat with Lou's parents, Christina and Henry, in front, close to the altar.

The funeral lasted seven or eight minutes.

Reverend Barry read the Episcopal service for the dead.

"Frequently," he then told the mourners, "it is the custom to deliver an address at a funeral, but it is the wish of the bereaved that this not be done. I am requested to say simply that there will be no eulogy because you all knew him."

Mom Gehrig wept. So did Bill Dickey and Giants manager Bill Terry.

When it was over, a hearse took Lou's coffin to a crematory in Queens.

Outside, hundreds of fans bid him a final good-bye.

In fifteen days, he would have turned thirty-eight.

2

Hollywood Beckons the Widow Gehrig

Within days, Hollywood's pursuit of the Gehrig story began.

Gehrig's life, and more important, his death, was the sort of heartwarming story that studios craved. World War II was expanding in Europe, and calls for the United States to enter it were growing ever stronger. Movies with inspirational and anti-Nazi themes were in demand as Americans stateside sought communion with a continent under mounting attack by the Third Reich. Nothing could suit the country's restive, fearful mood more than the story of a modest and tragic hero of the sport that was still the undisputed national pastime.

Eleanor knew little about Hollywood but her agent, Christy Walsh, did. Walsh was one of the first agents in sports, a tall, full-time hustler with slicked-back hair and three-piece suits who had been a ubiquitous figure in the sports world since the early twenties. Fixer, publicist, ad man, marketer, and agent, Walsh also organized the barnstorming tour of teams headed by Babe and Lou after the 1927 season that took them from Providence, Rhode Island, to California, with heartland stops like Sioux City, Iowa, in between. Walsh had shrewdly gauged that the star power of Ruth coupled with the growing allure of Gehrig (who won the American League Most Valuable Player Award in a season when Ruth had slugged 60 home runs) would be a hit across the country. And it was, attracting nearly 250,000 fans to see the Larrupin' Lou's play the Bustin' Babes.

Walsh also built a newspaper syndicate of about three dozen sportswriters who ghostwrote columns for baseball stars like Ruth and Gehrig and the World War I flying ace Eddie Rickenbacker. Walsh relished recalling how he snagged Ruth for the syndicate. Walsh had not met Ruth nor signed him to the deal that he had already guaranteed to a string of newspapers in early 1921. He had staked out the Babe's apartment at the Ansonia Hotel but Ruth kept eluding him. Then he posed as the delivery guy toting a case of beer from a nearby German deli to Ruth—the suds being what greased the hustle. Ruth signed, and Walsh quickly cashed in with the newspapers eager to print the Babe's first-person stories.

"I shall never forget the expression on Babe Ruth's face when I handed him a check for $1,000 at the Polo Grounds on the opening day 1921," Walsh crowed.

Walsh kept the syndicate running for fifteen years with dozens of writers and myriad stars, pairing them so the stars sounded on paper as if they could reasonably have written what was published under their names. He assumed that readers knew the players did none of the writing and insisted that he deceived no one.

"I never had Babe Ruth or any baseball figure pose in the act of typing for the simple reason he doesn't know how to type, but I have frequently posed stars dictating to a newspaperman-ghost, sitting at a typewriter," he wrote. "Such a picture is honest and logical exploitation."

Walsh's ghostwriting work might have led him to suggest the addition to the film of a pair of feuding sportswriters to represent the baseball press that traveled by train and dined with players and shared in the joint spoils of ghostwriting. Sam Blake (played by Walter Brennan, Cooper's frequent film sidekick) was Gehrig's fictional pal, traveling mate, and ink-stained protector; the cynical Hank Hanneman (Dan Duryea) took Ruth's side in every spat with Blake over Gehrig.

Walsh also concocted Hollywood ambitions for Lou in 1936, which may have been the first time Eleanor watched him work up close. Walsh saw an opening for Lou to play a character deeply different from his own. So after the World Series, Lou announced, through Walsh, that he wanted to play Tarzan, now that Johnny Weissmuller's contract had ended and MGM had lost the rights to the series.

"I read where Sol Lesser was looking for someone to play Tarzan," Walsh proclaimed. "I pointed out that Lou was the Iron Man of baseball, a good-looking fellow with a splendid physique and plenty of sex appeal for the box office. Lesser said he was interested so I sent him pictures of Gehrig who is in for the deal."

Those pictures showed the often serious Gehrig as a smiling, expressive Hollywood supplicant, willing to shed his Yankee flannels for Hollywood glamor. In some shots he posed in a Fred Flintstone–like caveman outfit, pounding his chest and looking almost seductive. In others he wore a tastefully large loincloth while leaning on a large club as if it were a Ruthian Louisville Slugger. In his jungle briefs, he displayed a sculpted, muscular body, including massive thighs, that offered vivid physical proof of his immense power. "I guess the public's entitled to look at my body," said Lou, who, beefcake imagery aside, might have been less interested in a Hollywood diversion than was the enthusiastic Walsh.

"This is not a joke," Walsh said. "Lou is dead serious about it and will take the job if it is attractive enough —that is, if they "kick in enough dough."

Walsh's publicity ploy irked the unimaginative editorial writers at the *Montana Butte Standard*, which wrote of Gehrig being made to "wear leopard skins, give a weakling and prolonged jungle version of the late Hughie Jennings famous baseball call of 'ee-e-yah' and have him swing from tree to tree."

Lou never slipped into the leopard skins of Edgar Rice Burroughs's famous jungle hero because his legs were too ample and muscular to be the fictional apeman's. He did eventually sign on for another role as a rancher named Lou Gehrig in *Rawhide*. The United Press's Frederick Othman wrote that after "knotty knees nearly spoiled his artistic career," he "foiled those gnarled members of his anatomy today by taking a movie acting job in which he will wear pants." He wore a cowboy's pants but not the mantle of a future star. One review said there was some pleasure in watching Gehrig "poke around a ranch and get tossed from a bucking bronco but any one of us would have done it as well. There is one thing about Lou, though; he wouldn't have much trouble substituting for the frog-voiced Andy Devine if that gentleman should be stricken suddenly with a bad case of laryngitis."

In the brash, entrepreneurial Walsh, Eleanor had a savvy guide through Hollywood at her most vulnerable time. She was not unsophisticated, but she was grieving and needed his help. He offered her his full devotion, writing her: "Anyway, El, you know that I consider it a pleasure and a privilege to be of the slightest assistance to you on this or any other thing that happens to come up. That's the way Lou would want it and that's the way I want it."

He fulfilled that promise, writing her regularly in gossipy, typewritten letters with multiple postscripts, handwritten asides, and typos that he fixed in pencil. He became her faithful, breezy, witty, and nosy confidant, offering her a front-row seat to the shooting in Los Angeles.

Walsh stepped gingerly around Eleanor's grief, uncertain when she would be comfortable talking about negotiating a film deal so soon after Lou's death.

"Not knowing how you have been feeling now that the shock is over," he wrote her three weeks after Lou died. She may have been concerned about her future but had no apparent problem partnering with Walsh. She called him in Los Angeles on June 24 to tell him of her upcoming meeting with *Gone with the Wind* producer David O. Selznick. He had news, too: He had just received a letter from 20th Century Fox asking to meet with two of its writers. When Walsh subsequently told sports columnist Joe Williams about those initial Hollywood contacts, he told the story a bit differently, in a staccato, Winchellesque rhythm:

"That night the phone rang in my apartment," he said. "It was New York. Eleanor Gehrig was talking. She had been visited by two different studio agents. They wanted to do a picture on Gehrig. I commented on the coincidence, the studio approach I had had that very afternoon. My advice was to agree to do the picture. The fact that three studios were interested indicated public appeal."

In his letter to Eleanor later that night, he advised her to be cautious. "Outside of suggesting 'terms,' I don't think there is really much I could tell you on the phone at this time," he wrote. "But Eleanor, for goodness sake, don't let anybody stampede you. I don't care how 'nice' they are or who they are. Take your time. This is not only a sacred and important subject…but it is a big undertaking. Make 'em wait until you take plenty of time to think it out."

He added, "Take your time and wear a poker face."

Walsh warned her against lofty dreams of a windfall, anticipating her worries about supporting herself with Lou gone. He solicited advice from Winfield Sheehan, a retired production chief at Fox, and told Eleanor that regardless of the "ideals and beauty of Lou's life and his brilliance at playing baseball, his life would lack the 'entertainment value' of Will Rogers." The assessment probably didn't surprise Eleanor; she knew that Lou entertained by what he did on the field and was not a performer like Rogers, one of the biggest stars of the era.

Sheehan suggested that the rights to Lou's story might be worth between $25,000 and $35,000, in line with the $25,000 Walsh got for Ruth in his goofy silent-film comedy *Babe Comes Home* and for great Notre Dame football coach Knute Rockne for participating in the 1931 drama *Spirit of Notre Dame*. Rockne died in a plane crash in Kansas while on his way to watch the filming. Walsh told Eleanor he had no idea how much Rockne's widow, Bonnie, received for the rights to a more contemporary comparison to the Gehrig story: the 1940 biopic *Knute Rockne, All American*, starring Pat O'Brien.

Eleanor and Walsh were awaiting offers while reading what was being said in the trades and newspapers about their project. The prospect of a Gehrig movie was not yet big news—and really would not be until its release—but on June 30, a story in the *Hollywood Reporter* piqued their interest. It reported that Selznick had secured an option and was trying to hire Richards Vidmer, a sports columnist at the *New York Herald Tribune*, to write the screenplay and had registered a title, *The Great American Hero*. A former college baseball and football player, Vidmer knew Gehrig well and claimed decades later to have been told by Lou's doctor that he had two years to live but never reported it. "Why should I?" he said in *No Cheering in the Press Box*, an oral history of sportswriters. "The public be informed, my ass! None of the public's damned business as long as he plays ball or doesn't play."

Selznick might have been drawn to hiring Vidmer because of what he wrote when Lou said farewell to baseball on July 4, 1939; Vidmer could have been offering Selznick a proposal for *Pride* when he wrote: "Throughout Lou Gehrig's career there was always the feeling that he lacked the mythical something called color. Perhaps he did. And yet now that his playing days are over he has more color than almost any athlete in the game. Somehow I felt that at the stadium yesterday they were honoring not a great baseball player but a truly great sportsman who could take his triumph with sincere modesty and could face tragedy with a smile."

Selznick, though, was not as eager to snatch the rights as the report indicated. Walsh thought the account was more guesswork than reality. He had met with one of Selznick's executives, Daniel O'Shea, who, by June 26, had failed to make an offer.

"As far as I am concerned (unless you should request it), I will not waste any more time on Selznick," Walsh wrote to Eleanor on July 2.

He was still waiting for a "respectable" offer from MGM, but Eddie Mannix, the number three man at the studio whose duties included keeping its stars out of trouble, was not willing to spend much. Walsh told Eleanor that Mannix doubted a film about Lou would be a "big picture" and summoned three "girl stenographers" to his office to prove his point. "Two of them said he was a baseball player and had died recently but the third one said that he was some kind of athlete and had died recently," Walsh wrote, describing Mannix's version of instant market research. He added: "Of course, you and I know that this is a ridiculous way of proving the case, and you may rest assured that I did use plenty of arguments to knock such a statement for a loop."

Walsh assumed Mannix told Dore Schary, an MGM executive who had shown more interest in the film, to "talk to me and try to chisel me down."

Walsh was roused from his brief disappointment when the gossip doyenne Louella Parsons telephoned him. He felt it was too early to hype his shopping of the Gehrig story, but she had read the *Hollywood Reporter* piece and wanted to learn more from Walsh. Listening to her must have given him a thrill: Here was one very big-time yenta whispering advice and encouragement into the wide-open ear of a less important one.

"By self-admission," he wrote to Eleanor, "she is no baseball fan but she is a sincere admirer of Lou's and thinks that the picture industry and the American public need just such a story at this time. She said "They ought to pay plenty.'"

"Queen" Louella had her own studio scouting report. She said Selznick "is O.K. but in the long run thinks you would be better satisfied with MGM. She says Selznick might sign up and then let the story lay for five or six years."

She was wrong. The answer would come quickly, and from another studio entirely.

3

The Tears of a Mogul

Samuel Goldwyn needed to be persuaded to make a film about Lou Gehrig, who played a sport that he did not know as a recreational pursuit, much less a subject for a movie. He got that push from Niven Busch, Jr.—a writer whose Hollywood aspirations led him to screenwriting and a job as story editor for Goldwyn. In 1929, he was still in New York, writing short takes about speakeasies and profiles of studio chief Adolph Zukor and baseball umpire Bill Klem for *The New Yorker*.

That summer, shortly before the Great Depression shattered the nation's economy and psyche, Busch had a new profile assignment—Gehrig—that sent him north to a classically suburban address, 9 Meadow Lane, in New Rochelle.

He climbed the steps of a house that had been Lou's first big purchase as a Yankee, a son's devoted gift to his parents. Lou also lived there, perpetuating the dynamic that Lou's mother dominated her only child and that he was too socially awkward to find a girl, marry, and break away from her. The modest house, on a quarter-acre, had a screened-in porch and built-in benches flanking the front door.

It wasn't the home of a wealthy man but that of an upwardly mobile ballplayer whose Yankee salaries would ensure a fine income through hard times.

Two months older than Lou, Busch was a well-dressed, handsome man with a broad face and slicked-back hair who was building a reputation as a writer in New York. He was working for *Time* magazine and *The New Yorker*, whose boss, Harold Ross, would reign for twenty-two more years.

Busch's hankering for Hollywood would cut short his journalism career. His father, Briton, had been the treasurer at Lewis Selznick's World Film Company; Lewis's son, David, the future producer of *Gone with the Wind*, was an errand boy at World's office in Manhattan "who once in a while let me sweep out a cutting room," Busch told film historian David Thomson. "And that was a big treat because of the smell of the film, for chrissake!"

From the opening words of the Gehrig profile, Busch's attitude toward his subject was contemptuous. If Busch was seeking someone recognizably cinematic, someone fascinating, he chose the wrong Yankee. Certainly, if Busch gave any thought to a ballplayer as a fascinating subject, he would have sought out Babe Ruth. Gehrig, he wrote:

has accidentally got himself into a class with Babe Ruth and Dempsey and other beetle-browed, self-conscious sluggers who are the heroes of our nation. This is ridiculous—he is not fitted in any way to have a public. I don't think he is either stimulated or discouraged by the reactions of the crowds that watch his ponderous antics at first base for the Yankees or cheer the hits he knocks out with startling regularity and almost legendary power.

Busch continued:

He was the sort of boy who laughed whenever you spoke to him. Big for his age, he had reached the period when the change from short to long trousers was imminent but he still wore short ones; their tightness exaggerated the size of his fat round legs.

The story took its title from the unfortunate nickname for Gehrig that had been used by the frat boys his mother cooked for: "The Little Heinie."

Lou was five full seasons into his career, two seasons past his astonishing MVP performance in 1927, when he hit 47 home runs, knocked in 173 runs, and batted .373. He was in the midst of a so-so '29 season, in which he would only hit .300, but Lou's reticence and lack of color had earned Busch's disdain. Busch's story compass gravitated to Lou's mother, Christina; he portrayed her as a strong, nearly heroic woman who "exercised a good deal of care on his upbringing"; who prized her son's time at Columbia University so much more than his baseball career that she sometimes called him "Columbia Lou." She was, to Busch, a hostess nonpareil, who continually cooked for her only surviving child: "apple-cake and cookies with raisins and pieces of bright red suet in them, making roasts and frying the fish and eels he catches in the Sound." Busch's picture of Pop Gehrig is very much like the one constructed in *Pride*: a Milquetoast nonentity and indolent worker who agreed reflexively with his wife for fear of angering her.

Busch wrote Gehrig off as an urban bumpkin and mama's boy whose teammates remembered him early on as "one of the most bewildered recruits that ever joined the club.…He was slow-witted—could find no comebacks for the wisecracks directed at him—and his schoolboy's peculiarities were an inspiration to the team wits and a source of worry to Manager Miller Huggins." One wonders how Busch, a baseball fan, could fail to connect with Gehrig on the sport Lou so excelled at, regardless of the ordinariness of his personality. Busch couldn't look past Gehrig's shyness and inability to be more like Ruth. When Busch failed to persuade Lou to confirm he had gone on a date to the movies with a "red-cheeked German girl who wore a bunch of flowers in her hat," he asked if he would ever marry.

"My mother makes a home comfortable enough for me," Lou told Busch—the only quote from him in the profile. That unsophisticated response reflected the limits of his life until then; it predated meeting and marrying Eleanor Twitchell and foreshadowed Lou's increasingly odd references in *Pride* to Mom as his "best girl."

There is no evidence that Busch encountered Lou again, except by listening to or attending games, or whether his view of Lou changed in the next dozen years when Lou had some of his greatest seasons. They soon moved apart geographically; Busch left for Hollywood in 1933, where he wrote screenplays, and, by 1941, he was working as a story editor for Goldwyn, whose track record in Hollywood was not impeccable but was filled with high notes like *Dodsworth, Stella Dallas, Wuthering Heights, The Goldwyn Follies,* and *The Little Foxes*.

"Goldwyn was not very smart on stories because he couldn't really envisage them," Busch said. "But he had a gut feeling about it. So he'd try this person's reaction about it and then that person's. He'd even get his comptroller, Reeves Espy, in there and he'd ask him. Somehow he'd precipitate a good judgment. And once he saw the film he was absolutely infallible. He knew what the audience was going to buy. I got to like him, but he was a tough old Jew."

Busch tested Goldwyn's ability to sense a cinematic story when he suggested that he make a film about Lou. Goldwyn didn't see the value in a baseball story—a game he thought was played with twelve bases on a field. So Goldwyn rejected Busch's proposal without listening to the details of the story. In one interview, Busch said that Goldwyn asked him, "Who's Lou Gehrig?" In another, he told A. Scott Berg, Goldwyn's biographer, that Goldwyn brushed him off with a now-famous declaration: "It's box office poison. If people want baseball, they go to the ballpark."

Beneath Goldwyn's ignorance was an intuitive judgment that sports, baseball in particular, was not yet a genre that Hollywood had explored much or done with broad success. By 1941, the category was a minor one sprinkled with films like Harold Lloyd's silent comedy *The Freshman*; baseball trifles by Joe E. Lewis; *Knute Rockne, All American*; the brilliantly wacky football sequence in the Marx Brothers' *Horse Feathers*; the boxing weepie *The Champ* and the boxing drama *Kid Galahad*; and Leni Riefenstahl's epic Nazi documentary *Olympia*.

Had sports films produced consistently profitable business, Goldwyn would have known about it and greenlighted a Gehrig film without undue prodding.

But there was no consistent track record—and Busch had to rethink the idea.

Which he did. He invited Goldwyn to watch the newsreels of Lou delivering his "luckiest man" speech on July 4, 1939, between games of a Yankees–Washington Senators doubleheader. Already suffering from amyotrophic lateral sclerosis, Gehrig shuffled to the field and stood in the heat to express his gratitude at a life that would end in fewer than two years. By any measure, the newsreels were emotional firepower, and Busch believed they would turn Goldwyn around, even more so because Lou had died just a month before he cued up the newsreels.

It was late June or early July at the Goldwyn studio lot in West Hollywood. The lights dimmed in the private screening room where Goldwyn viewed rough cuts and finished films. Goldwyn was likely humoring the talented, persistent, baseball-loving Busch. Maybe he would chastise Busch for wasting his time.

Something else happened, though, something like his tearful reaction at watching the scene in his silent 1925 production of *Stella Dallas* when Stella's daughter, Laurel, weeps upon realizing that no other schoolchildren will be attending her birthday party. "It's a beautiful woman's story," he said of the film.

The newsreels hooked him, and he saw the subject's potential for reaching women. He might have been fidgety and bored until the end, watching a marching band, brief speeches by McCarthy, New York City Mayor Fiorello LaGuardia, or Postmaster General James Farley, and the presentation of gifts that Lou could barely lift. But the speech, fewer than three hundred words that still move people nearly eighty years later, changed Goldwyn's mind. When the lights went up, Goldwyn was wiping the tears from his eyes.

"Run them again," he told Busch.

After the second viewing, he demanded that his top advisor, James Mulvey, a whip-smart, mild-mannered executive who had worked for him since the 1920s, be summoned on the phone. He told Mulvey: "Call Mrs. Gehrig. Tell her there's a remote possibility that we might be interested in the story of her husband."

It was, indeed, more than a remote possibility. It was a cinch.

Goldwyn and Mulvey quickly wrapped up a deal with Christy Walsh, and by July 9, he was helping Eleanor plan her trip west on the Union Pacific Streamliner to Los Angeles to sign the contract. Walsh had negotiated a $30,000 fee for Eleanor—$5,000 on signing, $10,000 the day that shooting started (which was originally to be in November, not the following February), and $15,000 when the picture was released (April 1942, not in mid-July, as it turned out to be). The other principal feature of the contract, Walsh wrote, was "the matter of delegating to me the approval or disapproval of all references to Lou in the film."

Walsh reminded her of the plan to stage the signing of the contract at three thirty p.m. the following Monday afternoon in Goldwyn's office to "break" in Tuesday morning papers. He advised her to avoid being photographed on the train so as to avoid unnecessary early publicity and told her not to take the train all the way to Los Angeles but to get off at San Bernardino early Sunday morning, where he would meet her, have breakfast with her, and then put her back on the train to Los Angeles.

"I am not only delighted but really SURPRISED at the deal," Walsh wrote to Eleanor. "Maybe Sammy has a little Irish in him or something. He apparently has secured some lowdown on me and in every meeting keeps giving me the terrific buildup…which of course I discount plenty. But even admitting he is full of 'Blarney,' the fact remains that he has backed his Blarney up with real money and a fine contract. All I can say is…he will never be disappointed."

Walsh told her about the contract he reached with Goldwyn (for more money than the producer expected to pay him) to orchestrate the film's publicity, play a role in story meetings, and secure releases from Lou's teammates to appear as themselves in the film. "I not only think any ballplayer would be happy to be included but he would be ashamed to refuse," Walsh wrote.

News of the signing did not overwhelm the press.

The coverage was modest, much of it parceled out in Associated Press items that suggested Goldwyn had prevailed in a bidding war against Selznick and MGM and that Eleanor was "under contract to assist prospective writers of the script and serve as technical advisor."

Within days William Wyler's name came up in the press as a possible director. Wyler had just finished *The Little Foxes* and would move on quickly to *Mrs. Miniver*, so he was interested in the Gehrig film as a change of pace from his recent films. As for the role of Gehrig himself, Eleanor quickly told the *Hollywood Reporter* that Gary Cooper was her husband's favorite actor, but that Spencer Tracy would be "ideal for the role which will stress the story of a brave, courageous man, rather than the career of a baseball player."

To Walsh, the only press clip that mattered was a short item from Queen Louella. "The biggest movie plum, for my money, is the life of Lou Gehrig," she wrote in her column. "I should think the story of Gehrig, clean living, likable, would make as great a picture as *Knute Rockne, All American*."

Now, she advised, it was time to make a splash with the casting of Gehrig.

"This," she wrote, "will be a job in which all the fans will have as much of a hand as they did in finding Scarlett O'Hara."

Goldwyn was also listening to Parsons. Days later, in a "Dear Sam" letter to Goldwyn, Parsons elaborated on her comparison between the nationwide search that led Selznick to pick English actress Vivien Leigh to play O'Hara in *Gone with the Wind*—a spectacle that brought Selznick enormous pre-release publicity—and the search for the right actor to play Gehrig. Parsons wrote:

It seems the whole world is interested in casting the Gehrig role and I think you should encourage the public to write to you. Certainly, *Gone with the Wind*'s searching for Scarlett O'Hara proved you can arouse interest in casting and there is no public hero so dear to the heart of the American boy as was Lou Gehrig.

A nationwide casting call would have been unnecessary except for the publicity it could generate, which appealed to Goldwyn and his crafty publicity chief, William Hebert. After all, Sam had the right actor under his control: Gary Cooper, who had one picture left on his deal with the producer. He had a testy relationship with Goldwyn going back to their earliest dealings in the mid-1920s and was eager to get his freedom. It is difficult to believe that Goldwyn didn't have Cooper in mind for the role, even as he was watching the Gehrig newsreel, or that he didn't think his biggest star could play the part. It certainly wouldn't have occurred to Goldwyn to deny Cooper the role because he couldn't play baseball—Goldwyn's towering ignorance of baseball would have precluded that judgment. And there was not yet any strong demand for actors who could credibly play sports.

Goldwyn embarked on his search, suggesting days after signing Eleanor to the deal that he was starting from scratch.

"Everyone wants to know who I think should play Lou and I haven't the faintest idea," he said. The search had begun.

4

In Search of Lou Gehrig

ary Cooper's performance as Lou Gehrig is so indelible that envisioning anyone else in the role is impossible. Had Cooper not played Gehrig, *The Pride of the Yankees* might not have been made. Or if Sam Goldwyn had signed another actor, *Pride* might have been a forgettable picture. Cooper's portrayal was as critical to the timelessness of *Pride* as Clark Gable's performance was to *Gone with the Wind* and Humphrey Bogart's work was to *Casablanca*.

Still, there were other candidates to play Gehrig—or at least names raised to pique the interest of the public. Despite her earlier thoughts on Cooper and Spencer Tracy, in a luncheon with reporters to celebrate her deal with Goldwyn, Eleanor kept her preferences to herself—already playing the publicity game.

"I have four or five different stars in mind but I do not wish to name them because I have confidence that Mr. Goldwyn will see to it that the film is properly cast," she told a group that included gossip columnist Hedda Hopper at Perino's, a Los Angeles hangout for Frank Sinatra, Bette Davis, and Cole Porter. "The reason I signed a contract with Mr. Goldwyn was because I always admired his productions and the good taste and popularity of them. I believe he is the man most capable of bringing the real picture of Lou to the screen."

Goldwyn, meanwhile, had been beating the publicity drum by soliciting the views of thousands of sportswriters and ballplayers. He asked fans to write the studio (where his publicist said the request was generating 1,100 letters a week). And he lined up a group of marketing allies—publications as diverse as the *Sporting News* and *Cosmopolitan* magazine, and the prestigious Gallup polling organization—that produced numerous names for the lead in *Pride* in addition to Cooper. Cooper was the biggest; at the time, he was being seen in theaters in *Sergeant York*, the true World War I story about a backwoods Tennessee army hero that would bring him his first Oscar.

As he began his Gehrig casting quest, Goldwyn issued a statement that spoke to the absurdity of his song-and-dance with a bold suggestion that science, not the typical Hollywood commerce he trafficked in, led him to produce *Pride*.

"The results of a Hollywood poll made confidentially by Gallup's American Institute of Public Opinion were made public today by Samuel Goldwyn, who announced that he was largely motivated to make his production of the life of Lou Gehrig by the findings of the survey," his studio announced in a momentous-sounding press release that was little more than standard-issue hyperbole.

The message: Forget the newsreels that Niven Busch showed Goldwyn and the tears that he shed when Gehrig declared his great luck despite being struck with a fatal disease. Now Goldwyn could publicly say: I've market-tested my baseball biopic—and it is precisely about the man and the sport America wants to see.

The results of Gallup's survey of theatergoers released in early October suggested that it had ignored its principles to please a demanding client who often felt the need to explain that *Pride* was not a baseball movie, but a romance. Gallup asked movie lovers which of seven professions they would like to see portrayed on the screen and—surprise—they said they wanted it to be a big-league baseball player. (Baseball was still the undisputed national pastime then, so it was no stretch to say that it would finish first in the poll.) And of all the candidates whose stories they wanted to see on the screen, they most wanted it to be Lou Gehrig—again, a surprise—over a stable full of Hall of Famers including Babe Ruth, Connie Mack, Ty Cobb, Walter Johnson, Christy Mathewson, and Grover Alexander, who brought up the rear. Boxing was at its peak of popularity, probably second to baseball at the time, and no fighter had more fans in 1941 than Joe Louis, whose remarkable ring skills and inoffensive personality extended his appeal across racial lines. But he was not mentioned in Gallup's poll.

Of the dozens of possible actors surveyed by Gallup to play Lou, Cooper was ranked first, followed by Eddie Albert, Pat O'Brien, Cary Grant, Fred MacMurray, Spencer Tracy, William Gargan, Brian Donlevy, and Big Boy Williams, a lanky Texan who brought comic relief to his Western roles but was known off-screen as the Babe Ruth of polo. So many of them were simply so wrong for the role, but their inclusion probably reflected movie-goers' feelings for their favorite actors. Grant was a terrific actor, but he would have to discard his trademark accent. Donlevy made his living as a tough guy, and O'Brien already looked too old for the part, even though he was only two years older than Cooper.

Big Boy was good-looking, but he was too little known to draw an audience.

Walsh was having a grand time playing the publicity game for Goldwyn. In early October, he sent a playful note to the writers covering the Yankees-Dodgers World Series that exclaimed: "WHO IS GOING TO PLAY THE ROLE OF LOU GEHRIG!" it asked, then continued: "In the interests of good reporting, let me say that Mr. Goldwyn has not and will not decide on the actor for some time to come. It may be Spencer Tracy, or Gary Cooper, or it may be a 'dark horse.' It is not impossible that one of several professional ball players might get the part."

This was, of course, pure hokum laid on a captive group focused on the Yankees and Brooklyn Dodgers playing their first Subway Series. A few reporters found it more interesting that Goldwyn had sent a camera crew to Yankee Stadium to shoot footage for *Pride* than in speculation about who would play Gehrig.

Walsh dropped his flack's persona in a letter to Eleanor a few weeks later, where he updated her on the search for "Lou Gehrig" ruse.

"That silly contest as to who ain't gonna play Lou still gets a lot of space," he wrote from his perch in Pacific Palisades. "You knew there was a row between the studio and Louella when she flatly announced Coop had the role about a month back." In scooping Goldwyn, Parsons had written that "there is every reason why he should have the part, for he is under contract to Sam and he is Mrs. Gehrig's choice."

Eleanor had, in fact, moved closer to endorsing Cooper, perhaps because she knew he would get the starring role. She told the syndicated columnist Bob Considine: "Why does it matter that he isn't the ballplayer Lou was. Who is? The important thing is to capture the spirit of Lou and I don't know anyone who would do it as well. I don't know Cooper well, of course, but he has a lot of Lou's manner and Lou's ways of expressing himself and Lou's outlook."

The *Sporting News*, the St. Louis–based bible of baseball, was central to Goldwyn's casting folderol. The weekly newspaper's authority in the baseball industry conferred credibility on Goldwyn, who would have been flummoxed by its pages of box scores and insider's take on baseball. It was also the ideal clearinghouse for fans voting on an issue that could still stir passions in the few months before the United States entered World War II. In mid-August, as voting began, the weekly newspaper wrote breathlessly:

If Sam Goldwyn, the movie producer, is finding it difficult to decide whom to cast in the role of Lou Gehrig for the picture depicting the late Yankee first baseman's life, it is not surprising.

In all, forty-four men were nominated by the newspaper's readers—twenty-three actors and twenty-one ballplayers—but Goldwyn was not going to hire a ballplayer to play Gehrig. It was too gimmicky for Goldwyn's bigger ambitions. Whatever credibility the search had was based on its sampling of actors. Cooper was among the *Sporting News*'s list of actors, with John Wayne, Lew Ayres (the star of several Dr. Kildare films), Ronald Reagan (coming off *Knute Rockne, All American*), Big Boy, Lionel Barrymore (at sixty-three, he was older than Elsa Janssen, who played Mom Gehrig), and George Tobias (a comic lug who in the 1960s would appear in *Bewitched* as Abner Kravitz, the cranky husband of Gladys Kravitz, Samantha Stephens's nosy neighbor).

One devout fan of Eddie Albert's was Barrow, the Yankees' president. Albert was a handsome singer and actor at that time, a quarter century before his best-known role in *Green Acres* as Oliver Douglas, the white-haired lawyer who leaves his Manhattan law practice for a farm where he finds himself surrounded by hicks, oddballs, and Arnold Ziffel, the celebrated thespian pig of rural Hooterville.

Hedda Hopper, Queen Louella's great gossip competitor, wrote that "Sam Goldwyn's had so many letters requesting that Albert play the life of Lou Gehrig that he started investigating and finds the man who's putting on the campaign is Ed Barrow," who had friends and relatives write to suggest Albert.

"You know," Hopper said, "it isn't such a bad idea. Eddie looks like Gehrig and given the part, he'd become a star, and a valuable piece of property." Hopper's affinity for Albert must have been blind, because he bore no resemblance to Gehrig.

Barrow, a shrewd judge of baseball talent, penned a scouting report for Albert's candidacy for Gehrig in early August that was half general manager's assessment, half fanboy mash note. Albert, he wrote, is "the actor who reminds me most of Lou. He has Lou's dimples. He doesn't have his build but he looks like a southpaw." Two weeks later, he wrote to Albert's manager, explaining that he "would like to see Eddie Albert get the name part in the coming Lou Gehrig film" but backed away from any further role in the casting. "In fact," he said, "I have already been accused of sticking my nose into something I know nothing about."

The next day, he wrote to Eleanor, saying Albert's manager had asked him to recommend Albert to Goldwyn, but it was a request "I did not feel like doing."

He wasn't the only fan of Albert's letting his or her opinion be known.

Regular folks were weighing in.

Bernard Sherling of Brooklyn told the *Sporting News* that Albert "has the same type of likable face, smile and dimples, and the sort of character resembling beloved Lou's." A woman who identified herself only as J. R. S. of Caldwell, New Jersey, wrote to Goldwyn, offering a casting double play: "I'm killing two birds with one stone. Eddie Albert for Lou and me for Mrs. Gehrig." Herbert Runion, of St. Louis, wrote: "In my opinion he is the only actor who resembles the immortal Gehrig. Maybe he isn't as good an actor as Gary Cooper, Spencer Tracy, etc., but I am sure that Eddie Albert could leave his conventional comedy roles and do a grand job about a 'never-to-be-forgotten man.'"

But Rae Robinson of Manhattan wanted Pat O'Brien to play Gehrig because "he is big and husky, a lover of all kinds of sport, especially baseball, and also has a pleasant smile and dimples and is good looking."

Dimples, it seemed, became a critical physical feature in the Gehrig hunt.

O. H. Lessin of Bridgeport, Connecticut, made a case for Cary Grant: "Since the late Lou Gehrig was left-handed, tall, good-looking, dark and dimple-faced, who else but Cary Grant could do justice to the role?"

A more personalized plea came from William Gargan's wife, Mary: "I know Bill would be terrific in the part. How do I know? He *is* Gehrig."

And some other votes were cast for unknowns.

Ray Henkel of Milwaukee nominated himself "because my friends have called me 'Lou' for a long time and begged me to write just to see what would happen." Clarence Culver of Malloy, Iowa, declared himself ready for the role because Lou tutored him during a visit to Des Moines in 1936. "It was there that he taught me to bat left-handed"—and the following year young Clarence hit .764.

One young New Yorker offered a pecuniary rationale for offering to step up to play Gehrig: "My girl won't marry me until I pay off my debts. I owe $600. I am 6 feet tall and possess personality traits similar to those of Lou Gehrig."

A Brooklynite named Arnold Dee offered Eddie Duberstein, a career minor leaguer (and first baseman) who had last played in 1939 for the Martinsville Manufacturers of the Class D Bi-State League. Dee declared that Duberstein "looks like and could act the part of Gehrig." Could he act? Who knew?

Walsh heard from Ripper Collins, a slugger with the 1934 St. Louis Cardinals, who were known as the "Gashouse Gang," who volunteered that a real player—like himself—would make a more authentic Gehrig than an actor.

And a Southern Pacific locomotive repairman from Tucson noted the resemblance between Gehrig and Washington Senators pitcher Steve Sundra: "Same shaped head," he wrote about the right-hander, who went 11-1 for the Yankees in 1939, sharing the clubhouse with Gehrig. "Same kind of chin. Same dimples. Don't let some ham actor muss the part. Take Sundra and train him for a month and he will do a good job, I'm sure."

The *Sporting News*—which reported in August that Cooper and Tracy were running neck and neck in its reader poll—felt it had a stake in *Pride,* at least as a guardian of historical accuracy. When it learned that Brooklyn Dodgers manager Leo Durocher might play a role in *Pride* as a teammate aware of Lou's illness, it pounced. Durocher knew Gehrig, as a teammate in 1928 and 1929, and he had tested for *Pride,* but Larry MacPhail, the

Dodgers' tempestuous president, was said to have ordered Leo not to wear the Yankee pinstripes.

Suggesting that Leo had any personal insight into Lou's sickness prompted an editorial chastising the attempted fictionalization of reality—a plot device that would become increasingly commonplace to biopics based on true stories and be used liberally throughout *Pride* by its several screenwriters.

"But now comes a proposal to place Leo in the picture as the man who discovered that something radically wrong has hit the Iron Horse and he was on the way out," a *Sporting News* editorial intoned. Not only was Durocher across town as player-manager of the Dodgers in 1939, it said, but manager Joe McCarthy and coach Art Fletcher first sensed "that there was something seriously amiss with Lou." To cast the feisty and brassy Leo the Lip "as the erudite, medically wise observer who first glimpsed the tragic turn in Gehrig would be incongruous," the paper said, and lack "the ring of reality to the Iron Horse's teammates, the writers and above all, to the fan public."

Durocher's proposed role might have been a rumor that sprang up when photographs of him at the Goldwyn studio appeared in the press, or some trial balloon from the studio to give Durocher, a wiseass who seemed to be playing a *Guys and Dolls*–like character come to life, a chance to play an inflated version of himself onscreen. But an analysis of the film's scripts show no such role for him.

Meanwhile, the "who-will-play-Lou?" returns were piling up—and the *Sporting News* was hyping them as if Goldwyn were ghostwriting its copy.

"Not since the speculation over the Scarlett O'Hara-Rhett Butler roles for *Gone with the Wind* has such a whirlwind of debate swept the country as the argument over who is best fitted to play the role of Lou Gehrig," J. G. Taylor Spink, the publisher of the *Sporting News*, opened his story on December 4, perpetuating the fantasy of a true talent search. Spread across the broadsheet page were photos of five men: Gehrig, Cooper, Chicago White Sox pitcher Johnny Humphries, Eddie Albert, and minor-league pitcher Al Hollingsworth. One can only imagine a theater marquee saying: *The Pride of the Yankees* starring Johnny Humphries.

Many readers voted for Albert, among the actors, based only on his physical resemblance to Gehrig, even though it is difficult to agree with what they were looking at. One reader said that Albert would be even better if he were built like the handsome actor George O'Brien, a heavyweight boxing champion of the Pacific Fleet during World War I whose credits included, coincidentally, a 1924 silent film called *The Iron Horse*. Cooper finished first in the voting among actors, his reputation as one of Hollywood's biggest stars known for playing dignified men no doubt having a significant effect.

Among the twenty-three ballplayers, the most votes for their fidelity to Gehrig's looks went to Humphries, with his dimpled chin, and Hollingsworth. The vote elevated an already productive season for Hollingsworth, who was in the midst of a 21-9 campaign for the fifth-place Sacramento Solons of the Pacific Coast League.

The remaining candidates included some odd choices that suggested readers were willy-nilly tossing in their favorite actors and ballplayers they might have seen as youngsters, from Eddie Duberstein to Ted North to Milton Galatzer.

Babe Ruth got some votes, but the Sultan of Swat looked like no one else, much less the better-looking Gehrig. Wally Pipp and Babe Dahlgren were on the slate, but their main distinction was their unique connections to Gehrig—Pipp preceded Lou at first base and Dahlgren succeeded him—not any resemblance to him. Lon Chaney, Jr., was inexplicably a candidate, but he no more resembled Gehrig than Gehrig resembled Chaney in *The Wolf Man*. The closest Chaney came to Gehrig was when he appeared with Cooper in *High Noon*.

The roster of would-be Gehrigs also included a handsome former Alabama running back named Johnny Mack Brown, who had a long Hollywood career, mostly in Westerns. The possibility of Brown as Gehrig intrigued Kieran, the sports columnist at the *New York Times*, a friend and neighbor of Gehrig's. Musing about various candidates, he wrapped up his analysis with Brown: "All-American football nominee. Played for Alabama in the Rose Bowl. Lou Gehrig was quite a football player for Columbia before he became famous on the professional diamond. Johnny Mack Brown might be the man—if he could hit an inside curve and play a good game at first base."

The women's vote coming from readers of *Cosmopolitan* gave Cooper a resounding victory, with 4,354 votes. Albert finished second, with 2,132 votes, with Reagan (1,025), Tracy (467), Dennis Morgan (398), and Gargan (356) rounding out the list.

Goldwyn waited until nearly the end of the year to announce his decision, delaying it for a week after naming Sam Wood to direct *Pride*. Sports editors got the word about Cooper when Walsh sent personalized telegrams on Christmas Eve. In his wire to the sports editor of the *Montana Standard*, the publicist wrote:

Here's something to put in your sports page Christmas stocking. Samuel Goldwyn formally announced today Gary Cooper will play lead in Lou Gehrig picture. Mr. Goldwyn's final decision, based on six months' sampling of public opinion with Cooper leading polls conducted by

Cosmopolitan magazine, *Movie and Radio Guide*, the *Sporting News* and consulting more than 1,000 newspaper sports writers. As you voted for Cooper, please accept my congratulations on your ability as a casting expert.

Happy Christmas, partner.

The casting was widely expected and landed with a thud on page twenty-seven of the *New York Times*, below news that the 86th Street Casino Theater in Manhattan was going to reopen Christmas Day with a revival of the Soviet film *General Suvorov*, and that three million people would have attended the Christmas pageant at Radio City Music Hall by the time it concluded its ninth engagement on December 30.

The news about Cooper was quickly eclipsed when the New York Film Critics named him best actor for *Sergeant York*, and *Ball of Fire*, Cooper's screwball comedy with Barbara Stanwyck, opened at Radio City in mid-January. Howard Hawks, who directed both films, understood Cooper as well as any director and echoed the prevailing view of the actor's minimalist skills.

"The grand thing about Cooper," said Hawks, "is that you believe everything that he says or does."

5

Babe on Film

Babe Ruth was nearing his forty-seventh birthday when he signed to play himself in *The Pride of the Yankees*. He was a lost soul, with no home in baseball. Released by the Yankees after the 1934 season, the Babe spent an unhappy two months with the Boston Braves, where, in one last Ruthian fusillade at the end of his run, he slugged three home runs against the Pittsburgh Pirates, one over the right-center field fence at Forbes Field. Days later, with a .181 batting average, he put an end to his career. He was bitter at being duped and mistreated by Braves owner Judge Emil Fuchs, who mistakenly believed Ruth's presence would salvage his dreadful team's finances.

"I don't want a thing from him—that dirty double-crosser," Ruth said as he parted. He said he quit. Fuchs said he fired him. The truth did not matter. The Babe was old. He ached. He was done as a player. And Fuchs was soon finished as an owner. The Braves ended the season at 38-115, the worst Major League record in nearly twenty years, saddled with debts that forced Fuchs out and the team into forfeiture with the National League.

Ruth had left Boston once before after the 1919 season, in an epic sale from the Red Sox to the Yankees. This ending in Boston was the unhappy conclusion of an astonishing twenty-two-season journey that demonstrated, to his great chagrin, that Ruth would never manage any team, not these desultory Braves nor his beloved Yankees. He and his wife, Claire, drove home to New York aware that no franchise thought enough of his baseball mind or his demeanor to let him skipper a team. He was paying for his orgiastic, booze-fueled, antiauthoritarian, narcissistic past.

If he couldn't manage himself, the line went, *how could he manage others?*

The indignities of his post-Yankee life continued, as if baseball had pulled the welcome mat out from under him. The indignities continued when he showed up at the Polo Grounds with Claire and his adopted daughter, Julia, for the New York Giants' 1936 home opener against the Brooklyn Dodgers. He was accustomed to being the enemy of the Giants, especially to manager John J. McGraw, first when the Yankees and Giants shared the Polo Grounds, then as rivals across the Harlem River, where Ruth's hitting and charisma justified Jacob Ruppert and Tillinghast L. (Cap) Huston's construction of Yankee Stadium.

So there he was, dressed in his civvies, ensconced in box twenty-seven, the focus of fans who wanted his autograph and newspaper and newsreel photographers who wanted to record his mug. A little like his golden days. But not really.

"Grin, sure I'll grin," he told reporters before the game. "What's that? You want me to look bewildered? Okay, okay, anything to please."

The attention was evanescent. "For fifteen fleeting minutes, minutes that must have thrilled him far more than the mightiest home run he ever crashed over the distant ramparts, Babe Ruth was baseball's idol and hero yesterday," the Associated Press reported. But once the 56,000 fans settled into the old horseshoe-shaped ballpark to watch the Giants win, 8–5, Ruth was no longer in demand.

He was just another middle-aged family guy struggling to find a place for himself after two decades as the *sine qua non* of baseball. Now "he was baseball's forgotten man," the AP wrote, sitting "virtually unnoticed the rest of the game."

Without a baseball job, Ruth spent his time golfing, bowling, hunting, and fishing, and wintering in Florida. He estimated that in one year he played 365 rounds of golf, which, given his passion for the sport, is believable. Personal appearances filled up the rest of his time.

Then came Goldwyn's offer in the fall of 1941 to play himself in *Pride* and re-enact the past with Gehrig, including their hug on Lou Gehrig Appreciation Day. It was important to bring Ruth to the film; his name would look good on a movie marquee near Cooper's.

The movie wouldn't be the same without the Bambino.

George Herman Ruth had spent his life playing a rollicking character named the Babe, a rambunctious kid placed by his parents in a Catholic orphanage, where he learned to play baseball from a Xaverian brother; who started his Major League career as a pitcher with the Boston Red Sox, then turned to full-time hitting and became the greatest and most influential ballplayer of his time, or ever. His appetites were as prodigious as his home runs—yet as insatiable and incorrigible as he could be, he was often recalled as a well-intentioned, overgrown kid who lacked the nurturing of loving parents and could not follow the rules that ordinary, civilized adults obeyed.

Having mastered playing himself, it was natural to become Babe Ruth in Hollywood. It was a part-time job, at best, that began in silent films during his first season with the Yankees. In 1920's *Headin' Home*, he was a trim, fictional character named Babe Ruth. Next, he was a minor-league Los Angeles Angel named Babe Dugan with a tobacco-chewing problem in 1927's *Babe Comes Home*. The latter was shot partly at Wrigley Field in Los Angeles, where Ruth would be for the on-field action in *The Pride of the Yankees* fifteen years later. Babe's participation in *Babe Comes Home* was followed intently by Marshall Hunt, one of Ruth's leading chroniclers for the New York *Daily News*. In one installment of his coverage, Hunt wrote:

But yesterday, while rehearsing a home run blow, he connected with a ball with such power that the club was split from end to end [a foreshadowing of Robert Redford's cherished bat, Wonderboy, shattering in his final at-bat as Roy Hobbs in *The Natural*]. A piteous expression wrinkled the features of the Babe. His head dropped. He trudged disconsolately to a chair. Smelling salts were applied....

Babe returned to the silent screen soon after, playing himself in *Speedy*, a comedy starring Harold Lloyd, who, with Charlie Chaplin and Buster Keaton, formed a triumvirate of comic genius in the early twentieth century. It is not a starring role but a meaty five-minute cameo that captures Ruth after the glorious 1927 season when he hit 60 home runs, drove in 165 runs, and hit .356.

Ruth is first seen tossing signed baseballs to orphans at an asylum on First Avenue in Manhattan when the hapless cab driver,

Speedy, pulls up, and Ruth beckons for a ride. Speedy is shocked but thrilled at Ruth's summons.

"Gee, Babe, you've done more to baseball than cheese did to Switzerland," Speedy, turned backward in the driver's seat to talk to Ruth while ignoring the cars and trolleys in his path uptown, tells Ruth in the dialogue card. "Gosh, Babe, this is the proudest moment of my life," he adds.

"If you don't look out," Ruth says, "it'll be the last."

That begins a ride where Ruth, without overacting much, conveys his anxiety over Speedy's hair-raising driving. Babe wipes mock sweat from his brow. He closes his eyes, fans himself with his cap, and angrily gesticulates.

When the adventure ends in front of the ticket booths outside Yankee Stadium, Ruth gets out, puffs out his cheeks, and leans against the cab.

"If I ever want to commit suicide," he says, "I'll call you."

As they speak, Lou Gehrig walks by, looks at the camera, and moves on, presumably on his way to the Yankee clubhouse, where Babe must hasten.

Ruth appeared in a few short talkies in the 1930s, including *Fancy Curves* (1932), with Ruth as a women's baseball coach facing a men's team. The most notable aspect of the eight-minute film was seeing him come off the bench in a wig to hit a game-winning homer. His hip-swiveling scam is revealed as he tips his cap, which removes his wig, and he escapes on the roof of a car, waving good-bye.

Babe was so eager to be a credible version of his former self in *The Pride of the Yankees* that he put himself on a diet. Playing himself from 1925 to 1939, the Babe could afford to show up with his trademark pot belly but anything more would risk making him look ridiculous. A half century later, John Goodman lost a great amount of weight to play Ruth in *The Babe*, but he still looked too obese for the role that took him from his teenage years to his retirement. Ruth's weight-loss plan worked. He took off nearly fifty pounds in a couple of months. He showed off his slimmer physique at a publicity event for *Pride* in late December along with Eleanor Gehrig and screenwriter Paul Gallico at the Rainbow Club in Rockefeller Center. Those who knew him were cheered to see him no longer a corpulent figure.

"He looked to me exactly as he did the last year I saw him play and I think he will make a very good impression in the picture," Gallico wrote in a letter to Goldwyn. "It will really look like the well-known, baseball-playing Babe Ruth, not the old fat caricature of him. I was pleased with his appearance and told him so."

A few days later, shortly after midnight, Ruth was rushed from his Manhattan apartment to an undisclosed private hospital in New York, a scene that reminded Ruth watchers of the illness in 1925 that delayed his debut until June. Gallico, who had covered Ruth for much of his newspapering career, responded as if Ruth's alcoholic excesses once again required emergency medical attention.

"My suspicion is that that he went on a bender and was dumped in there to sober up," he said in the letter to Goldwyn, written from his New Hope, Pennsylvania, farm.

The Babe's doctor diagnosed him with an "upset nervous condition," unrelated to boozing. "Ruth has not been looking quite right for several weeks," the doctor said. "Perhaps he was trying to take off too much weight in too short a time in preparation for his forthcoming picture work."

Ruth had also been in a car accident shortly before in Westchester County in which he was forced off the road while trying to avoid hitting another car. Newspaper reports suggested that he had had some sort of breakdown. But he was home in two weeks and by the end of January was packing for his train trip to Hollywood.

"I never felt better in my life," he said in his apartment, moving trunks around to show his renewed strength and boasting that he had cut back on his bowling and golfing but not his cigar-smoking. "I weigh two twenty-three, less than I've weighed in fifteen years. If they keep taking all these young kids in the army, I guess I'll have to go back into baseball. That's if I can get someone to run for me."

He promised that he was not worried about his work on *Pride*. "I'm an old actor from way back," he said, listing his Hollywood credentials.

Babe and Claire were greeted at Union Station in Los Angeles on February 8 like the First Family of *Pride*, even if the title more properly belonged to Cooper and Teresa Wright. Walsh had spent a week trying to arrange the perfect greeting for his longtime friend and client: an orphan band to play him off the train. When he called the Nazareth House in Van Nuys, he was rebuffed by a nun, a recent immigrant from Australia with a "gorgeous dialect," Walsh wrote to Eleanor. Walsh's instinct to bring in an orphan band struck at Ruth's sympathies as a child of parents who sent their incorrigible son to St. Mary's Industrial Home for Boys, where he lived for twelve years, learned to make shirts and play baseball and, sort of, came of age.

Walsh drove to Van Nuys to sell the nun on letting him take the band to the Babe. "I found the reason was that she didn't know what Babe Ruth was!" he told Eleanor, incredulous. "Yes, she had heard the name...but that was all. Finally I showed her the publicity value...and she said 'Yes.' "

Walsh had a bus pick up the uniformed band at six a.m. for

the trip to Los Angeles, where they handed roses to Claire and held up signs welcoming Ruth. Knowing Ruth, Walsh probably realized the strong nostalgic note he had plucked with the band; in 1920, Ruth's first season with the Yankees, Babe brought the St. Mary's band to Major League stadiums to raise money to rebuild the school's main building, which had been destroyed in a fire. Ruth could not have helped thinking about the school's influence on him as the boys from Nazareth surrounded him with music from their horns, tubas, and drums. In one picture, he wields a baton. Filling up the station were soldiers who clamored for his autograph.

"A crowd gathered and the old Babe (give him credit) did his stuff like a million dollars," Walsh wrote. At Walsh's prodding, Ruth invited the band to a breakfast at the Roosevelt Hotel with Bill Dickey and Bob Meusel, two of the Yankees who were playing themselves in *Pride*, sportswriter Grantland Rice, and Babe Herman, the former left-handed-hitting Brooklyn Dodger who doubled for Cooper in long shots at bat in the film. Two dozen kids and a dozen adults had their ham and eggs. Walsh had all the players sign balls for the boys in the band.

Once finished with the orphans, Babe went in search of a pair of his beloved white pants with blue stripes, which he wanted to wear to a round at Lakeside Golf Club that day, according to *Los Angeles Times* columnist Dick Hyland. He tore through the steamer trunks that arrived belatedly from the train station before an amused audience that included Claire, Meusel, and Walsh.

No pants.

"That man!" Claire harrumphed in the Babe's direction. "I just found my white ermine wrap on the floor with his dirty baseball gloves and things on top of it." Only after Claire emptied the Babe's white leather handbag were the pants discovered. "Take him out of here!" she told his posse. "Make him play fifty-four holes."

The Babe's antics were doubtlessly amusing and worthy of the gossip-filled letters that Walsh tapped out on his typewriter, though Eleanor didn't care much for Babe news, or the Babe at all. Walsh wrote her about the missing trunks, the Ruths' two-bedroom, $200-a-month suite, and the Babe's concern that he couldn't immediately find his golf clubs. Eleanor was tired of the Babe, who had overshadowed Lou in their time together. The two men had not talked for a few years until Gehrig's farewell ceremony.

One reason suggested for their distance had it that Mom Gehrig—who doted on the Babe, who loved her German cooking—had questioned why Claire dressed Dorothy, Babe's adopted daughter from his first marriage, so poorly while she lavished fine clothing on her natural daughter, Julia, whom Ruth adopted after he married Claire. But as the Ruth biographer Leigh Montville wrote, the real enmity might have been over Lou's suspicion that Eleanor had once slept with the sybaritic Ruth.

Now that Eleanor was on her quest to preserve Lou's image for the ages, she didn't want Ruth anywhere near *Pride*. It was impossible and impractical to keep Ruth out, though; he was still a major name and was being counted on by Goldwyn as a big draw to movie-going baseball fans. The best Eleanor could hope for was to limit the Babe's time onscreen regardless of how central Ruth was to Yankee history.

Walsh was pragmatic and deferential with Eleanor in assessing Ruth's importance to the movie. Ruth, by any measure, ranked third in importance in *Pride*, below Cooper and Teresa Wright.

"To tell the life story of Lou Gehrig without some reference to Babe Ruth would be suicide from a box office or the critics' standpoint," he wrote her. "But you can rest assured his inclusion will only be in conformity with your wishes, which I have always found extremely reasonable, no matter what your emotion."

Walsh knew her animus toward Ruth could not be allowed to hurt the film.

Eleanor confided her feelings soon after in interviews with Gallico as he prepared to write the movie's outline and initial screenplay. They worked together in San Francisco, where she poured her heart out about Lou, his mother, his health, and her sheltered life in Chicago that unraveled because of her father's financial fall and philandering. Over thirty-eight pages of notes typed out by Gallico, she provided the biographical template for *Pride*. Her dismal view of Ruth is clear.

"He should not appear in the flesh," she told Gallico. "Feeling that he would make a further mess of baseball and ruin the beautiful tribute to Lou, who represented the clean side of the sport."

Her thoughts moved her in various directions, from suggesting that an actor play Ruth and portray him positively to showing how the real Babe was a mentor to Lou early in his career. She also cuttingly suggested using Ruth early in the film, then drop him out of the story "just as he was dropped out of baseball."

If the real Babe was in the picture, she conceded, "use him as necessary atmosphere, as the man that Lou looked up to in the beginning of his career."

She believed, with some rancor, that Ruth would be a scene-stealer.

"Babe himself would be a menace in the picture," she told Gallico. "There would be all kinds of trouble" and "Mrs. Ruth would undoubtedly end up supervising every inch of the picture and the outcome would be 'Ruth Glorified.'"

Eleanor told Gallico that Lou was not jealous of Ruth's

publicity but was envious of Ruth's ability to hit 60 home runs and bothered "that he could get away with all the things he did and remain on top." She said that Lou had vowed that if it was necessary to live that way, "he didn't want to be famous."

Still, she said, Lou watched Ruth with "amazement and amusement—a man who could have five affairs in a night!"

She could not resist poking at both Babe and Claire.

Recalling how Babe embraced Lou on Gehrig Appreciation Day, she said, "There was nothing Lou could do about it. Perhaps Ruth had some honest emotions, but Mrs. Ruth controlled all his actions." She added: "Ruth was probably scared of his wife but really loved Lou. Perhaps he was honest when he cried before Lou's casket." And, she added: "He was drunk at the time."

More than thirty years later, in her autobiography, she was not as tough on Ruth. "He seemed to be a pot-bellied, spindly-legged, good-natured buffoon," she wrote, and added:

There was no whispering about him because he did everything out in the open. He loved the bottle, he loved to eat, he was an uncommon ladies' man when he was unattached, and he was absolutely tremendous at bat and in the field. You had to look at him and feel that you were watching one of the wonders of the world.

Those words were written at a distance. In the heat of creating The Pride of the Yankees, Eleanor's emotions about the Babe were tough and raw. She was protecting her husband, at least in her private thoughts about Ruth, none of which could be discerned in the finished film. Walsh knew her feelings about Ruth, and it created a conundrum for him. He began representing Ruth in his ghostwriting syndicate in 1921, and became his agent and the promoter of his barnstorming trips with Gehrig. Ruth was a publicist's gift that kept giving for two decades. Gehrig was also Walsh's client, and after his death, Walsh's frequent correspondence with Eleanor showed a desire to keep her informed and play the friendly go-between with Goldwyn. Until the film, Gehrig brought him prestige but not the profits that Ruth did.

A letter from Walsh to Eleanor in late November of 1941 alludes to what seems to have been something of a showdown with Goldwyn over Ruth's use.

"In the beginning," he wrote, "you opposed Ruth in the picture. After many days of controversy, you finally conceded the point but on the condition that Ruth would not be there alone but as one of a group."

She did not get her way, and *Pride* is better for it.

Even Goldwyn and, to a greater extent, director Sam Wood, an amateur ballplayer as a young man, placed a real value on Ruth's presence. For $1,500 a week, Ruth was going to do more for *Pride* than embrace Gehrig. He would not dominate the film, as Eleanor feared, but in his several scenes, he enlivened the film and showed the same ease at playing himself that he showed in *Speedy*, all the while lending credibility for the audience.

Not All Yankees Welcome

6

It was only November 1941, and Samuel Goldwyn was furious over the first script for *Pride*. It had too much baseball. Shooting wouldn't start for more than two months, but Goldwyn blew up at Paul Gallico and Collier Young, insisting that they were not keeping to his concept of a romantic, heroic film about Gehrig. Always easy to enrage, Goldwyn's pique was misguided, driven by his ignorance of baseball. The baseball scenes in the script served, as he had dictated, as the backdrop to the story of Gehrig's childhood, his rise to greatness in baseball, his marriage to Eleanor, and his fatal illness. But with so few sports movies in Hollywood's past, measuring what was too much was inexact, and Goldwyn could only see too much of what he didn't understand or want.

So he erupted at the screenwriter Gallico and Young, who was one of his story editors. In Gallico and Young, Goldwyn was facing off against hired hands with considerable baseball knowledge. Gallico was a prominent former sports columnist whose time at

Columbia overlapped with Gehrig's. Young was a big baseball fan who happily played nursemaid to Babe Ruth—that is, he said, he drank copious amounts of booze with the Sultan of Swat—during the filming of *Pride*.

Walsh, who was never far from *Pride's* action or gossip, ran into Goldwyn at the studio on the morning of November 24, when, "with no previous warning," he told Walsh: "I am dropping all the baseball players from the script, except Ruth," because the script was "too heavy" with the presence of several ex-Yankees, a peculiar complaint because only Ruth and Dickey had roles with any consequential lines.

He added, "I'm cutting Ruth's part in two."

Goldwyn's anti-baseball choler surprised Walsh, a staunch Babe partisan who felt that Cooper needed more than just Ruth and Dickey with him for any credible portrayal, however fleeting, of the Murderers' Row Yankees team.

So why, having already enlisted Walsh to hire some of Lou's teammates, did he want to summarily nix everyone but Ruth?

"It seems illogical," Walsh wrote to Eleanor, "to have Ruth in person and alongside of him some actors playing *Lazzeri, Dickey, and Meusel*... actors who probably will walk like toe-dancers and swing a bat like it was a bamboo cane."

Goldwyn's demands were short-lived or forgotten. Walsh heard nothing further, and the casting of former players began. Walsh set about bringing in Dickey, Bob Meusel, Mark Koenig, and Tony Lazzeri for as little as Goldwyn would pay them to create a sampling of the old team Ruth and Gehrig had anchored. It was a balancing act: Hire too many players and Goldwyn would flip; bring in too few and the credibility of the biggest scene in *Pride* might be imperiled. Walsh was the right man for the job with his experience in putting together barnstorming teams and talent for self-promotion. His short, self-published memoir is packed with a series of group photos taken annually with those whose names were on the ghostwritten column: Ruth, Gehrig, Ty Cobb, John J. McGraw, Walter Johnson, Rogers Hornsby, Grover Cleveland Alexander, and others—stars in uniforms and Walsh, always in a suit and sometimes a fedora.

Dickey's closeness to Gehrig made him, surprisingly, reluctant to participate. A modest man, Dickey could not relate to anyone else posing as Gehrig. After the 1941 World Series when Eleanor told him that he would likely be asked to be in the picture, he told her, "Good God El, I can't look at Cooper and call him Lou." His importance to Lou kept Walsh and Eleanor trying to change his mind.

In November, Dickey wired Walsh: "Would rather not appear. But will come if you and associates feel it necessary." The *Times's* Kieran surmised that Dickey preferred to stay home in Little Rock, Arkansas, rather than "have himself flashed on the screen in the guise of a movie actor."

Lazzeri demanded $500 a day to appear—many times what Goldwyn was willing to pay—and priced himself out of a role.

Babe Dahlgren, who replaced Lou at first base, proved elusive. Dahlgren wasn't a Yankee great, but he was a part of the Gehrig saga. The role did not require much—leave the visitors' dugout when Gehrig permanently removes himself from the lineup in Detroit and say something brief. After ignoring several of Walsh's letters seeking a release to let Goldwyn use his name, Dahlgren arrived at Wrigley Field as filming began.

"To put it briefly," Walsh told Eleanor, "he ABSOLUTELY REFUSES to give a release for use of his name unless he appears in the picture in person for which he demands ONE THOUSAND DOLLARS to say two words." Dahlgren cornered Dickey at the ballpark and told him "if the studio uses his name in any way, he 'will make trouble for Goldwyn.'"

Walsh added: "There's a louse for you."

Dahlgren was insulted by the $75 a day he was being offered and threatened to take action with Judge Kenesaw Mountain Landis, baseball's commissioner, if *Pride* hired anyone else to portray him. "When a company such as Wheaties can pay ball players from $200 to $1,000 a year for just endorsing their product, it makes Mr. Goldwyn appear mighty small in his offer to me," he told Walsh. He vowed that the film would not refer to him as "'lad,' 'kid,' or even 'buddy,' call it what you may—anything as a cover-up to get away from using my name."

Dahlgren lost his fight (although his grandson, Matt, believes he was paid for the use of his name). He ended up as a character in the film, but was played by Rip Russell, a chubby-cheeked infielder with the Chicago Cubs, who had already been hired to play the all-but-invisible role of Laddie. Russell had one small task: Act surprised at McCarthy's call to replace Gehrig and say "Thanks, Lou" when Cooper tells him "Good luck" as they cross paths on the dugout steps. Russell received no credit except for being listed in production reports.

Wally Pipp, who lost his job to Gehrig in 1925, did not ask to be in *Pride* (nor was he asked), and was reported to be working at Ford's Willow Run auto plant in Ypsilanti, Michigan, which was producing B-24 bombers. But on January 21, he telegrammed Goldwyn from Grand Rapids, urging him: "IMPORTANT YOU PHONE ME TODAY BIG STORY READY TO BREAK GEHRIG PICTURE."

On behalf of Goldwyn, Walsh spurned him ("Glad to know big story is breaking on Gehrig picture and will certainly watch for it with interest"), but Pipp wrote back, detailing a proposal by an associate, Sam Westerman, that Goldwyn donate all profits from *Pride* to war relief agencies, which Pipp would announce to the press, pending the mogul's approval. "There is no selfish motive in his proposal," Pipp insisted. "He feels that under the present emergency, with fellows like Hank Greenberg, Bob Feller, Ted Williams, Joe Louis, Tom Harmon and others in the sport world making costly sacrifices to help our war effort, Mr. Goldwyn will be deeply interested in the above-mentioned suggestion."

Goldwyn did not respond to Pipp. But he told Walsh, "This guy is nuts."

Walsh wrote to Eleanor: "I'm not even going to acknowledge his communications from now on. Let him suffer in silence."

In all, four Yankees were hired to be themselves: Ruth, the highest paid at $1,500 a week; the reluctant Dickey, who bonded with Cooper over their love of hunting; Meusel and Koenig, whose $100 daily rate was for a few days' work. Meusel and Koenig did not have much to do; Dickey had a little more of a role.

Ruth, as usual, was the central force, the irrepressible sun around whom all others revolved. For the Babe, this was a reunion with a few pals and one more opportunity to wear the pinstripes, talk baseball, play a little bit, and drink. It didn't hurt to be a star again, swinging a bat in front of thousands of extras and getting his full head of slightly graying hair primped by doting stylists.

He had not stopped being a character even if he had been shunted aside by baseball. Walsh dished to Eleanor, and God knows who else, about his friend and client. One night soon after Babe and his wife, Claire, arrived in Los Angeles, he arrived back at the hotel at eleven thirty p.m., two hours later than he had promised after a night out with the alcoholic actor John

Barrymore and sportswriter Grantland Rice, who rewrote his baseball poem, "Game Called," for Ruth after the Babe's death ("The Big Guy's left us lonely in the dark/Forever waiting for the flaming spark").

Returning home from revels at eleven thirty must have seemed absurd to a veteran carouser like Ruth (whose best partying was probably well in the past), but Claire was angry. Walsh's retelling of the story must have confirmed to Eleanor that the Big Bam was, more than ever, just another henpecked, middle-aged husband.

"You ought to hear what the 'old woman' said to him," Walsh wrote on a sheet of paper on which he scrawled a fat heart and typed "Valentine's Greetings" inside. "He told us, he told her if she didn't lay off, she could pack up and go home…Thurs. night we went to annual stag dinner" and "she raised H- - - again. Anyway, Babe was ranting and threatening and telling Dickey, Meusel and me how he was going to be in charge from now on but all the time we were splitting our sides laughing and Meusel and Bill were winking at me on the side. The chances are when he went home that night he pussy-footed in with hat in hand. SPECIAL BULLETIN: Mr. Ruth officially announces that he and his 'old woman' now sleep in separate bedrooms!!!!"

The Babe's star was on the rise again—whoever he was or wasn't bedding.

7

The Producer and the Star

One hundred years from now, when the history of Holly-wood is written, it will tell of a man by the name of Samuel Goldwyn who made a baseball picture without a man by the name of Harry Ruby, who was considered the greatest authority on baseball of his time. Prosperity will look upon this as the greatest blunder since the "Charge of the Light Brigade."

—telegram to Samuel Goldwyn from Harry Ruby, fanatical fan and co-songwriter/screenwriter behind the Marx Brothers' films Horse Feathers, Duck Soup, and Animal Crackers

n Hollywood there was no starker contrast between baseball fans and baseball know-nothings than Harry Ruby and Sam Goldwyn. Goldwyn was utterly ignorant of the sport, and Ruby, a native New Yorker, was dubbed America's Number One Baseball Fan. For Ruby to hear that his friend Sam was making a film about Lou Gehrig without him—and which would not have much baseball in it—must have felt like a Bob Feller beanball to his temple. Ruby's fandom was so deep that he asked God why He let someone else write "Take Me Out to the Ball Game." Ruby aspired to a Major League baseball career. He collected uniforms. He played second base for the Washington Senators in an exhibition at the invitation of his friend, the pitcher-turned-manager Walter Johnson. But after blowing a double play he was waived by the owner, Clark Griffith. He also played several games for the Hollywood Stars and Los Angeles Angels of the Pacific Coast League that found their way into official records of the authoritative Baseball-Reference.com.

Ruby had the right background to write and score *Pride* if *Pride* were the baseball film he dreamed of making. He had cinematic sports experience as one of the writers and composers of 1932's *Horse Feathers*, one of the best pre-*Pride* sports films, albeit an anarchic Marx Brothers comedy. Ruby and the Marx Brothers satirized amateurism in college sports, a continuing joke to this day. In the film, Professor Quincy Adams (Groucho Marx) addressed a gathering of academics at fictional Huxley College by impertinently declaring, "And I say to you, gentlemen, that this college is a failure. The trouble is, we're neglecting football for education."

Helping to make *Pride* would have let Ruby slip on Yankee pinstripes, play second base, pal around with Cooper and Ruth, and take a few swings from the minor-league pitchers hired for *Pride*.

Eleanor and Lou *may* have fallen in love to one of Ruby and his songwriting partner Bert Kalmar's hits, such as "I Wanna Be Loved by You."

Instead of recruiting Ruby, Goldwyn signed a group of screenwriters, including Gallico and Herman Mankiewicz, who were laden with baseball knowledge. And he persuaded Irving Berlin, his card-playing and backgammon pal, to license "Always," which he wrote for his wife, Ellin, as the love theme of *Pride*.

Had the irascible Goldwyn hired him, Ruby might have chafed under his friend's autocratic ways, as many others did, and sought solace in famous lyrics from one of his songs in *Horse Feathers*: "Your proposition may be good/But let's have one thing understood/Whatever it is, I'm against it!"

Of course, Goldwyn wasn't asking for permission to make *Pride* his way. *Pride* would follow his fiats. He never hid his nonsporting intentions—rather, he was excited to announce that in matters of *Pride*, baseball was tangential.

"First of all, *The Pride of the Yankees* is not to be, in a strict sense, a 'baseball picture,'" he wrote in a letter to a Hollywood reporter. "I have not been motivated, for example, by the fact that baseball is America's greatest sport that no ambitious motion picture has ever been made with big league baseball as its background, or that 1941 was 'baseball's greatest year.'" That last phrase suggests someone was helping Goldwyn with baseball history; 1941 was indeed the season when Joe DiMaggio hit in 56 consecutive games and Ted Williams batted .406.

Gallico, Goldwyn's first hired hand to create the story, accepted the producer's dictum. Gallico, who adored the Babe and wrote often about the national pastime as a columnist for the New York *Daily News*, surrendered to Goldwyn's vision nonetheless, saying, "Baseball on the screen is dull. That's because the game is a drama in itself, with its own heroes, villains and clowns, its own conflicts and its own suspense. You can't show all that in a picture; all you can show is a long shot with little figures galloping around the diamond. So in *The Pride of the Yankees*, we treated baseball as simply one man's profession."

He added, "The game itself is incidental."

Goldwyn, who fled Poland as a teenager, alone and virtually penniless, might have felt some affinity for Gehrig, the son of German immigrants. Goldwyn said the story is "in a broad sense, the story of the opportunities that America offers every boy and of the whims with which life sometimes favors a few and then destroys them."

In another exchange about the film, Hollywood correspondent Thornton Delehanty asked Goldwyn about the diminution of baseball in *Pride*.

The exchange is bizarre, at best.

Delehanty asked: "What is there so repellent about baseball that you exclude it so rigorously from a picture purporting to be about our national pastime or am I to understand that the allusion to Yankees has to do with the aborigines who infested New England shortly after the landing of the *Mayflower*, Mr. Goldwyn?"

They parried in a way that suggested the hands of a ghost-writer and publicist at work in Goldwyn's responses:

Goldwyn: There is nothing aboriginal about this tribe or about the picture either. In fact, it is based on an unaboriginal story by Paul Gallico but hardly more than 5 percent of it has anything to do with baseball.

Delehanty (speaking with what he said was "devastating irony"): I see, you are afraid that if it should leak out that the picture had anything to do with baseball, no one would go to see it.

Goldwyn: There are fifty million people in this country who don't go to baseball games.

Delehanty: All right, then, so it's not about baseball—what's it about?

Goldwyn: That's what I've been waiting to tell you. It's the story of a young American and his struggle upward to fame. It's the story of a modest hero and his love for the woman who stands by him through his trials and triumphs. It's a love story. It's a success story. It's the kind of story that could happen only in this land of equality and opportunity. It's a tender, moving, touching romance.

No one could predict that focusing so much on Gehrig the man, his relationship with Eleanor, and the testing of their romantic bond when he faced death would work. It had elements of standard melodramatic fare, but would people care about a ballplayer and his girl? This was Goldwyn's only path; he was not persuaded by childhood sentiment for baseball. Had he seen *Knute Rockne, All American*, he would have seen the effective use of emotionally manipulative situations like the deathbed wish of the star Notre Dame running back George Gipp (Ronald Reagan) that Rockne's team "win one for the Gipper," and the mourning over Rockne (Pat O'Brien) after he dies in a plane crash. But he also would have seen too much of a reliance on scripted football action starring actors like Reagan who were well past their college-age athletic prime.

Goldwyn's gut craved commercial success, not fidelity to a sport he had no affinity for. He longed to produce movies of class, but there was a division in Hollywood about whether he had a creative impulse. Did the so-called "Goldwyn touch" really exist as an artful force, or did he simply drive artists to produce good work? The writer Alva Johnston profiled Goldwyn and concluded that his films bore certain hallmarks: "The characters are consistent; the workmanship is honest; there are no tricks and short cuts; the intelligence of the audience is never insulted."

Daniel Mandell, who edited Goldwyn films like *Wuthering Heights*, *Meet John Doe*, and *Pride*, suggested that Goldwyn's greatest skill was knowing when something onscreen was wrong. But, he said, "I never knew what the Goldwyn touch was. I think it was something a Goldwyn publicist made up."

No publicist could manufacture the depth and unintended comedy of Goldwyn's baseball ignorance, which fueled tales alleging he didn't know which direction a base runner took from home or how many bases were on a diamond.

Mankiewicz joked that Goldwyn wanted to cut the baseball rulebook standard of three strikes and four balls to two strikes and three balls.

"Can't we do that, Mank?" Goldwyn asked Mankiewicz.

"No," the screenwriter said, "I don't think that's going to work, Sam."

Walsh delightedly pointed to Goldwyn's lack of baseball bona fides a few days before filming began.

"And honest to goodness," Walsh burbled with delight to Eleanor in a lengthy letter, "you would have rolled on the floor in tears to have heard Goldwyn in his first meeting with [Bill] Dickey," Lou's closest friend and Yankee teammate:

Bill and I (also Dorothy Parker) were in Sam's office. Sam started explaining the "big scene" at [sic] end of picture when Lou will walk down the dug-out steps. Well, I give you my word of honor, Goldwyn took 20 minutes looking into Dickeys' [sic] eyes and explaining what a dugout is…what a players [sic] bench is…and a few other "secrets" Dickey has known for 20 years. And Goldwyn kept calling the Stadium the "Polo Grounds." Dickey and I never cracked a smile but he has told it to 50 people since. Sam also kept calling Dickey "Paul Dickey" and Hug [Yankees manager Miller Huggins] "Muller Higgins."

Goldwyn started life far from the American sandlots depicted in *Pride*, but his immigrant's story is remarkable, a tale of long travels, hard work, and determination told by his biographer A. Scott Berg.

Born in Poland as Schmuel Gelbfisz, Goldwyn was the eldest of six children living in Warsaw with little expectation of seeing his lot improve in the Jewish ghetto. At age sixteen, with his father dead and his relationship with his mother distant, he set out for America—walking three hundred miles to the Oder River; paying to be smuggled to Germany; walking to Hamburg, where he learned glove-making; taking a boat train to England, first to London, then to Birmingham, where he became a blacksmith's apprentice, and selling sponges before sailing from Liverpool to Canada. Briefly he found himself in Manhattan before he boarded a train to upstate Gloversville, New York, a company town north of Johnstown that dominated the United States manufacturing of gloves.

He learned to make and sell gloves, rising to sales manager of a firm that uprooted itself for New York City. One day in 1913, he recalled walking home from his office when he stepped into a nickelodeon theater and was mesmerized by a cowboy, "Bronco Billy," jumping from his horse onto a moving train. It was a revelation, he said, that "brought me into a whole new, exciting world and I wanted to be a part of it."

With an excess of ambition, arrogance, and guile, he willed himself to become one of Hollywood's shrewdest operators. As the Americanized Samuel Goldfish, he entered silent-movie production with his brother-in-law, Jesse Lasky, a mild-mannered producer and ex-vaudevillian. As their company, Famous Players-Lasky, grew, Goldfish became increasingly testy. Lasky, whose sister had by now divorced Goldfish, was deputized by their other partners to show him the door. Showing the bullheaded resilience that marked his career, he formed a new company with theatrical brothers named Selwyn. They created Goldwyn Pictures, a new corporate name carved out of pieces of theirs, and Goldfish eventually adopted Goldwyn as his new name, branding himself and leading the Selwyns to sue him. Federal judge Learned Hand ruled in favor of Goldfish-turned-Goldwyn, writing, "A self-made man may prefer a self-made name."

Goldwyn created yet another company and spotted an opportunity in providing pictures that United Artists—the superstar studio owned by Charlie Chaplin, Mary Pickford, and Douglas Fairbanks—could distribute. He made dozens of movies for the studio over nearly two decades. He amassed increasingly more power but ran afoul of them (Pickford, in particular, loathed him), and after a long boardroom fight, Goldwyn's distribution contract was canceled and he received several hundred thousand dollars to go away.

"They called me the lone wolf, and I have been called some other things," he told an interviewer, explaining his difficulties working with peers. "I had partners but I discovered I was spending more time trying to explain to them what I was doing than in making pictures."

He began anew, again, with Samuel Goldwyn Studios.

Ronald Colman, Vilma Banky, Eddie Cantor, Verna Zorina, David Niven, and Danny Kaye topped Goldwyn's marquees over Goldwyn's career.

But no Goldwyn star was bigger than a lanky Montana cowboy who came to Hollywood with the name Frank Cooper, soon to become Gary. He was a stuntman and actor in bit parts, including two with a dog, when he arrived at Goldwyn's office in 1926 and filled out a biographical card where he listed his education (three years in England and Grinnell College in Iowa), ambition (director), favorite author (Alexandre Dumas), and address (Carlos Avenue). Not much stood out except for the hobby he listed after freehand drawing: taxidermist.

There was serendipity in his move to Hollywood, which was kick-started by his father's move from Montana to Los Angeles, leaving the judicial bench for lawyering. In late 1924, he met a group of Montana cowboys who picked up extra money as stuntmen and extras in low-budget Westerns. He quickly picked up work, but it was more an accidental profession than what he had planned to do. "I had planned to do my suffering over an easel in the privacy of a garret," he wrote. "I had not planned to be an actor and make a public spectacle of my troubles." With good looks and plenty of horse-riding and stuntman skills, he caught on, and by 1926 was unexpectedly elevated from a minor role to a major one in *The Winning of Barbara Worth* when Harold Goodwin was not released in time from his role in the film *The Honeymoon Express* to play Abe Lee.

Watching a scene with the inexperienced Cooper, Goldwyn told director Henry King: "Henry, he's the greatest actor I have ever seen in my life." Before shooting a subsequent scene, where he was to die in Ronald Colman's lap, Cooper was advised by the older actor: "Easy does it, old boy. Good scenes make good actors. Actors don't make good scenes. My own feeling is that all you have to do is take a nap and every woman who sees the picture is going to cry her eyes out."

Cooper said he followed the advice, napped in Colman's lap, and nearly wept as he watched the rushes.

"How easy can acting get?" he asked himself. "I had yet to learn."

The relationship between Cooper and Goldwyn was productive but occasionally tempestuous. Cooper had a clear idea of his rising value in Hollywood during the shooting of *Barbara Worth* in the Nevada desert and let Goldwyn know it. They haggled via telegram, with Cooper demanding $200 a week to make one picture in his first year. Goldwyn's trusted aide, Abe Lehr, agreed to yearly options of $10,000, $15,000, $25,000, $40,000, and $45,000, "providing his father, who is a Los Angeles attorney, approves terms." But the terms changed in Goldwyn's favor within two weeks, and Cooper wired Goldwyn his acceptance of a $125 weekly salary and options of $9,000, $12,000, $15,000, $25,000, and $40,000.

In his telegram to "Garry Cooper," Goldwyn ordered him to sign the contract within four days of returning to Los Angeles.

A decade later, with Cooper now a major star, Goldwyn wanted him to star in his retelling of *Hans Christian Andersen*, about the Danish children's storyteller, whose possibilities as a film were starting to obsess the producer. Goldwyn was about to release another Cooper film, *The Real Glory*, an action film set in the Philippines after the Spanish-American War, when he sent Cooper a script for *Andersen*.

"I believe the possibilities of *Andersen* are enormous, providing we get the right script," he told Cooper. Cooper never made the film. Eventually, Goldwyn piled up thirty-two scripts before assigning it to Moss Hart for a musical starring Danny Kaye, a very different actor from Cooper, in 1952.

Later in 1939, Cooper rejected the script for a Goldwyn film tentatively called *Vinegaroon* (it would be renamed *The Westerner*) because his character, Cole Harden, "was still inadequate and unsatisfactory for me." He was angry that, as the putative star of the film, his role was smaller than that of Walter Brennan, who was playing the hanging judge Roy Bean. "I have a position to uphold," Cooper wrote to Goldwyn on November 18, 1939. "My professional standing has been jeopardized from the beginning." Goldwyn threatened to sue Cooper for $400,000 for expenses, then blame him for lost jobs if he didn't report for work.

Cooper reluctantly and angrily wrote to Goldwyn:

I bow to your threats, since normal reasoning and friendly relations mean little if anything to you... Your reaction serves as confirmation that my experience since the beginning of the contracts had been consistently unsettled, insecure, lacking inspiration and enthusiasm and it is, therefore, best for you to realize that our association is incompatible, holding small hope for any mutually happy solution and I fail to see how we can profitably continue this strained relationship.

He showed up on the morning he was due in Tucson and did as he was told—he was getting $150,000 a picture, regardless of the size of the part or his happiness with it. He was castigated by Alsatian-born director William Wyler, who compared him with ensemble-oriented European stars who didn't demand rewrites to beef up their modest parts into leads. Cooper admitted that the criticism made him feel "pretty small" but insisted that he was protecting his image, not being boorish. He apologized to Goldwyn, who responded with gratitude expressed in the mangled English he was known for.

"Glad to hear you feel that way, Gary," Cooper recalled the

mogul saying. "It wasn't much fun the other way. Relations were getting pretty strange."

Cooper had assessed the situation well. When the film was released in 1940, it was neither his nor Brennan's (who won his third Oscar for Best Supporting Actor for the film). Brennan had the better part. "My part is such that it cannot help but steal the spotlight," Brennan said.

That would not happen again to Cooper.

Over the next two years, during film reunions in *Meet John Doe*, *Sergeant York*, and *Pride*, Brennan's roles were subordinate to Cooper's, even in *York* as the powerful, bushy-browed Pastor Pile. "Ordinarily, I play hellers," Brennan said. "Bad ones, too. Now I find myself warning Gary Cooper that the devil has him by the shirt tails and exhorting him to wrestle him, wrestle him like he would a b'ar."

In *Pride*, he defined utter subservience to Cooper. As Sam Blake, he played several roles wrapped in an idol-worshipper: a reporter who ghostwrote Gehrig's columns, scouted Gehrig for the Yankees, introduced Lou to Eleanor, traveled in a train compartment with Lou, and accompanied Lou to the clinic where he was diagnosed with amyotrophic lateral sclerosis. He was the classic sidekick.

8

Eleanor: Defender of Lou's Legacy

ore than thirty years after Lou's death, Eleanor sent a short proposal for her autobiography to her lawyer, George Pollack. At five pages, the proposal was a first draft, a hodgepodge of topics, but it was just a taste. She promised Pollack a longer version with more details: about "a trip around the world, during which I attempt to patch up the Ruth-Gehrig feud aboard ship. Lou's biggest hold-out. Lou starring in the horse opera *Rawhide*...Never before told why he left baseball; his commissionership of parole under LaGuardia."

Then: "Decline and death."

Her proposal was tantalizing and faithful to the personality of the woman Lou fell in love with—strong-willed, candid, sarcastic, and self-aware.

The chapter "Baseball Bride" opens cinematically in the kitchen of their apartment, where she posed for photographers as the new Mrs. Lou Gehrig.

"Hold it! Just one more. Keep the pot closer to the stove.'

Click. "That's the girl." "Bend over," she wrote, describing her dutiful but reluctant assent to endure the wedding day ritual. "'Adjust the vacuum cleaner.' *Click.* 'Give us a big smile.' Smile, hell. It was my first press conference dressed to the hilt in a strange uniform called an apron. Sports writers, to this day, with this lack of imagination, descend on baseball brides. The next day's headlines screamed LOU GEHRIG WEDS. That frump on the inside page—holding the frying pan—was me."

Gehrig watched this uncomfortable "sweaty session" in their apartment "convulsed with laughter" (it is easy to see Cooper and Wright re-enacting this scene), knowing of his wife's unfamiliarity with housework and his own understanding of helping his mother at his Columbia fraternity, from cooking to delivering the laundry she did for extra money. Without a segue, Eleanor snarkily asked, "Where was Pop? He was the sporadic janitor with a great taste for beer."

Lou and Eleanor's union was one of an introvert and extrovert; a wallflower and a party gal; a poor boy and a girl whose family knew wealth for a time but lost it; a sheltered star with limited outside interests and his more worldly mate.

She became the curator of Lou's career—an adoring, sharp-tongued, candid overseer of his memory. You see her work in her book proposal, which became *My Luke and I*, written with *New York Times* reporter Joe Durso; in the interviews she did with Gallico that formed the basis of the *Pride* story; and in the scrapbooks of his career, which she donated to the Baseball Hall of Fame.

The scrapbooks were thick and meticulously maintained—and too heavy to use in *Pride*. Instead, Teresa Wright leafs through a single prop scrapbook in scenes in her house and a hotel suite. She looks at Lou's public school diploma, a picture of young Lou (Douglas Croft), a photo of Cooper uncomfortably fitted in a Columbia football uniform and headlines like "WHY THEY CALL HIM TANGLEFOOT" and "LOU GEHRIG WEDS." Wright lingers over the latter, smells a flower she once pressed into the book's pages, and glues a new article, "BASEBALL WORLD MOURNS MILLER HUGGINS, YANKEE MANAGER." Moviegoers probably didn't notice that whoever produced the scrapbook got the wrong years for a story about Ruth leaving the Yankees (1935, not 1934) and Lou becoming Yankee captain (1935, not 1936).

The prop is a far more expedient version of Eleanor's grand effort. No one watching the film would have easily recognized its other historical inaccuracies or sloppiness, since Wright only flipped to a few pages that looked their best. The articles were largely phonies unconnected to the headlines *Pride*'s camera zeroed in on.

Below the headline "REUNION WITH BABE CLIMAXES GEH-RIG TRIBUTE" are the details of a burglary. The story attached to the photo of Cooper with the headline "STARS ON COLUMBIA ELEVEN" leads into an account of electric shovels moving sand and gravel. And below a headline "DANGEROUS YANKEE LOU" is an article that starts, "If two city employees, spreading salt on icy streets from a D.P.W. truck, accidentally shovel some salt on the windshield of a passing automobile, thus obscuring the vision of the motorist and causing him to crash into another car, should the city pay the damages?"

Some of the prop work was authentic. Lou's note to Eleanor, "From Tanglefoot with love," which accompanied the roses Wright receives in the scrapbook scene, is there. So is a telegram—"AFTER SUCH A PLEASANT TIME HATED TO LEAVE. WILL MISS YOU, LOU"—that did not appear in the film.

Goldwyn was proud of the prop. In a letter to the Baseball Hall of Fame, where he agreed to donate it, he wrote, "We made the scrapbook itself an important part of the story," and "we duplicated each item and photograph telling of the progress of his career and arranging them just as they were arranged in Lou's book."

Not true, but it was good enough to get by.

Eleanor Twitchell Gehrig was the First Widow of the Yankees. There were other Yankee widows, but she was the original star widow, preceding Claire Ruth by seven years. As she aged into elderly widowhood, it was easy to forget she wasn't the frump she self-effacingly described but an attractive woman with full cheeks, an upturned nose, and a slight smile. She was slender and wore long, tailored dresses.

"Auburn-haired, brown-eyed, vivacious and urbane," wrote Ray Robinson, a Gehrig biographer, "with her hair cut in a Dutch-boy bob in the manner of the Twenties' movie star Colleen Moore, and she applied lipstick and rouge faithfully."

She was not a wallflower, either. About her Prohibition years, she wrote:

You could say I fiddled while Chicago burned. I was young and rather innocent, but I smoked, played poker, drank bathtub gin along with everybody else, collected $5 a week in allowance from my father, spent $100 a week, made up the difference from winter book jackpots at the racetrack that filled a dresser drawer with close to $10,000 at one point and learned to become a big tipper.

In her proposal, she focused on two main parts of her relationship with Lou. The first was how she broadened his cultural horizons—introducing him to opera, like Wagner's *Tristan and Isolde*, which he understood in German, orchestral music, and "books without pictures." She said that her Iron Horse, a "sensitive and even soft man," wept when she read *Anna Karenina* to him.

Second, she grasped that part of his story—which became *their* story—was coping with his mother, Christina. It was obvious to Eleanor how difficult it was for Lou to break away from a mother to whom he felt he owed so much. The umbilical cord between them was unusually strong, even steel-reinforced; she knew it had to be severed for their marriage to survive. To Eleanor, Mom was an extreme caricature of the overprotective matriarch. More like a monster.

"It was I who was to inherit as a mother-in-law this domineering, massively built, shouting, hit-below-the-belt specimen," she wrote. "The Matriarch of Baseball." She added:

Everything was over-sized; eat everything on your plate; from an overwhelming thick vegetable soup, to a suckling pig with an apple in its mouth, to a double slice of apple pie, all washed down with her strong, home brewed elderberry wine. Babe Ruth wolfed down her pickled eels between innings and she became famous for that dish alone.

She saw herself as the woman who could make up for the privations of Lou's childhood. "What he badly needed was confidence, building up," she wrote in her book. "He was absolutely anemic for kindness and warmth. He had never known closeness or close love before, and when he found it, he grew frightened to death that he might lose it. So he needed constant reassurance and I'd prop him up again and again until his next sinking spell."

She added: "This was my man, maybe my man-child, Luke."

With her book well in the future, her desire to protect Lou—and tell his story, her way—is seen vividly in her collaboration with Gallico. They worked together in San Francisco for several weeks, producing thirty-eight pages of notes that toggled between her early life and her eight married years with Lou. She talked about her frivolous youthful life of golf and horseback riding, of hanging around with older married men and being surrounded by "a number of parasites and playboys of pre-1929 gaiety." Her single life was very unlike Lou's, she wrote: "I could hold my liquor, even though I was pretty far from converting to an apprentice lush. I don't remember too many days when I missed playing eighteen holes of golf or riding horseback for an hour or two, no matter how late the party had lasted the night before."

She observed Gehrig at Comiskey Park before they met and, while taken with his good looks, rooted "like hell against him" and screamed at him to "break a leg or strike out." Reflecting on the differences between her upbringing and Lou's, she told Gallico: "There had never been any gaiety or frivolity in Lou's life before he married." Her conspicuous lack of seriousness—which competed with an interest in the works of Sigmund Freud and Thornton Wilder—contrasted with Lou's unwavering work ethic, a trait burned into his soul by Mom Gehrig.

Her Prohibition-era lark was not made to last. Her father, a politically connected concessionaire in the Chicago parks system, embarrassed his family when he was caught in a public adultery scandal. He eventually lost his catering contract and saw his real-estate holdings rapidly dissipate in value. The changing times changed her, maybe inadvertently, into the type of woman Lou would take seriously. She took a six-month business course, found a $30-a-week job as a file clerk at Saks Fifth Avenue, then rose to director of personnel by the time she lost her job in 1931. She hooked up as a secretary at the Chicago World's Fair, and it was at that time, at a friend's party, that she met Lou.

He was quietly smitten, and in most accounts walked her home afterward—he needed to be back at his hotel by curfew—but she told Gallico that she drove him to his hotel. Then she returned to the party, where her friends told her how crazy he was about her. At four a.m., she called his hotel room to say good night, but he snapped at her. "Good God, do you know what time it is?" he asked. But the next morning, she looked out her window at the World's Fair and heard him calling to her. "She ran downstairs as fast as she could to join him," Gallico wrote.

Once married, she introduced herself as Mrs. Lou Gehrig, which rankled some other Yankee wives who felt she was pushy. Tony Lazzeri's wife, Maye, recalled putting Eleanor in her place, reminding her, "Listen, Eleanor, I'm only married to Tony Lazzeri. I have nothing to do with all the home runs and the honors. I'm just lucky I've got him. And the quicker you learn you're not Lou Gehrig, the better off you're going to be."

She did have higher aspirations for Lou than other teammates' wives. He was the star of the team, with Ruth fading and then gone by 1935. She wanted Lou to make more money off the field. With help from Walsh, he had a deal to be the first athlete on a Wheaties box, and endorsed Camel cigarettes and Aqua Velva aftershave, ventures that would eventually lead to Hollywood, where he auditioned for Tarzan and a role in the Western *Rawhide*. She also shared a songwriting credit with Fred Fisher in 1935 on "I Can't Get to First Base with You"—with sheet music showing Lou in a home uniform, a cigarette in his right hand, and Eleanor, in an inset photo, in a flapper coif, looking directly at him. The song was dedicated to Lou, but it is not exactly an ode to their love, now two years into their marriage. Indeed, it ends sadly with the lyrics: "You got me crying, alibing, making me blue/I can't get to first base with you."

Eleanor was eager to talk to Gallico, not just to fulfill her contractual duties, but to give heft to his scriptwriting with information that the average fan, and maybe even Gallico, who covered the Golden Age of Sports, did not know. She may have seen participation in the film as a way to settle scores with her mother-in-law and shape Lou's posthumous image with nearly free rein.

Lou, she told Gallico, was "supersensitive" to hurtful remarks from her, and he would sulk for days before coming back to himself. She revealed that "he took a New Rochelle girl out a few times," but when he refused her request that he kiss her good night, "she accused him of being queer." He also "had a terrible fear of blackmail" from aggressive women; she told him to send designing harlots to her, and she would deal with them. In one instance, a woman named Mercedes called him and claimed that he had taken her to various cities. Babe Ruth would have invited her to his room and asked if she had a few friends. But a frightened Lou summoned twenty teammates to his hotel room, as witnesses to his fidelity. Mercedes's threat was a false alarm. She never showed up.

There were little things, too. Sometimes he spoke too loudly or was so physically playful that he hurt Eleanor's back—but in an impromptu boxing match she knocked him cold with a blow under his chin. He loved beer. He played bridge. He was a very good dancer. He read Tolstoy and Schopenhauer.

He also had a fierce temper that came out in road rage: She said he would "chase taxicabs to argue with drivers who had annoyed him" and demanded that other offending drivers get out of their cars to explain their actions to him.

And she told Gallico that Lou "seemed to have a premonition" that his life would be over at thirty-five. Tragically, he was right. He was nearly thirty-six when he was diagnosed with ALS at the Mayo Clinic.

She was furious when people described Lou as colorless; perhaps he had once been, but she felt he no longer was, not in his time with her. While still shy, he was no longer a drab little brother to Ruth. Gallico translated that perception of dullness in his first screenplay into a failure of self-confidence that flares when he is accused by a newspaper writer, ghosting for Ruth, of continuing his consecutive games streak as a ploy to get attention. The scene never advanced to subsequent scripts.

Lou: He's right I'm not good. I've been thinking about myself instead of the team—I've never been any good. I ought to get off the Yankees and let a real player take my place.

Eleanor: Don't you dare say such a thing. Don't you say those things are true. They're not! You're not a grandstand player. There isn't anybody in baseball who has his team more at heart than you have. How can you sit there and say that Babe is right and that you want to quit baseball. You're not selfish and you're not stuck-up. How can you let someone say such things about you?...You sit there and say that you're selfish yet you can hold a little boy in your arms and coax the spirit back into his body! It was you who brought the Babe to see him because you're so modest and unselfish you think of everybody and everything but yourself. Oh...you...you...big—you big slow-witted lovable idiot. You're not to let people walk over you anymore and push you around. You're sweet. You're honest, good and clean.

Do you hear me?

Eleanor tantalized Gallico with her memories of Mom Gehrig and Lou's pre-Yankee days—including a drunken bender as a minor leaguer that required a script-room showdown to eliminate from *Pride*. She brought a similarly open approach to the proposal for her book, wooing publishers with her acidic view of Gehrig's mother and her attempt to maintain her grip on her son. Eleanor recounted a visit to New York in 1933 after she and Lou were engaged. Eleanor soon wanted to flee.

"Mom started to plan our honeymoon" and "counted herself in," she wrote. There were "endless bickerings"—in German—and a jabbering parrot that irked her. She tried to end the engagement: "Lou cried, I cried, Mom yelled, Pop slipped into a far corner and the parrot joined in. Mom suddenly put her hand to her head and wobbled. 'It was the changes,' she said. I jumped into my car bound for a friend's house in Long Island, and Lou followed. I stayed there for the remainder of my visit, and Lou was a daily visitor. We found an apartment in New Rochelle."

Eleanor's harshest comments to Gallico about Mom never found their way near the film. The romantic, uplifting tone of *Pride* would not allow for her characterizations of Gehrig family dysfunction to advance beyond Mom's dual disapprovals of Lou's desire to play baseball and of his choice of Eleanor. Eleanor vented to Gallico, presenting a portrait of a toxic household that perhaps only a strong-willed wife, like her, could help poor, meek Lou to escape.

"Lou was raised in an atmosphere of abuse and hatred," Gallico wrote after talking to Eleanor. "Father had no understanding of raising a sensitive son. All disputes were settled with a smacking blow of the hand. Never had any real affection from his parents." Later, Gallico wrote: "When Lou told his mother that his wife came before his mother, she couldn't understand it. It festered in her mind that Eleanor was the cause of it—a smoldering hate which still exists."

Gallico created a scene that fell well short of that rancor but suggested that Lou was in the middle of a love triangle that had one too many people in it.

Mom: You like Mama's cooking, don't you, Lou?

Lou: You bet I do, Mom. Nobody in the world can cook like you.

Mom: Lou wouldn't be happy if he didn't have my pickled eels and rostbraten und dumplings.

Lou: Maybe you can teach Eleanor some of those things, Mom. Mom's famous for her pickled eels. All the boys come here to eat them. They think it helps their hitting.

Eleanor: Lou told me about your wonderful parties, Mrs. Gehrig. And how close you've been to him.

Lou: Mom's been a pal to me. I've always told the newspaper boys she was my sweetheart, haven't I, Mom?

Lou: Boy, wait 'til they find out I've got a new sweetheart. [Mom picks up her head sharply, but says nothing; Eleanor looks concerned.]

In another scene that could have been dictated by Eleanor but didn't survive to *Pride*, the couple breaks up and Lou walks disconsolately to Mom's house.

Mom: Lou, she ain't the kind of girl you ought to have anyway. Mit her ideas, und a servant in the house—und she can't cook neither! Vot you get iss a gut substantial girl, Lou, somebody who will—

Lou [cuts her off]: All right, Mom, I know. I know.

Eleanor won the battle for Lou but was not free of Mom Gehrig until the older woman died in 1954. Before that, she saw Lou's will bequeath his parents $205 a month, only to get into a squabble with them over the estate that troubled her almost from the moment she signed the deal to make *Pride*.

"I am down here nursing the worst heartbreak a woman will ever have to bear," she wrote her lawyer, Milton Eisenberg, after an intermediary for Mom and Pop Gehrig demanded additional money, "but there are certain limits to what I will accept from trouble makers." Eisenberg suggested offering the Gehrigs $1,000 to $1,500 for cooperating with the movie but told Eleanor that Mom and Pop could be threatened with having their assets frozen because they were German subjects at a time when Nazis were trampling Europe.

Eventually, the elder Gehrigs sued over the distribution of Lou's estate. They were seeking almost $5,200 and interest, and settled out of court.

The serious Gehrig family discord—the loathing between Eleanor and Mom that began so soon in their relationship—found its way into *Pride*, but not in such sober or legal terms. The two Mrs.

Gehrigs would fight over Lou, and over home furnishings, but their squabbles were softened and whitewashed.

And all the fights were instigated by grim-looking Mom—a perfect setup to make the young and beautiful Teresa Wright a sympathetic Eleanor.

Years later, Eleanor expressed her comfort with being Mrs. Lou Gehrig.

"I had the best of it," she wrote. "I would not have traded two minutes of my life with that man for forty years with another."

9

Teresa Wright Will Not Do Cheesecake!

Teresa Wright's odyssey as Eleanor began with a telegram.

On January 19, 1942, a wire arrived at Eleanor's home in the Bronx carrying news: Teresa Wright would be playing her in *The Pride of the Yankees*.

"WANT YOU TO BE THE FIRST TO KNOW THAT T.W. HAS BEEN SELECTED TO PORTRAY YOU AFTER VERY CONVINCING TESTS," wrote William Hebert, Samuel Goldwyn's aggressive and creative publicity chief.

Wright was quickly becoming a major star: Her first movie role, in *The Little Foxes*, brought her an Oscar nomination for Best Supporting Actress; her second role, in *Mrs. Miniver*, which she had just wrapped, would earn her another in the same category. Now signed to play Eleanor in *The Pride of the Yankees*, the twenty-three-year-old Wright was moving into rare company, shifting from supporting roles to co-starring opposite Gary Cooper, one of Hollywood's elite actors.

"I don't believe anyone is surprised that Teresa Wright has been selected by Sam Goldwyn to play Mrs. Lou Gehrig," gossip queen Louella Parsons wrote. "It was in the bag, so to speak, days ago—just as Gary Cooper was chosen long before the public announcement was made."

A Hollywood career was not Muriel Teresa Wright's intended career path. Her upbringing presaged a troubled, psychologically compromised future.

Her father, Arthur, was a traveling insurance salesman. Her mother, Martha, was a prostitute who had sex with men while her daughter was in their apartment, wrote Wright's biographer, Donald Spoto. Her parents may never have been married. But her father had the good sense to take Muriel from the house and send her to live with friends in New Jersey, later enrolling her in boarding school and supporting her financially. Eventually, her mother faded from her life.

Wright started acting in school and coveted an onstage life like Helen Hayes's. At eighteen, she watched Hayes play the title role in *Victoria Regina* on Broadway and was further inspired. She performed in high school and two summers at the nonprofit Wharf Theatre in Provincetown, Massachusetts, advancing her ambitions—until they hit overdrive with an invitation to meet the cast backstage at the original Broadway production of Thornton Wilder's *Our Town*. It wasn't long before nineteen-year-old Muriel—she soon dropped her first name to avoid confusion with a Muriel Wright in Actors' Equity—was understudying the Emily Webb role in the play, then going out on the national tour.

In late 1939, shortly after she turned twenty-one, she took the stage at the Empire Theater as Mary Skinner in the Clarence

Day comedy *Life with Father,* which would run for more than 3,000 performances—straight through World War II. *New York Times* drama critic Brooks Atkinson said that she "plays a young lady with uncommon charm as a person and willowy skill as an actress."

Soon after *Life* opened, Katharine Hepburn congratulated Wright backstage at the Empire Theater and suggested that she would be ideal to play the leading lady in *The Outlaw,* which was being produced and directed by her friend Howard Hughes, according to Spoto.

Wright, bent on a theatrical career, told Hepburn: "Oh, I couldn't. I don't want to make movies. I want to be a legitimate actress." The role went to Jane Russell, who wore a specially designed cantilevered bra to best showcase her breasts. Wright stayed with the play for two years, through more than six hundred performances, afraid to take a day off or leave for a vacation.

"Everyone else did but I was sure that if I took a vacation and stopped saying the words, I'd never be able to go on saying them again," she said.

Late in her two-year stint as Mary Skinner, *The Little Foxes* playwright, Lillian Hellman, stopped by on a scouting mission for Goldwyn to find an actress to play Alexandra Giddens, the seventeen-year-old daughter of Regina Giddens, who was being played by Bette Davis in the proposed film. Hellman was impressed with Wright's performance and told Goldwyn, who flew to New York. Goldwyn waited for Wright to return to her dressing room after the cast took its curtain calls and recalled: "I had discovered in her from the first sight, you might say, an unaffected genuineness and appeal."

He signed her immediately to a contract for $500 a week, for the first forty weeks of her employment, which covered *The Little*

Foxes. When the long-term option kicked in, her weekly pay escalated annually to $750, $1,000, $1,500, $2,250, and $3,000. Years later, in an oral history interview at Columbia University, she said that she had other offers in addition to Goldwyn's.

"I wasn't interested in any of them, but I was interested in this part," she said. She passed her screen test, returned to *Life with Father* for a little while, then filmed *Foxes* with Davis, Herbert Marshall, and Richard Carlson, and directed by William Wyler, who elicited great performances out of Davis.

During a break in filming, Davis implored a reporter to meet Wright.

"And don't mind if she twists her fingers," she said. "She's nervous."

Indeed, Donald Hough of the *Los Angeles Times* found her in a black evening dress, doing a costume test. Wright was smiling, Hough wrote, "But it was a nervous smile. One corner of her mouth kept twitching a little. I did not look at her hands, but I knew what she was doing. She was twisting her fingers. I glanced down and saw that her knuckles were white." When Hough told her that Davis thought she was a fine actor, Wright said, "She didn't say anything like that!"

He further assessed her state of mind, writing: "Miss Wright was—and is—more wistful than forward, more doubtful of herself than sure. Her class at one of the schools she attended voted her least likely to succeed."

Goldwyn was often smitten with young actresses and lavished great attention on them. He watched Wright closely during the filming. One day, he called out an instruction to her from behind the camera to persuade her to loosen up. A. Scott Berg wrote in *Goldwyn*, his biography of the producer.

"Teresa," Goldwyn exhorted her, "let your breasts flow in the breeze."

Little Foxes over, Wright worked with Wyler again on *Mrs. Miniver*, a story about an English family trying to survive the early days of World War II in a rural English village. Wyler, one of the best directors in Hollywood (whose credits included *Wuthering Heights* and *Dodsworth*), worked deliberately, like a stage director, which appealed to Wright. Wyler also worked with cinematographer Gregg Toland, whose deep-focus camera innovations were seen in *Citizen Kane*.

"Wyler was the first one out there, so far as I know, really to use a certain amount of stage technique to doing a film," she said in the oral history at Columbia. "He would rehearse for two weeks, which is unheard of in most places. He knew by the time we got there exactly what he wanted from us in the ways of performances, and we knew, too, what he wanted."

Wright played Carol Beldon in *Mrs. Miniver*, who marries Vin, the son of Kay Miniver (Greer Garson). Goldwyn had lent Wright to MGM for the film but *Variety*'s review reminded him of Wright's broadening appeal.

"Miss Wright," the trade magazine wrote, "has many of the fine screen characteristics of Miss Garson and will undoubtedly prove b.o. gold to Samuel Goldwyn, to whom she is under contract."

Playing Eleanor in *Pride* elevated Wright to a new level. She was now a co-star, although Cooper's fame and experience eclipsed hers. She was nearly twenty years younger than Cooper, about a foot shorter (remedied in part by her wearing high heels to bridge their height difference), and possibly more ignorant of baseball.

"I never knew anything about baseball and never cared," she said.

Goldwyn was willing to play that up.

"If you queried Miss Wright carefully," studio publicity offered as a story peg, "you would probably discover that she thinks they play polo in the Polo Grounds in New York. Such is the power of illusion." If William Hebert had asked Goldwyn the same question, the answer would likely have been similarly erroneous.

Wright was a year into her Hollywood career and, while critically acclaimed, was not well known. Being in *Pride* was an assurance that that would change. Her intelligence and reverence for the stage probably made her cringe at the sort of silliness published in one of Hollywood gossip Sidney Skolsky's columns: "She despises bananas...She reads all the time and eats all the time. She constantly chews on a candy bar or a piece of fruit but never puts any weight on...She wrinkles her nose when she smiles, has dimples, walks with her toes pointed in and likes to keep her hands in her pockets."

Hebert put out word about Cooper's kissing, with comments from Wright and Virginia Gilmore, who plays flirty Myrna at *Pride's* fraternity dance. "As a woo pitcher," the release said, "Cooper is reported to be a better first baseman."

In Cooper's assessment of Wright as an actor, he sounded a small note of 1940s-era condescension: "This little girl's a natural and even though she's been in Hollywood a year, she has it all over most actresses who've been here ten years."

Hebert, upping the ante, reminded reporters that Wright had twenty-eight changes of costume in *Pride*, eight more than Vivien Leigh had in *Gone with the Wind*.

Wright was happy to puncture expectations that she would do anything more than basic publicity about her films for Goldwyn. Studio moguls loved to turn their female stars into sex symbols in low-cut dresses or bathing suits. Glam was an essential tool in the Hollywood marketing machine, but Wright wanted nothing of it. In her contract with Goldwyn she inserted a clause that guaranteed that she would not let the studio exploit her—an early feminist stance that Goldwyn grudgingly accepted.

In her original, anti-cheesecake language, the clause read:

I will not pose for publicity photographs in a bathing suit—unless I'm doing a water scene in a picture. I will not be photographed on the beach with my hair flying in the wind, holding aloft a beach ball. I will not pose in shorts, playing with a cute cocker spaniel. I will not be shown happily whipping up a meal for a huge family. I will not be dressed in firecrackers for the Fourth of July. I will not look insinuatingly at a turkey on Thanksgiving. I will not wear a bunny cap with long ears for Easter. I will not twinkle for the camera on prop snow in a skiing outfit, while a fan blows my scarf. And I will not assume an athletic stance while pretending to hit something or other with a bow and arrow.

Wright's bathing suit scene in *Pride* was sanctioned by this being a scripted scene, not a publicity shot. She and Cooper wrestle playfully on a beach during spring training as others look on, including a black extra, one of the few African-Americans in the cast. Wrestling was the most physical part of their onscreen story and this scene, which is hardly salacious, sends them into fits of giggling on the sand brought in to simulate a beach on a soundstage. Cooper pins Wright and out of nowhere, Brennan's Sam Blake darts into the shot, wearing business clothes, and raises Cooper's left arm in victory.

"The winner!" he declares. "Not only that, you just handed

me my next story on a silver platter, 'How I Beat My Wife,' by Lou Gehrig."

Cooper, showing Gehrig's newfound confidence as a happily married man, says "Nix" to the story proposal and tells his side-kick to lay off his private life.

While she and Cooper are lying prone together, Wright is struck warmly by how he shielded their lives from Brennan's intrusion and deflects any regret that they've never honeymooned.

Stroking his arm softly, she says, "We've never had anything else."

It is one of the most romantic, genuine scenes in the film.

The mores of the time did not prevent *Collier's* magazine from spending the first few paragraphs of a profile on the fact that Wright's stockings were usually wrinkled around her ankles; how a bellhop in Detroit left her a note after a performance of *Our Town* praising her personal appearance save for her stockings bunching up and how Wright had done nothing about it. Writer Kyle Crichton's verdict: "It must be the contour of the Wright limb." In view of the frumpiness caused by her serially wrinkled hose, the writer noted that her employment by Goldwyn "is in the nature of a phenomenon" because of the producer's "atten-dance at the altar of glamour."

Goldwyn's only excuse for tolerating Wright's poor stocking maintenance?

"She is an actress," Crichton added.

Wright's screen persona was fixed as an intelligent, pretty, blue-eyed girl-next-door who could hold her own against Bette Davis, Greer Garson, and, as audiences would learn, Cooper. Their chemistry is at the center of *Pride*—a traditional romantic couple in a 1940s film but a joining of screen equals: Cooper, the big star, playing a quiet man with dignity, and Wright, portraying a loving girlfriend and wife with a sense of humor and flashes of willfulness. As the Hollywood biographer Scott Eyman said: "She incarnated a domestic radiance."

Her job, if not easy, was simpler than Cooper's: He not only had to incarnate Gehrig, but learn to play baseball for the first time in his life.

10

Becoming Lou: Cooper Learns to Play Baseball

Major League Baseball was still years from arriving in California when *The Pride of the Yankees* began filming in early February of 1942 at Wrigley Field. The hometown Angels played in the Pacific Coast League, a successful and potent minor league with eight teams along the West Coast, from San Diego north to Seattle, and superstar alumni like Joe DiMaggio and Ted Williams. With *Pride* shooting at Wrigley, the baseball season was starting early in Los Angeles for the Angels and their local rivals, the Hollywood Stars, immediately transforming the atmosphere. There was Cooper, a movie star at the zenith of his popularity, in his slightly baggy Yankee uniform. And there was Babe Ruth, happy for a return to the spotlight that shone brightest when he hit 60 home runs in 1927, when he also filmed *Babe Comes Home* on the same field.

The Angels were, for now, an afterthought. They were coming

off a losing season in 1941 and were still a few weeks from starting spring training an hour east in Ontario, California. Their roster was packed with future Major Leaguers like Peanuts Lowrey and Eddie Waitkus—whose career was interrupted in 1949 when a deranged young woman shot him in a Chicago hotel room, an incident that apparently inspired a scene in Bernard Malamud's novel *The Natural* and the 1984 film based on it. Fay Thomas, who pitched without distinction for the 1941 Angels, was cast as Christy Mathewson in *Pride,* but his role didn't make it to the final cut or wasn't filmed at all.

On his first day at Wrigley, Cooper filmed scenes largely invented to describe Gehrig's first game with the Yankees in 1925. In one, he is too tongue-tied to speak to Ruth when the Bambino asks him for a ball that has bounced his way ("Come on, son, give me the ball—would you give me the ball?"); in the second, he waves his glove to acknowledge Blake, who is watching from the press box; and in a third, he listens intently to manager Miller Huggins (played by Ernie Adams, whose gauntness matched Huggins's) tell him to keep his eye on the defensive skills of first baseman Wally Pipp. Behind Adams and Cooper, thousands of extras filled all the seats in the camera's line of sight.

Sitting upstairs in Wrigley, Elsa Janssen (Mom Gehrig) scanned the field for Cooper as he emerged from the dugout and into foul territory, and asked Ludwig Stossel, playing Pop, why there were "pillows" on the field.

"They are bases," Stossel says. "You slide into them."

"I slide into them?" Janssen asks, still chagrined at Lou's occupation.

"Just watch, Mama," he says, sucking on his cigar. "Just watch."

On a gloomy day a few days later in February, shooting moved inside, to Stage 3 at the Goldwyn studio, for a scene in the Yankees clubhouse, where a starstruck Cooper enters and slowly moves from one locker to another, seeing Ruth's name, then Mark Koenig's, Bob Meusel's, and Tony Lazzeri's before coming upon his own, written in a script that suggested his newness among the big-name veterans. (A small faux pas: Lazzeri did not join the team until 1926, the season after the one depicted.) Lou's quiet time is interrupted by the boisterous entrance of the players, the last of them Ruth.

Before the first take on the set at Stage 3 of the Goldwyn studio, Sam Wood instructed Ruth on the handling of one of his favorite foods.

"Now, in the first scene, you walk into the dressing room gulping a hot dog," says Wood, "because everyone remembers how you used to love 'em."

"Gee," says Ruth, who had, for years, famously overindulged on cooked sausages. "My wife won't let me eat 'em." He then ate five before the first take.

He hadn't lost his zest for them, chomping on a dog for the camera as he responds to a teammate's question about whether he has hit 38 or 39 home runs.

"Don't know," he said. "But I'll hit 'em and you count 'em."

Cooper silently looks on, his eyes wide, gobsmacked in Ruth's presence, a goofy, almost beatific smile on his face. His Yankee uniform—white flannel with pinstripes—looks fresh. His Yankee cap, although blue, appears a stark black with the interlocking NY contrasting in white. From this first shot of Cooper as a Yankee, the plan by production designer William Cameron Menzies to showcase Cooper crystallizes: Cooper had to look heroic, maybe even angelic.

"When Cooper is in uniform it will always be a clean, white one," he said. "All will tend to glorify the man, Gehrig, in the eyes of the audience—and yet the audience won't realize that the lighting, the mood and the general design of the production have all been worked out in advance to make them think and feel the way they do." He went even further: "Gehrig was not just a great first baseman—he was a great American—and everything I have done in designing the production was intended to point up this fact."

The Pride of the Yankees—produced by a man, Goldwyn, who knew nothing about baseball, starring a man, Cooper, who had never played baseball, and shot by a cinematographer, Rudolph Mate, who was also new to baseball—would portray baseball as a bright and shining sport. In the early 1940s, that wasn't far from a broad truth. Baseball was still the undisputed national pastime, although the Majors excluded African-Americans until 1947, when Jackie Robinson broke the color barrier with the Brooklyn Dodgers.

The Yankees, thanks to Gehrig, Ruth, and DiMaggio, and the architectural gigantism of Yankee Stadium, were the premier franchise in baseball and probably in all sports. Pro football was two decades from challenging the hegemony of baseball. DiMaggio, Ted Williams, Hank Greenberg, and Bob Feller were extending baseball's hold on fans from the superstars of the 1920s and 1930s.

One of *Pride's* goals was to idealize baseball—even while showing relatively little of it—through its worshipful treatment of Gehrig. Goldwyn himself had become so enamored of the Gehrig story that, through the magic of movie publicity, he retroactively pronounced himself a baseball fan who had waited a dozen years to make *Pride*—well before Gehrig's marriage and illness, the life events that made Gehrig filmworthy. Once invested in *Pride*, Goldwyn understood that the film could not be ignorant about baseball, that however few the baseball sequences, they had to look reasonably authentic.

The quest for authenticity began the previous fall. On September 22, 1941, second unit director Arthur Rosson took a film crew to Comiskey Park in Chicago, home of the White Sox, the favored team of Eleanor Gehrig, a daughter of Chicago. While only the ballpark's brick exterior would be shown in *Pride*, interior footage was likely needed as reference for the matte painters who re-created the look of the distant outfield and faraway seats of the Comiskey grandstand.

The cameramen spent three days at Comiskey before heading east to New York City, where Rosson and Jim Mulvey, Goldwyn's top aide, scouted for a ballpark in Brooklyn that could double for Comiskey. They found only Ebbets Field and a lot of sandlots that looked nothing like Comiskey.

Then it was off to Yankee Stadium to film the first two games of the World Series between the Yankees and Brooklyn Dodgers, their first meeting in the Fall Classic. There were more than 66,000 fans attending each game in the Bronx, and the four cameramen brought back crowd shots that were used sparingly in *Pride*, nearly all interspersed in scenes that were set at other stadiums. Inconsistencies like that mattered little back then. Reasonable authenticity was the goal, but absolute fidelity to baseball truths was not. Few if any people had the inclination or equipment to parse these scenes to locate the fraying seams and inaccuracies in the contrived reality.

The next stop for the crew was Ebbets Field for at least one of the three remaining games of the World Series that the Yankees would win in five. What they shot apparently did not get into *Pride*—and they would certainly have had no reason to use footage they might have shot of Dodger catcher Mickey Owen's famous fumbled third strike in Game 4 that would lead to the Yankees' victory.

Rosson's group made one more notable stop while they were in New York, at Columbia University, where Gehrig played baseball and football. Over two days, they shot outside Low Memorial Library, with its statue of Alma Mater, which became the establishing shot of the sequence at the school; the Journalism Building; the Sigma Chi fraternity house; and South Field, the stadium on the campus in Morningside Heights where the Lions baseball team played through the 1923 season before moving uptown to the capacious Baker Field.

"On old South Field," the *Columbia Spectator* wrote, "'The Iron Horse' will be seen hitting the longest home run in the history of Columbia baseball, a blast that soared from the plate, which was then located where the tennis court is now situated, over the stands in center field, hitting the steps of Journalism on the fly."

A home run by Gehrig on May 19, 1923, was described by the *New York Times* as the longest home run ever bashed at South Field—and may have been the one the film wanted to depict. It "rose gently until it was above the border of the infield and outfield," the article said, "then sailed on a straight line over the entire field fence into the small campus surrounding the School of Journalism building."

Rosson, an Englishman who led a second unit on *Gone with the Wind*, told the student paper: "We're taking these shots now since we intend to superimpose the main action to be filmed later against these true backgrounds. It would have been impossible to bring the actors and actresses to the campus."

The film did not re-create any of Gehrig's Columbia homers; while it showed Cooper swinging a bat, the destination of any balls was left to the imagination. An overhead shot of South Field was superimposed in a scene with Sam Blake and the Columbia football coach in the foreground when a ball "hit" by Cooper smashed through a school window. Several Columbia buildings, and a flagpole, were visible in the background behind Cooper as he took a couple of swings for Brennan.

Working at Wrigley was not new to Cooper. The ballpark was the location for the chaotic rally at the end of *Meet John Doe*, where Cooper's character, Long John Willoughby, an inadvertent populist hero to Depression-era masses, was to expose his former patron, the manipulative publisher D. B. Norton, who instead denounces Willoughby as a fake. Wrigley was unrecognizable as a ballpark after being transformed into the equivalent of an outdoor political convention with sprinklers suggesting a rainy nighttime spectacle.

Now, two years later, Wrigley was a backdrop for baseball, a sport that was not a passion for Cooper, though it was not a subject entirely alien to him. In 1939, he joined other investors, many of them celebrated stars, in buying the Hollywood Stars in time for their move into newly built Gilmore Field. Stars, indeed, owned the Stars. Led by Robert Cobb, the owner of the Brown Derby restaurant (where the Cobb salad was said to be invented), the group included Bing Crosby, a future part-owner of the Pittsburgh Pirates; Jack Benny; Cecil B. DeMille; Robert Taylor; and Walt Disney, whose company would in the distant future acquire the Angels long after they were a Major League franchise. Nearly two decades earlier, another Hollywood star, Fatty Arbuckle, bought control of the Vernon Tigers, another PCL team, and owned it for a year before his career unraveled in a sordid rape-and-murder scandal.

Cooper, who brought rectitude to his roles, was scheduled to catch co-owner Robert Taylor's ceremonial first pitch on the opening day of the ballpark that March in an exhibition game against the Chicago White Sox. But he could not because the filming of *Beau Geste* kept him busy at Paramount. We do not know, without the tutoring he would receive to play Gehrig, if he knew how to catch a ball or was going to wear a catcher's mitt.

His daughter, Maria, recalled attending games with her parents at Gilmore Field but was unaware if her father's involvement with the team was anything but passive. "He loved sports—boxing, tennis, golf, skiing," she said. "And I would assume, given their friends and their interests at the time, also baseball."

By playing Gehrig, Cooper was much further invested in baseball than as the owner of a sliver of a minor-league team. He knew he could mold a fictional character to his personality—but could he turn Gehrig into a role fans would accept, with Gehrig's image still so clear to them? At Wrigley he stood out as a novice among old pros and young players who could perform as he could not. His inability to play baseball made him vulnerable to the sort of criticism that he had been inoculated from by portraying fictional characters or historical figures, like Marco Polo, who were not contemporary.

He was in the midst of a hot streak playing characters that he felt comfortable with. *Doe* was followed by *Sergeant York*, in which Cooper played the Medal of Honor–winning World War I hero Alvin C. York, whose fame peaked a quarter century before and who was not as recognizable to Americans as Gehrig. Then, Cooper shifted to screwball comedy in *Ball of Fire*, where he played a reserved scholar toiling on a slang encyclopedia with seven brilliant eccentrics who gets mixed up with a slang-spewing stripper (Barbara Stanwyck, his co-star in *Doe*) and mobsters (one of them, Dana Andrews, was considered for the role of Bill Dickey).

Now, as Cooper attempted to meld his screen personality to the Gehrig character, he could not know if his one glaring and undeveloped deficiency, playing baseball, would be a hindrance to *Pride*. He would be tested at Wrigley, a million-dollar stadium built by chewing-gum magnate William K. Wrigley, Jr., who owned the Chicago Cubs and the Los Angeles Angels, the Cubs' top minor-league club.

This was the *other* Wrigley—not to be confused with the one in Chicago, where the Cubs were on the verge of a thirty-fifth season since last winning a World Series. This newer Wrigley was for a time considered a modestly grand ballpark with its Art Deco design; red-roofed, double-decked grandstand; fifteen-foot concrete wall in left field where ivy grew; and a clock tower at its entrance.

"NEW DIAMOND, BUILT BY GUM, IS PERFECT," the *Los Angeles Times* cooed when it opened in 1925, near the end of the seven-month PCL season. "Big league baseball with big business trimmings was dished up for the fans yesterday in Mr. Wrigley's new steel and concrete home-run dispensary on South Park Avenue," the paper wrote after four homers were hit in the Angels' 10–8 win over the Seals, one by Paul Waner, a future Hall of Famer nicknamed "Big Poison."

Cooper, a sophisticated man who was one of the highest-paid actors in Hollywood, may not have been overwhelmed by the unfamiliar surroundings, but he nonetheless fretted over whether he could play the sport even for the modest amount of time required by the script. Anything outside Yankee pinstripes would be easy and familiar: romantic scenes with Teresa Wright or those where he tried to break away from overbearing Mom Gehrig. But Cooper had no natural baseball IQ. His scene as a pitcher-turned-hobo in *Doe*—in which his chronically painful right shoulder made his motion awkward when he fired imaginary pitches to Brennan, his unshaven sidekick—impressed no one.

Cooper's athleticism was embodied in being a skilled horseman, a talent natural to his upbringing in Montana. In silent movies, he was a trick rider who specialized in falling off horses despite a hip that had been broken, but never set, after a car accident when he was a teenager. He needed help that he could not find in the script. It wasn't a baseball movie, but Cooper needed to learn enough baseball to be credible with a bat or glove in his hands.

He could not wear Gehrig's number four and play like a klutz.

So in the six weeks leading up to the filming, he took classes in batting, fielding, throwing, and sliding from Lefty O'Doul, a former National League batting champion who was managing the San Francisco Seals, a rival of the Angels in the mighty PCL. If O'Doul's tutelage didn't pay off, Cooper would likely embarrass himself and hurt box office receipts if baseball fans shunned *Pride*. While the bar may not have been set very high for actors playing athletes in the early 1940s, Cooper had to show reasonable competence on the field. Some critics were still raising their doubts about Cooper's baseball competence, perhaps to demonstrate their loyalty to Gehrig's memory. The Tinseltown gossip columnist Jimmie Fidler wrote, without showing proof: "Baseball fans and writers are protesting Gary Cooper as Lou Gehrig on the screen because Lou was left-handed and Gary isn't."

Cooper's lack of affinity for playing baseball came naturally. During three of his formative years out west, his parents

sent him and his older brother, Arthur, to live in England, to learn to become young gentlemen and cast off the wildness of their Montana boyhood; he returned at age twelve. "When I came back to Montana, the other kids were so far ahead of me at playing ball, I just never got started and stuck to football and track instead," Cooper recalled. Helena was also 1,500 miles west of St. Louis, Major League Baseball's westernmost market, making it inaccessible to Cooper in the time before radio unified the nation.

Cooper tried to be diligent even when he and O'Doul were apart. At a dinner party at his house with Jack Benny; his wife, Mary Livingstone; and the stars Barbara Stanwyck and Robert Taylor, who were married to each other, Cooper picked up a glass ashtray and tossed it from his left hand to his right, then returned it to his left.

"Do it all the time from force of habit," he told writer Harry Evans, who was one of the guests. "Have to practice throwing with my left hand."

O'Doul, the benefactor of that persistence, was suited to play the coach of a Hollywood star. He loved the limelight—and he loved hitting. "When I was playing ball in the big leagues my bats would be jumping up and down in the trunk," he said. "Couldn't wait to get to the ball park and grab that bat. Big crowd, sock a triple, nothing like it! Maybe I was a ham. What's the use of doing something when nobody's looking. But a packed ballpark, crowd roaring, the guy throws you a great breaking curve, you hit it on the nose and drive it over the outfielder's head. What a thrill!"

Frank Joseph O'Doul, whose memorable wardrobe earned him the nickname "The Man in the Green Suit," started as a pitcher for the Yankees but was never very good at it. One day, with his arm injured, he announced to his Salt Lake City Bees minor-league manager, "I am now an outfielder," and so became a prolific left-handed hitter who finished his Major League career with a .349 batting average, the fourth-best in baseball history. He did not have enough great years to be elected to the Baseball Hall of Fame, but in a span of four seasons, he hit .398, .383, and .368. In that in-between year, he hit .336.

"If I had to do it all over," he said, "I'd be a ballplayer again without pay. Yeah, without pay. I loved it. That's why I never squawked when I didn't get big salaries. I liked to play too much."

Cooper presented an unusual challenge for O'Doul, who adeptly schooled minor leaguers in the Pacific Coast League and players in Japan during trips to the country in the years before and after World War II. He is credited with giving the Tokyo Giants their name and helping to create the first Japanese baseball league.

Now came Cooper, a dapper six-foot-two-inch cowboy with a bum hip, a right arm he couldn't raise above his shoulder, and no sandlot games in his childhood. O'Doul's mission was not just to teach him baseball in a few weeks but to turn the right-handed actor into a decent left-handed facsimile of Henry Louis Gehrig.

"No mean feat in itself," Cooper said.

Perhaps Cooper's ignorance of how to play baseball worked in his favor when O'Doul began his classes. He did not have to alter any bad habits because he had none, save for his poor throwing in *Meet John Doe*. But among all the skills in sports, hitting a round ball with a long, cylindrical bat is the hardest—harder still if you're a right-hander learning from scratch and trying to imitate one of the greatest left-handed players ever. Greatness was not an option for Cooper.

Mediocrity was a reasonable goal.

"If that Cooper doesn't get in there and play ball like Gehrig," O'Doul said, probably overstating his worries, "I'm going to be in the doghouse for sure."

After seeing Cooper throw, O'Doul's verdict was sharp and negative.

"You throw a ball like an old woman tossing a hot biscuit," O'Doul said.

O'Doul could not have been thrilled to watch Cooper hit, either. He had no muscle memory for hitting and none of the hand-eye coordination that is critical to making contact with a ball. But O'Doul developed a plan, maybe just for Cooper specifically or perhaps adapted from how he helped his players recover from slumps.

The lessons took place mostly behind Cooper's Brentwood mansion before the filming of *Pride* began—a luxurious spring training site where the neighbors were Tyrone Power, Cesar Romero, Frank Capra, William Wellman, Van Johnson, and film editor J. Watson Webb, an heir to the Vanderbilt and Havemeyer fortunes.

Cooper learned to throw left-handed by tossing pebbles, then larger rocks, before graduating to baseballs. O'Doul had him bowl and hit a boxer's speed bag with his left hand. For hitting, O'Doul reasoned the batting stroke was close enough to chopping wood, so he instructed Cooper to hit by comparing the action of a Louisville Slugger to that of an axe. Fortunately, the right-handed Cooper chopped wood naturally from his left side. Photographs show O'Doul taking Cooper through his wood-chopping/batting lessons while attired in forties Hollywood casual: collared shirts, sweaters tucked into high-waisted trousers, and dress shoes.

O'Doul did not expect to turn Cooper into a Major Leaguer, but he joked, "We'll make him look like one for the camera or I'll break his arm."

O'Doul brought his sessions to the ski resort in Sun Valley, Idaho, where the Coopers had a home in what had become a fashionable getaway for celebrities like Ernest Hemingway, Cooper's closest friend, and Clark Gable. In late January, the weather was so warm they trained on a patch of ground clear of snow. One day, O'Doul said, "A bunch of soldiers showed up. One of them, a sergeant, came over to Gary and saluted. 'From one sergeant to another, Sergeant York.'"

The studio saw the Cooper-O'Doul sessions as promotable fodder, one of many aspects of the production that were enthusiastically hyped by William Hebert, Goldwyn's crafty publicity chief. Some releases were fanciful, some were based on verifiable fact, and some were a hybrid of both. Describing the first day of filming at Wrigley, Hebert wrote that a microscope would be required to see the differences between the transformed ballpark and Yankee Stadium (an exaggeration, given the differences in size and design, and the movie magic that was yet to occur).

Hebert played up the notion that Cooper was learning baseball from scratch. It was a great hook for a publicist seeking every drop of ink he could get. All red-blooded American boys and men in love with the national pastime knew how hard it was to play baseball, let alone convert all hitting, throwing, and catching from one's natural side to the other one. The arduous task of turning a star of Cooper's magnitude into a left-handed copy of Gehrig almost defined the hero's journey, at least in Hollywood. Wrote Hebert: "Cooper attempts a form of mimicry infinitely more difficult than anything he has to do as an actor."

Rousing success in the Great Cooper Experiment was declared in a yarn discovered in Hebert's fat publicity file for *Pride*, which detailed an astonishing occurrence at 11940 Chaparal Street when a titanic clout flew out of Gary and his wife Rocky's estate. It was more than Ruthian or Gehrigesque. It was Bunyan-like.

"Presently up the walk of the Tyrone Power home came a tall, sheepish man with a baseball bat," the release began, and described Cooper's walk of shame to Power's front door. There he was met by a well-informed housekeeper who could only have been conjured by a studio's central casting, or a creative publicist:

"I told you this was going to happen, Mr. Cooper," she told him, as if she were a disgusted manager taking his ineffective pitcher out of a game.

Cooper scratched his head, took the ball, and looked at the hole in the library window. "Didn't think I could hit it this far," he said, aghast at what he had done.

The maid reminded Cooper of a similar smash of his a few days before that crashed through the Powers' patio window while Tyrone and his wife, the French actress Annabella, were having breakfast. Power was almost conked in the head.

Cooper apologized in the hesitant manner known to his fans. The story, fabulous already, climbs a higher rung of studio fiction when the maid tells Cooper to direct his dingers elsewhere.

"Why don't you knock it over in that direction, toward Jesse Lasky's house?" she said.

Here now was a maid who either subscribed to *Variety* or eavesdropped on industry gossip. Her suggestion that Coop aim for the Lasky house suggests a level of cattiness that your average housemaid might not exhibit. Lasky and Goldwyn were hardly friends. They were former brothers-in-law, but more important, the low-key Lasky had helped engineer the bombastic Goldwyn's ouster from the Famous Players-Lasky studio a quarter-century earlier.

"Reckon I'll have to," Coop said. "And, uh, I'll pay for the window."

(The scene evokes the opening scene of *Pride*, when young Lou's long hit smashes a delicatessen's window, requiring his mother to pay the deli's owner.)

Maria Cooper Janis, Cooper's only child, considered for a moment the story—that her father, in just a brief period of tutelage by O'Doul, clubs the sort of meteor shot associated with Mickey Mantle. She said that if her father were even capable of such a batting feat, he and his sidekick, O'Doul, had to have been in the "south 40" of the family's seven-acre property to be reasonably close to Chaparral Street, a fairly wide street that the blasted ball would have had to cross before it passed over the Powers' driveway and crashed through their patio window.

"It might have been apocryphal," she said, with understatement.

Doubts about Cooper's ability to play baseball well, let alone smack a baseball like Gehrig, persisted until he took the field in Los Angeles. If O'Doul could transform Cooper into Gehrig, one writer wisecracked, "The millennium is just around the corner for sure." On the Sunday before shooting began, the *Oakland Tribune* carried a gossipy story that bore the headline, "BASEBALL FILM BAFFLES GARY." Cooper was described as spending his nights watching a slow-motion film of O'Doul and Herman "batting and throwing in the left-handed manner that Cooper, as Lou Gehrig, will have to employ in *The Pride of the Yankees*. Right-handed Cooper is going crazy trying to turn into a southpaw."

The story might have been planted by Hebert, whose goal was to lure moviegoers into theaters, even if some of the truth was shaded. Putting out the word about Cooper's struggles might have been a way to entice Gehrig fans eager to see a movie about their hero if he could perform credibly as a player. O'Doul, at least, believed he had done a good job. Late in their sessions, as O'Doul was looking toward the start of his PCL season, he told an interviewer:

Cooper hardly knew one end of the bat from the other when we started. Now he has a smooth swing that makes him look good even when he's striking out...He didn't know a first baseman's glove from a bat, either, but he's learned to catch a ball pretty well...He throws like a shot-putter pushes the ball so we'll have to straighten that out.

Word of O'Doul's teaching reached the oversize ears of the baseball sage Casey Stengel. Stengel was then managing the Boston Braves, who were on their way to another awful season with only 59 wins. Talking to reporters in Chicago, Stengel said, "I see where Lefty O'Doul is taking a lot of bows teaching Gary Cooper to hit." But the eccentric Stengel said O'Doul was wasting his time crowing about coaching a movie star, when he should have been boasting of his working with Nanny Fernandez the year before. Nanny was indeed an early-season phenom, hitting .356 when Stengel bragged about him.

By season's end, though, his batting average had tumbled to .255.

Cooper ultimately had the better season, which would culminate in an Academy Award nomination for playing Gehrig. Fernandez missed the next three years because of military service and never played full-time in the majors again.

11

Did Cooper, a Right-Hander, Become Gehrig, a Left-Hander?

Cooper stopped to light a cigarette one day as he and Babe Ruth came off the field at Wrigley. Ruth, casting himself in the role of doting nanny, watched to see if Cooper was lighting up as he had instructed.

"That's fine," Ruth said proudly. "You did everything left-handed. Swell."

When Ruth rushed off to call his wife, Claire, Cooper said, "He's got me using my left hand for everything. I even light matches left-handed, hold my cigarettes left-handed-conscious, like Lou. Between him and Lefty O'Doul, I haven't much chance to get crossed up, trying to be more like Lou Gehrig." Ruth, he added, "rides herd on me."

The final cut of *Pride* suggests that Cooper learned his lessons fairly well as a batter and fielder, considering that he had started from scratch as a ballplayer. He didn't make anyone watching forget the brilliance of Gehrig; Cooper's job was not to turn into a Major Leaguer. He was forty, with a bum hip, a bad shoulder, and only six weeks of baseball instruction. Nor was his athleticism required to carry the picture; for all his training with O'Doul, Cooper the ballplayer is rarely seen, and when he is, he does little hitting, catching, or throwing.

Director Sam Wood and editor Daniel Mandell might have sifted through many other shots to find the few good ones, possibly protecting Cooper from criticism. Or they were simply obeying Goldwyn's order to minimize baseball and focus on Gehrig the man. *Pride* did not need much baseball from Cooper if Ruth was around to bring back some thrills from the past.

Cooper did more batting than fielding in *Pride*. Gehrig was, first and foremost, a ferocious hitter, with a .340 career batting average and 493 home runs, and third all-time in on-base plus slugging percentage (OPS), a statistic that came into vogue long after Gehrig's death. So establishing a plate presence for Cooper was important even if it meant that he swung a bat without connecting with a ball.

If O'Doul was correct, Cooper's natural aptitude to chop wood as a left-hander was going to help him to learn a left-handed batting swing. Establishing his bona fides on the field was not as critical; Cooper was not going to be burdened with learning to stretch at first base to scoop up an errant throw in the dirt or throw a runner out at home. He only had to hint at catching and throwing.

In Cooper's first scene as a batter, he is at Columbia, taking his swings in front of Blake and a school official. Cooper checks his swing on one pitch. On the second swing, Cooper swings away, but we do not see any contact. Still, we are led to believe that he hit a long shot by the reactions of his observers.

Cooper's next batting sequence is more demanding: a montage

that shows his progress as a minor-league player in Hartford. It is a succession of quick shots that is meant to show him hitting, sliding, fielding, and catching. It flits by so rapidly that it may have been difficult for moviegoers in 1942 to see how little he was actually doing. He is shown catching a ball at first base with the presumed instruction of a coach or teammate, but it is Babe Herman, the former Brooklyn Dodgers star, who, like Gehrig, was a left-handed batter and fielder. Herman's face is barely seen, but enough of him is visible to identify him.

The next scene, which is meant to show Cooper sliding, lets someone else (probably Herman) do the dirty work before it cuts to a close-up of Cooper on the ground, acting as if he had done the sliding. But the seam is there. When it appears that Cooper is nimbly moving to snatch grounders in the next shot, it is Herman, whose lanky body is like Cooper's, making him an ideal double. Herman, thirty-eight, was born a week after Gehrig, and was still active, hanging on with Cooper's own Hollywood Stars after a Major League career with a stellar .324 batting average.

When batting, Cooper appears to cleanly line one pitch but is framed in such a tight close-up on the next shot that it is impossible to know if he hit the ball, save for the accompanying sound effect. His throws are also cropped so severely that their strength and accuracy cannot be determined.

In his first at-bat as a Yankee on the road, portrayed as taking place at Comiskey Park in Chicago in front of his future wife, Eleanor (Wright), and her father, Cooper is shown in the batter's box. The camera cuts to a long shot of Herman with his natural left-handed swing, who hits a single to left field and rounds first base. After Wood cuts to a smiling Wright, who minutes earlier had taunted Gehrig by calling him "Tanglefoot," the follow-up shot is of Cooper heading back to first to avoid the tag, then glancing at Wright, the first glimpse of their chemistry. By now, it is easy to pick out the differences between Cooper and Herman. Herman, a terrific player in his day, moved with grace. Cooper ran with an awkward gait, moving like a man with a bad hip.

Cooper's next turn to show his batting skills is at a carnival arcade in Chicago. He is dressed in a tuxedo and patent leather shoes, out on the town with Wright in *Pride's* version of Lou and Eleanor's first date. With slow pitches coming at him, his swings are fluid and his contact solid, proving that Cooper had learned the basics of hitting. O'Doul sent Cooper to the Venice amusement pier to prepare for the scene.

"The machine would pitch out the ball and I'd whang at it, left-handed," Cooper said. "That kind of business." Taking cuts against easy mechanical pitches in a carnival booth was a bit less challenging than hitting two home runs in a World Series game for Billy, the hospitalized kid. In the longest baseball sequence in the film, Cooper and Herman took turns being Gehrig, but Herman was handed the harder parts.

First, Ruth had to hit the home run that *he* had promised to Billy. Even as he approached fifty, Ruth could still look like his younger self while wielding a bat. From a long shot taken from above home plate, Ruth's dramatic, uppercut swing still appears true—but all that is shown is the Ruthian cut; there is no evidence that he actually hit the home run. He had not hit a home run in seven years.

Wood was apparently willing to wait patiently for thunder from Ruth's bat.

During filming one day at Wrigley, Wood called for Ruth to step up and swing for the fences. "I want a genuine home run," Wood told him. "We're not going to fake it when we're paying you for the real thing." Facing off against a minor-league pitcher, Ruth needed five pitches before he "makes the ball sail like only Ruth can make them sail, right where the doctor ordered."

After Ruth's home run for little Billy, it is Cooper/Herman's turn. The sequence begins with an establishing shot that was not filmed at Wrigley but lifted from film made by *Pride*'s second unit during the 1941 World Series at Yankee Stadium against the Brooklyn Dodgers. The stadium's familiar dimensions are visible, as is the gravestone-like monument to Gehrig in deep center field that was unveiled on July 4, 1941, the two-year anniversary of the "luckiest man" speech. A monument to Miller Huggins was already there, too.

The player at bat in the footage is a left-handed Yankee but not identifiable. Then, from a low angle, Cooper is seen, in his stance, at Wrigley. Following a cut to the St. Louis pitcher's delivery, Herman re-enters and clubs a home run (its flight is unseen) before being replaced by Cooper for the trot around the bases.

Cooper's next two at-bats are swinging strikeouts, sequences captured in medium shots and close-ups. In two swings, he spins around awkwardly, as if he is looking for one pitch and gets another.

Then, for the final at-bat of the game—for that second home run for Billy—the Cooper/Herman tandem returns. First, Cooper takes three balls in succession, prompting Blake to stand and decry St. Louis for walking Gehrig without allowing him to try for the second homer for Billy, and Huggins mockingly suggests that Lou take a walk. The camera cuts behind home plate; the swing on the 3-0 count looks like Cooper's, but the bat whips too quickly and the ball is hit too hard for it not to be Herman slamming the opposite-field home run that fulfills the promise to Billy. Herman's blow is followed by a long shot of a runner racing to first base that is from a newsreel of the second unit's World Series footage.

Cooper takes two more swings in *Pride*. The first is another Cooper/Herman effort that comes after Lou and Eleanor's wedding. A long shot of Herman is followed by medium and close shots of Cooper (when the rival catcher asks, "What are you doing, Lou, knocking the rice off your spikes?"). Then in a long shot, Herman homers to right field and tips his cap as he approaches first base on his trot. The camera returns to a close-up of Cooper, giddy, looking backward at Eleanor and shouting, "Thank you for marrying me!"

The final swing is the saddest, and it's all Cooper. He is in spring training in 1939, his body deteriorating, increasingly unresponsive to his brain's commands. Following an inside pitch that sends him reeling, almost helplessly, into Bill Dickey's arms, Cooper hits a fairly sharp grounder but is thrown out at first base. He laments that it should have been a hit and runs off to take a few laps around the field as the end nears for his career and his life.

The end is close.

Since the film's release, a myth, or at least a near-myth, has persisted that Cooper had failed in his efforts to play baseball credibly from the left side. Instead some believed he performed as a natural right-hander and the film negative was reversed. If that were true, it would have required considerably more planning to pull off the trick.

Some of it could appear to be simply executed, such as having Cooper run to third base instead of first. It gets complicated beyond that. The lettering of his road uniform would have to have been sewn backward to read "ЯЯOY WƎИ." The jersey lettering of all other players in the scenes with him would have had to be reversed as well. Infielders would have had to wear left-handed gloves in order for them to look right-handed on the film, essential for any second basemen, third basemen, and shortstops who shared the camera with Cooper or Herman. Such planning would not have been beyond the ability of cinematographer Rudolph Mate or the production designer, William Cameron Menzies, one of the best in the business.

Indeed, some base-running legerdemain was done; to deal with the sun casting shadows at inconvenient times at Wrigley Field, some runners ran to third, instead of to first, and the film negative was reversed. *The New York Times* wrote:

Thus, when Sam Wood wanted to shoot a scene of Gary Cooper running to first base from home, the first base line shadows would be all wrong, for it was morning. So, quite simply, Cooper ran from home plate to third base and was safe just as the third baseman caught the ball thrown from first. Then—the film was reversed and moviegoers will see Cooper scooting like mad down the first-base line.

The story of a more extensive film flip has been told by various people over the years, among them Cooper and *Washington Post* columnist Shirley Povich. Making the film-reversal work well would have been a surprisingly audacious scheme for such an early entrant to the sports-film genre and one that was only secondarily a baseball picture.

Two days before the film's July 15 release, Povich wrote:

A heap of hokum came out of Hollywood concerning the efforts of Lefty O'Doul to teach Cooper how to throw and catch a ball left-handed. O'Doul, the old Giant who is a left-hander himself, was supposed to have converted the right-handed Cooper into some semblance of a left-handed first baseman, but apparently it didn't work out very satisfactorily. In *The Pride of the Yankees*, you'll see Cooper as a left-hander, wearing the first baseman's mitt on his right hand, taking throws pretty well and throwing the ball left-handed, but chums, it will be an illusion. Everything you see Cooper doing left-handed, he's actually doing right-handed.

He went on to write that the reversal of the lettering on the right-handed Cooper's jersey transformed "YANKEES" into "ƧƎƎꓘИAY"—an error that should have been caught because no Yankee uniform says "YANKEES"; the Yankees' home uniform added an interlocking NY to the pinstripes in 1936; the Yankees' road jersey then said "NEW YORK" across the chest of each player.

Years later, Cooper confirmed some of the film-flip story, saying that after training with O'Doul, he was able to raise his right arm above his chronically painful shoulder so he could reasonably duplicate Gehrig's throwing motion. That would have indicated that the negative reversal was planned all along, not decided only if Cooper's efforts to be a left-hander had failed. He added that "the letters on my uniform were reversed as it is in mirror-writing and the film was processed with the back side to the front. My right hand thus appeared to be my left."

Yet another version came from film editor Daniel Mandell, a former acrobat and vaudevillian who won Academy Awards for *Pride*, *The Best Years of Our Lives*, and *The Apartment*. More than thirty years later, he recalled the frustration of Goldwyn and

Menzies over converting Cooper to a southpaw to Goldwyn biographer Carol Easton:

I said, "Well, put the letters on his shirt backwards, and the number backwards, and when he stands up at the plate right-handed, we reverse all the film. We'll have him run to third base instead of first base." Then we covered it by showing a double running like hell and sliding into a base, and cut to a close-up of Cooper getting up.

The conflict over what was or wasn't done can be heard in contradictory accounts given by Herman Mankiewicz, who co-wrote the final screenplay, to his wife, Sara, and son Frank. Sara Mankiewicz told her husband's biographer, Richard Meryman, that it was "very hard to get a left-handed actor," and that they had trouble teaching Cooper "but he trained and he did it." But Frank Mankiewicz, as much a baseball fan as his father, recalled to Meryman that the uniform lettering was reversed "because they couldn't make him left-handed."

Cooper, Mandell, and Mankiewicz were integral to the production of *Pride* and had no reason to lie. Povich, as a journalist, had to depend on an insider's knowledge of the production. Either version would have been acceptable to moviegoers at that time in the evolution of the sports-film genre. Had Cooper achieved a level of respectable baseball skill as a left-hander, he would have seemed almost heroic. On the other hand, if some film and wardrobe magic were required to achieve the illusion that Cooper could play baseball left-handed, isn't that what Hollywood does?

So what was the truth?

In 2013, Tom Shieber, the senior curator of the Baseball Hall of Fame, examined *Pride* frame-by-frame to determine if the film-reversal story was true. His expertise involves studying the minutiae and anomalies of baseball equipment and garments to authenticate them, whether it's a smudge on a bat, a button's placement, an *S* on a jersey worn by the Bustin' Babes, Ruth's barnstorming team, that was sewn a bit low, or the alignment of pinstripes on a uniform.

For his study of *Pride,* he inspected more of his craft's fingerprints: shirt plackets, the double layer of fabric that held the buttons of the uniform jerseys; the Louisville Slugger brand and Powerized logo on Cooper's bats; the way zippers are sewn on the flies of uniform pants; a bandage on the palm of Cooper's hand; and the mystery of a coach who pitches left-handed in one shot during Gehrig's minor-league sequence and right-handed in another.

His verdict: Based on the final cut, there was almost no flipping of the negative. He found that in the scenes with Cooper in his Columbia and Yankee uniforms, there was no reversal at all. He says that the plackets in all instances are correctly positioned; that is, the buttons were attached to the right portion of the shirt. And if the Goldwyn wardrobe crew went so far as to create a backward-buttoning jersey for Cooper (with reverse lettering spelling out "AIBMUJOC"), they would have had to custom-tailor a backward-buttoning jacket and vest for Walter Brennan, who stood behind the backstop talking to Cooper.

Shieber argues persuasively that Goldwyn's crew was even less likely to order bats from Hillerich & Bradsby to produce Louisville Slugger bats with backward lettering and an angled Powerized logo in a mirror image. It would have taken some astonishingly crafty wardrobe, design, and prop workers at Goldwyn to think of so many ways to fool moviegoers—yet miss the fact Cooper's baseball pants had a zipper-fly that lay precisely as Gehrig's did.

Shieber conceded that if any negative flipping occurred, it was during the Hartford montage. That makes sense because the scenes depicting Gehrig's minor-league career were filmed largely in May at Wrigley, two to three months after much of the work at the ballpark had been done. A judgment might have been made that Cooper's earlier left-handed fielding at Wrigley was substandard, so it would be easier to have him switch to his natural side than have him retrained.

In the scene where Cooper is being coached at first base, the coach wears a right-handed glove. Yet the coach is clearly the left-handed Herman. When Cooper steps in, he makes a nice catch coupled with a sweeping tag, which is clearly suspicious. If the right-handed Herman and the suspiciously slick left-handed Cooper weren't tip-offs to the flipping, there was a third clue to the deception: The same coach who throws left-handed to Cooper and Herman in one scene throws right-handed with the exact same motion in another, a triumph of reversing the negative, not ambidexterity.

Shieber discerned more flipping in the final portion of the montage, when Cooper throws the ball. Here, the right portion of the shirt placket rested on top of the left, the opposite of the norm, suggesting that Cooper threw the ball right-handed and Mandell reversed the negative. This particular throw was similar to Cooper's pitches in *Meet John Doe* and was awkward enough to believe that his troublesome shoulder made it too painful to throw better. It was the only one in the montage where Cooper's jersey was not covered by a sweatshirt, which means the other shots of him throwing were almost certainly flipped.

Without living testimony or outtakes, the understanding of the depth of Cooper's baseball education is incomplete. In six weeks, he did learn, however awkwardly, to play baseball. That he was able to swing a bat, whether from his natural right-handed side or as a converted left-hander, suggests some innate athleticism. Perhaps Cooper was told that as a batter, he only had to build a swing, not show the ability to connect very often.

"Even for most ambidextrous athletes, it usually takes years and years of dedicated practice to approach a real level of proficiency," said Rick Wolff, a former minor-league ballplayer, coach, and psychologist to Major League Baseball teams. "Some top athletes—no matter how hard they try to develop their other-side abilities, just never seem to make any progress at all." If Cooper could learn to throw, bat, and field left-handed, his less-dominant side, "that might have been one of the greatest athletic accomplishments of all time. It's possible but not probable."

Mama's Boy

12

ou Gehrig was too young to serve in World War I and deceased by the time the Japanese attacked Pearl Harbor. Yet in *The Pride of the Yankees*, he was immediately depicted as one of America's fallen, a soldier in Yankee pinstripes who had suffered a tragic death.

Hollywood's films were already reflecting the country's war footing by the time *Pride* was released in July 1942, depicting European battlefields and the plight of the people whom the soldiers left behind. So Goldwyn hired Damon Runyon, the wisecracking Broadway writer and sportswriter whose short stories would years later be adapted into *Guys and Dolls*, to write a patriotic foreword to the film.

Runyon covered sports for the Hearst syndicate and reported on Gehrig and Ruth, whom he dubbed the "Beezark of Kerblam." Writing about the 1927 World Series between the Yankees and Pittsburgh, he wrote, "Mr. Ruth and Mr. Gehrig are warm friends, despite the fact that Mr. Gehrig seemed to be infringing on Mr.

Ruth's copyright during the greater part of the season. I am told, however, that the Columbia young man operated under written permission from Mr. Ruth who felt that there were enough home runs in the American League pitching—60 from Ruth and 47 from Gehrig—"to be cut up several ways."

By 1941, Runyon was a writer-producer for RKO, following years of selling short stories to studios. While Goldwyn was preparing to make *Pride*, Runyon was adapting two of them, "Little Pinks" and "Piece of Pie" into what became *The Big Street* with Lucille Ball and Henry Fonda. The Runyon voice was full of righteous patriotism in one column after Pearl Harbor: "We have not yet come to view the Japs as Asiatic barbarians who will not observe any of the ethics of civilization in war or otherwise. We are still in the beatific state of mind of not hating our foes which is a lovely thought that can get your brains knocked out in a bear fight."

The attitude might have appealed to Goldwyn, who seemed to feel a need for a dose of scene-setting patriotism to match the anxious national mood—even in a romantic movie about a baseball hero. The words that unfurled in a slow-moving scroll, with Irving Berlin's song "Always" playing behind them, bore Runyon's name if not his idiosyncratic voice:

This is the story of a hero of the peaceful paths of everyday life. It is the story of a gentle young man who, in the full flower of his great fame, was a lesson in simplicity and modesty to the youth of America. He faced death with the same valor and fortitude that has been displayed by thousands of young Americans on far-flung fields of battle. He left behind him a memory of courage and devotion that will ever be an inspiration to all men.

The Gehrig-as-military-casualty theme faded quickly as *Pride* shifted to its Horatio Alger story: The surviving child of poor German immigrants in Manhattan grows into one of the greatest ballplayers of all time.

The story begins with eleven-year-old Lou (Douglas Croft) wending his way through a clotted Goldwyn backlot posing as a New York street, with horse-drawn carts and other vehicles posing as obstacles to his reaching a sandlot with other kids playing baseball. The field is bordered by wooden plank fences and surrounded by the billowing laundry lines of adjoining tenements. Croft, who played the first screen Robin in the *Batman* serial a year later, is the outsider looking to join in what the screenplay called these "ragged, tough, yammering New York gamins" for the first time.

Snitch Mulligan, a character in an early script, whose name suggest an alternate life as a Bowery Boy, taunts Lou: "Oh, a Dutchie, eh? I betcha you're for the Kaiser!"

"No, I'm not. I'm an American," says Lou, a young patriot.

Croft's turn at bat is secured after one of the kids is summoned home by his mother for a music lesson (that's some tough gamin!) and surrenders his Sweet Caporal tobacco trading cards as the ransom for a place in the game. He gets to keep his rookie Babe Ruth card, one of which sold for $575,000 a century later.

Croft steps to the plate, and on the first pitch, slams a pitch that shatters the window of an Italian delicatessen.

The screenwriters originally had something more dramatic in mind to elevate childhood glory into legend: a fantasy sequence that begins as Lou looks at the mound, where the pitcher dissolves into Christy Mathewson, the great New York Giants right-handed pitcher. Around Mathewson, the field of scruffy young boys turns into a Polo Grounds full of Giants during the World Series.

The fantasy was concocted by Paul Gallico, who had left sportswriting a few years earlier. He had never written a screenplay before, but more than a decade as a columnist and sports editor for the New York *Daily News* gave Eleanor comfort that he had the background the film needed.

Gallico was a dreamer himself, accustomed to turning his fantasies into reality. In 1923 he was so fascinated by Jack Dempsey, and what it must have felt like to be hit by the heavyweight champion, that he persuaded Dempsey to let him in the ring with him for a round. Gallico described being whacked by the "Manassa Mauler" as "a ripping in my head, then a sudden blackness, and the next thing I knew, I was sitting on the canvas with my legs collapsed under me." He would fulfill his fantasies many times in the future, paving the way for another enterprising writer, George Plimpton, to box and play goalie and quarterback for his art.

The idea of turning a kid's at-bat into a baseball fantasy was as irresistible to Gallico in his treatment as it was months later to Herman Mankiewicz and Jo Swerling, who preserved it in their final script, dated mid-February 1942. When Lou connected with Mathewson's first pitch, Gallico wrote that the home run "sails out of the park, perhaps even of the city"; he describes Lou's teammates hoisting him to their shoulders; being feted by the mayor (in a high silk hat and long white beard); a band of beautiful girls bearing flowers and banners; and a city selectman presenting Lou with a car.

Mankiewicz and Swerling were seasoned screenwriters—Mankiewicz and Orson Welles collected the Oscar for Best Original Screenplay for *Citizen Kane* early in the filming of *Pride*—who tempered Gallico's first-timer's histrionics. They described the "perfect rhythm and timing" of Lou's swing against Mathewson. The crack of the bat "is like a pistol shot," they wrote. As Lou runs to first base, the fantasy ends—the Giants "are kids again. They're yelling as Lou runs, but the sound of the crashing glass of a bakery's window is heard before he reaches first base."

Now we see what Wood filmed: the kids scattering but a cop snagging Lou and shepherding him home, where his disappointed mother pays the baker, and Lou contritely accepts the blame.

The ambitious Mathewson sequence appears to have been abruptly scratched even though the era's technology could have handled it. Walsh provides the only available explanation of the scene's absence when, at the end of a letter to Eleanor before production started, he added a handwritten postscript: "I think Gallico is going to find things missing or added by Sam Wood. Example: I think the sandlot 'dream' sequence (Mathewson, Cobb, etc.) is going be entirely eliminated. I thought it was a swell idea but apparently it is not practical on the screen."

The decision was Wood's, and Walsh agreed with it. He did suggest that if Gallico had stayed in California longer and not returned to his budding career as a novelist and magazine writer, he might have been able to save it.

Still, Wood had prepared for such a sequence, which would have provided a vastly different opening to *Pride*. He hired an aging pitcher named Fay Thomas to play Mathewson. The thickly built Thomas was nearing the end of a long career, mostly in the minor leagues; but he had a few flings in the majors, the first a nine-game stint with the Giants in 1927. Thomas was probably nearby: He had played much of his career for the PCL's Los Angeles Angels. Even though his sequence was never filmed, Thomas must have thought it would be; he appeared one day at the sandlot set to be photographed pitching to the gamins with one of the kids riveted on his wind-up.

Croft's window-shattering home run brings us to the Gehrigs' shabby walk-down apartment, where we meet Elsa Janssen as Lou's careworn mother, Christina, and his father, Heinrich, a well-dressed unemployed janitor, played by Ludwig Stossel. Janssen is stout, her gray hair in a bun, and fixated on her son becoming an engineer, like his uncle Otto. Any deviation by Lou from his future as an engineer, any signs that he loved baseball more, was cause for a reminder, if not a reproach, from Mom Gehrig that he had to return to Otto's career path.

Otto exists only in a framed photograph hanging on a wall in the apartment, his face as stern as Janssen's maternal demeanor is unyielding.

Late in the film, after Lou is an established superstar and Mom has enthusiastically accepted that her son will not be an engineer, Janssen scoffs, "Otto, schmotto!," and reveals that he only dug ditches. Indeed, Eleanor stressed in a letter to Walsh that Otto was a fictional relative. "Lou's real uncle has been dead many years," she wrote. "He was a chef and he has a daughter and wife still living who are out and out chiselers. They have been dogging me for money for months." She didn't mind the make-believe Otto's occupation in the script.

"It certainly is not libelous," she added, "to make a chef into an engineer."

Janssen's Mom Gehrig is the dominant figure in the family, a woman who lost three children (which the film says nothing about), but her strong, respectful Lou survived. She smothered him with her overwhelming attention—for good reason. Niven Busch witnessed that when he profiled Gehrig as an adult, passive in his mother's presence; the screenwriters imagined the excessive doting as the avenue to portraying the movie's main tension between Mom and Eleanor. Mom wants to control every aspect of his life, from his career to his diet to whom he dates—she tries to midwife a romance between Lou and Hedwig, a butcher's daughter, in an early script—to how Lou and Eleanor will furnish their home.

Gallico initially describes Mom as an "enormous hausfrau with arms like a wrestler, big bosom and rear end," with her "thick hair done up in a knot." Teamed with a veteran screenwriter, Earl Baldwin, Gallico turned Mom into an offensive immigrant caricature speaking in broken English ("Gott im himmel, it fires! Vawter!"). By late 1941, when Gallico and Abem Finkel (who, a year earlier, wrote *Sergeant York*) devised a detailed outline of the story, Mom's screen personality was gradually softening and would be softened further into a tough but conciliatory character who gradually learns to get along with Eleanor, something she never did in real life. "Mom will not be written as a whining scold or a bullying nag but as an honest hardworking woman who is trying to keep her family together and bring up her boy," Gallico wrote.

Croft, meanwhile, grows up quickly in *Pride*, sprouting from the kid whom Mom smacks on his butt for breaking the store window to Cooper, the student at Columbia who waits tables at the same fraternity his mother cooks at and hopes the snobs will admit him as a member. Cooper was forty, playing a character half his age, trying to join a frat whose toffs look a decade too old to be undergraduates.

Despite the look of someone too old for the part, Cooper movingly conveys the joy of receiving his pledge pin over the objections of the snobbish frat leader Van Tuyl (Hardie Albright, thirty-eight at the time)—and getting Janssen to notice the pin while she's cooking. Cooper's Gehrig is flirty with his mother, and tells her, as he would several times more in the picture, that she is his "best girl"—an Oedipal comment that reflects their relationship but is less sweet with each mention, and which gets more disturbing each time he says it.

Until Teresa Wright enters the picture, the most constant relationship Cooper has is with sportswriter Blake, who first appears in the Columbia athletic director's office when Lou, unseen, smashes a ball through *his* window, prompting Brennan to suggest that the Yankees could use a hitter like him. The athletic director wants to keep Gehrig, who is also a star running back—a "line-plunging fool"—but Brennan is adamant that he will let the Yankees know about him.

Brennan is inescapable, playing a role based on sportswriter Fred Lieb, but also acting as Cooper's advisor, driver, train berth companion, matchmaker to Eleanor, interpreter of romantic talk, ghostwriter for newspaper columns, Yankee scout, and pal when Lou gets the news from the doctor that he is dying. Gallico's intent was not to give Blake so many roles. While he would have known journalistic sycophants during his time as a columnist and sports editor, he also knew Paul Krichell, the Yankees scout who discovered Lou in 1923 while watching Lou hit two home runs during a Columbia-Rutgers game in New Brunswick, New Jersey. But Krichell disappears after an early script, replaced by Blake.

Writers were closer to players in those days, but Brennan's character is far too much of an intimate, a composite character whose behavior verges on a besotted fan's. It can't withstand the credibility test. Until the final script, Blake was a minor character who replaced Chuck Frawley, Lou's fictional coach at the minor-league Hartford team, who follows him to the majors.

Brennan meets Cooper at the frat house to tell him of the Yankees' interest in him. It is the culmination of two scenes: one, a fraternity dance where he meets flirty Myra (Virginia Gilmore)—"vivacious nitwit," wrote Gallico—who cozies up to Cooper at frat leader Van's insistence. Cooper dances his first-ever dance with her. She pretends to be impressed with the great ballplayer, who confesses he will follow his mother's goal that he be an engineer. "You're going to do what your mother wants?" she asks. "Well, that's just adorable."

Here are the first stirrings of Cooper the romantic, who will eventually tear away from Mom's umbilical cord. He enjoys Gilmore's attention (while his frat brothers are listening to the couple flirt). After she gives him a flower to remember her by, he heads to his room and preserves it between the pages of a book—a rather feminine act but one he might have learned in a home dominated by a very strong mother. He is so smitten—and, well, this is Gary Cooper pressing a flower—that there is a sort of shy dignity to the act. Then, as he whistles "Ain't We Got Fun?" to himself, he uses his sport jacket to pretend he is dancing with her.

The next day, the frat boys torment Cooper as he serves them—reinforcing the class differences between rich young men in suits and Lou handing out lunch to them dressed in a waiter's smock—snidely reprocessing the sincere words they heard him say to Gilmore. Enraged, Cooper leaps across the table to attack Albright, leaving a dish-breaking mess, and follows him underneath to grab him by the legs. When told by another frat member amid the tussle that someone from the Yankees is there to see him, Cooper thinks he's being played and hustles the bewildered Brennan out of the house.

In the film, Brennan heads to South Field at Columbia the

day after getting the bum's rush to assure Cooper of the Yankees' interest, which mimics Krichell's actual trip to the campus where Gehrig hit a tremendous homer and pitched the Lions to a 7–2 win. But in the film, that epiphany of early greatness was replaced by Lou's rejection of Blake's offer to sign with the Yankees.

"Gee, that's wonderful," Cooper says, with a smile that disappears quickly. As he bows his head to mask his disappointment, he says, "But I'm going to be an engineer."

He walks away, but not before tantalizing Blake with a long smash.

"An engineer," Brennan harrumphs.

The engineer contrivance is the axis upon which the early part of the film revolves. Mom Gehrig did not, in reality, put such an unforgiving obstacle in his way. But in the film, Lou struggled to satisfy his mother even if it meant sacrificing his happiness. Cooper shows Lou's inner conflict whenever he reasserts that he will be an engineer. He never says it happily, but he says it respectfully. That resolve wavers when Mom gets sick and needs expensive hospitalization. Her sickness, undefined in the film (her lungs filled with fluid in an early script, suggesting pneumonia or a heart problem), compels him to sign with the Yankees to get the money for her medical care. Before director Wood settled on a brief scene showing Cooper signing his contract in Huggins's (played by Ernie Adams) office, the story line first sent Lou off to earn money for Mom's medical bills as a dishwasher, longshoreman, crate handler, and night porter before Pop reminds him of the Yankees' offer. Mankiewicz and Swerling also wrote a scene that described him as motivated to sign with the Yankees for $1,000—enough to pay for his mother's care—after seeing a headline that says, "YANKEES LOSE AGAIN."

Cooper's treatment of Brennan at the frat and his sudden rush to sign the contract makes Adams think of him as a little daffy—maybe too odd for the Yankees.

"Maybe he signed with the wrong team," he says. "He's nutty enough to play with the Brooklyn Dodgers."

Eleanor was displeased with this scene. She was reading scripts and sent at least three lists of corrections to Goldwyn through Walsh. She was not only a one-woman truth squad in service to her late husband, but a baseball fan who grew up rooting for the Chicago White Sox. She knew that Barrow, the Yankees president, and not Huggins, should be shown signing Gehrig.

"Huggins is seen seated behind the desk giving Lou the $1,000 and later telling him to sign the contract," she wrote. "This is never done in baseball, that is, the field manager never signs up a player. It is always some executive."

Her attempted correction was ignored.

She told Walsh that she was concerned about the liberties being taken by the writers in this clash between reality and Hollywood storytelling. *Pride* was an early example of the based-on-a-true-story genre, where details of central personalities' lives are changed, history is condensed, and characters turned into composites to suit a studio's desires. Whatever Eleanor understood about Goldwyn's contractual rights to use Lou as moldable clay for *Pride*, she was going to stand up for the truth of her husband's life.

She wrote to Walsh that "all sorts of poetic license can be taken with the dramatic scenes and the romantic ones but one garish slip (and there are many to follow in this letter), and you will have millions of fans hooting at the picture and the writers will say, 'Leave it to Hollywood to attempt to rewrite the records of a national game.'"

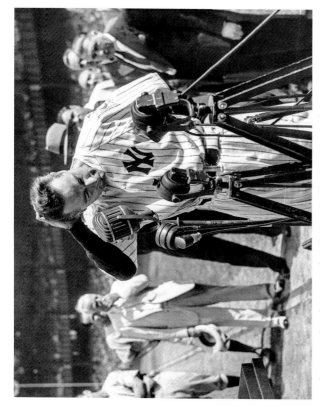

A photograph of Lou Gehrig's iconic "luckiest man" speech shows him struggling to continue, overcome by his emotions. The man standing behind him to his right is only a suggestion of how much solidarity he had. *The Stanley Weston Archive/Archive Photos/Getty Images*

Eleanor Gehrig (center) poses for a staged phone call with Joe DiMaggio and Yankees manager Joe McCarthy at a press event in for the film in 1941 while Ty Cobb (seated left) and Paul Gallico (seated right), who co-wrote the outline and first script of *Pride*, listen in. *Photograph furnished by Samuel Goldwyn Jr. Family Trust*

Producer Sam Goldwyn, who himself knew nothing about baseball, pretends to swing a bat at the head of Gary Cooper, as if out of frustration at all the work required to teach Cooper how to play the game. Babe Ruth (left), who knew better than anyone how much damage a bat could do, seems to watch nervously. © *Photofest*

Lefty O'Doul, a former National League batting champion, who was managing the San Francisco Seals at the time of the making of *Pride*, leads Cooper in a crash course on how to swing a bat. Tasked with turning the right-handed Cooper into reasonable facsimile of the left-handed Gehrig, O'Doul looked to unconventional techniques. *Photograph furnished by Samuel Goldwyn Jr. Family Trust*

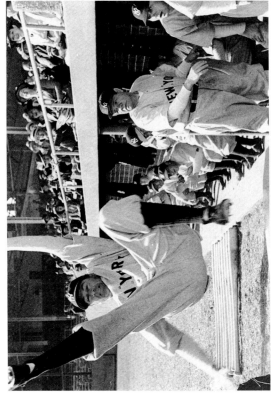

Cooper in mid-pratfall as, in his haste to get to home plate, he tumbles over the bats laid out in front of the dugout. Cooper's flop earned him the nickname "Tanglefoot" from Teresa Wright in the film, but research shows it was probably writer Westbrook Pegler who had actually dubbed him "Tanglefoot" for his early struggles to right his footwork at first base. *Photograph furnished by Samuel Goldwyn Jr. Family Trust*

Cooper poses with the two Eleanors. Eleanor Gehrig (right) was uncertain about Teresa Wright playing her. Though she voiced pleasure with the portrayal, decades later she suggested to Blythe Danner, who played her in the 1978 movie *A Love Affair*, that she act tougher than Wright and less sweet. *Photograph furnished by Samuel Goldwyn Jr. Family Trust*

Fay Thomas, a career minor league pitcher, was cast as the New York Giants ace Christy Mathewson for a dream sequence that was never filmed. But Thomas showed up at least once on the sandlot set where a young Gehrig dreams that he slugs a home run off one of the toughest pitchers of his era. *Photograph furnished by Samuel Goldwyn Jr. Family Trust*

Director Sam Wood (right) coaching Cooper and Wright through a scene of playful wrestling on the beach in St. Petersburg where the Yankees held spring training. It was a prelude to another wrestling scene in which a stabbing pain in Gehrig's shoulder illustrated the first sign of his fatal illness. *Photograph furnished by Samuel Goldwyn Jr. Family Trust*

A former amateur ballplayer, Wood (standing) appears to be showing Cooper (right) how a close pitch should send him reeling backward. © *Photofest*

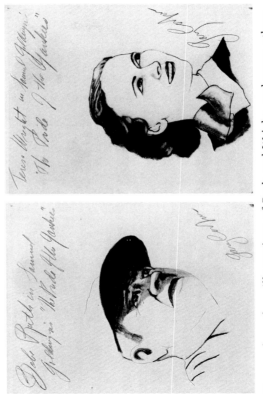

Cooper drew these illustrations of Ruth and Wright—and many others—during the filming of *Pride*. As a teenager, he aspired to be a commercial artist and drew cartoons for the *Scarlet & Black*, Grinnell College's student newspaper. His talent was unmistakable; he just happened to have more talent as an actor. *Photographs furnished by Samuel Goldwyn Jr. Family Trust*

Taken while filming the scene of the Gehrigs' wedding ceremony, this shot shows the newly united family's surprise and disdain when their service is interrupted by workmen. Though Eleanor pointed out to Goldwyn that Mom and Pop Gehrig (portrayed third from right and fifth from right respectively) did not in fact attend the ceremony, he did not heed her. © *Photofest*

Connie Mack (third from left), the venerable owner and manager of the Philadelphia Athletics, who was born before radio, film, or television, visited the Goldwyn lot where he spent time with (from left) Ruth, Cooper, and producer Samuel Goldwyn. © *Photofest*

Wright and Cooper's undeniable chemistry is never more apparent than in the scene invoked in this publicity shot when, with tears in her eyes, Eleanor watches her husband fumble as he tries to loop his bow tie, owing to his loss of dexterity to amyotrophic lateral sclerosis. © *Photofest*

At the end of *Pride*, Cooper and Wright gather in the tunnel leading to the dugout, from which he would emerge to give the "luckiest man" speech. Showing them from a different angle than the scene does, this shot was probably a publicity photo or part of a scene envisioned by the screenwriters but never produced in which they meet after the speech and leave together. © *Photofest*

Cooper as Gehrig is presented a trophy from his 1939 teammates after delivering his "luckiest man" speech. Owing to the popularity of *Pride* as well as the lack a reliable transcript or newsreel footage of the speech, Cooper's rendition ended up largely defining the event that inspired it. *John Springer Collection/Corbis Historical/Getty Images*

In late 1943, Cooper went on a USO tour of the South Pacific as an entertainer. At one point, soldiers asked him to recite Gehrig's "luckiest man" speech. Surprised and unprepared, he excused himself to jot down what he remembered, then reemerged on the stage to deliver it. At every subsequent stop of the tour, he delivered the speech again. © *US Marine Corps*

Gallico was more sanguine about what he was doing for Goldwyn.

"I will tell you, Baby," he said, in an overly friendly greeting when he wrote Eleanor, "no matter what I know we are going to catch hell from the sports writers so we might as well face it. None of the boys will ever understand what we were up against in trying to make baseball fit into a Sam Goldwyn movie." He added that they had all been well paid, and "can afford to take a little abuse."

When Lou is sent by the Yankees to play with their Hartford farm team, Cooper lets Janssen think he is studying engineering at Harvard, which thrills her—and he happily leaves her and Pop (who knows the truth) to start his baseball career. To hell with Uncle Otto.

The film tells us little of the time Gehrig spent with the Hartford Senators, offering only a quick-moving montage of Cooper hitting, fielding, sliding, and throwing, accompanied by a succession of increasingly encouraging newspaper headlines ("GEHRIG TIRELESS WORKER—SAYS MANAGER," "HUMAN DYNAMO NEVER TAKES IT EASY," "GEHRIG RECALLED BY YANKEES"). The clips of Cooper playing baseball constitute the most continuous action he experienced as a ballplayer in the movie—and probably enough to satisfy most moviegoers of the day.

Left out of *Pride's* trip to the minor leagues was Gallico's attempt to use what Eleanor told him about Lou's brush with boozing.

She was frustrated by the assumption that Lou was colorless, and during her meetings with Gallico, she told him a few stories that would make you think twice about considering Gehrig a dullard. Eleanor recalled an incident, apparently when Lou was a teenager, when he was arrested with other boys for skinny-dipping in the Hudson River. The judge whom Lou faced asked him, "Didn't you know enough to wear trunks?" She also recounted the time when he was in an apartment with "ten burlesque belles," drinking and carousing, and one of the guys slapped a girl. "Lou and several others got out quick." All but Lou were served with court papers, but Lou still hired a lawyer.

In Hartford, one of his teammates got him some gin, which had a salubrious effect on his hitting. "He went out and murdered the ball," Eleanor told Gallico. Emboldened, Lou bought himself some gin and kept drinking it every night for two weeks, believing it would keep him hitting. But manager Pat O'Connor cautioned him off the liquor, telling him, "You're going places in baseball and this stuff is going to slap you down."

Gallico expanded on the yarn, placing Lou in a speakeasy, getting blotto with teammate Carl Johnson. When Lou reports for the game the next day hung over, Johnson offers even more booze, calling it his "cough medicine." Lou is fuzzy throughout the game. At bat, he sees two pitchers and two balls coming at him, then three pitchers and three balls. But as he swings desperately at the trio of balls, he "connects with a terrific clout that sends the ball over the right field fence for a home run." Before the next game, the coach, Frawley, catches him sipping gin, then warns him that the booze might help him now but "you'll be hitting from the gutter in about two years from tomorrow."

Mankiewicz and Swerling also played out a scenario that portrayed Lou as a naïve boozehound. In a scene submitted in late January 1942, one of Gehrig's teammates, known only as Bugs, slips Gehrig a bottle of liquor from his glove and advises the struggling young batter to use it to relax.

"What is it?" Lou asks.

"It's whiskey," Bugs says. "It's the best medicine in the world for guys who ain't hitting. You try it and see."

"Hitting medicine?" Lou says, sniffing at the open bottle.

Bugs says, "It's not in the guidebooks. But it works. You take it in large doses before and after every inning."

Later, when both men are drunk in a speakeasy, Lou says, "Bugs, if we don't run out of hitting medicine, I'm going to end the season batting .600."

The scene was derived from what Eleanor called Lou's "two-week drunk" at Hartford. But in a film about a recently deceased hero, was it conceivable that any scene depicting reprobate behavior would survive?

The question ultimately reached Goldwyn during an early February meeting with Walsh; Lefty O'Doul, Gehrig's hitting tutor; Wood; and several writers.

Goldwyn turned to Walsh and asked, "What do you think?"

"What exactly is the question you want me to answer?" Walsh responded. "Is it a question of referring to liquor or eliminating it?"

Further discussion did not resolve the liquor issues, and Walsh spoke again.

"Mr. Goldwyn," he said. "I don't know anything about story construction but I do know a lot about what the American public thinks about Lou Gehrig and his ideals and character. I don't want Lou to be painted like an angel. And I am not a prohibitionist. But if it's a question of excluding or including a liquor scene, I vote to exclude it."

Goldwyn dismissed Walsh's concerns.

"We don't want the public to think Gehrig was a sissy," he said. "We want them to feel that he was a man."

Walsh was not ready to give up.

"I'm an old bastard fifty years of age and I haven't yet had my first drink," Walsh said, "but I'm just as much a man as anybody in this room." As long as he was being paid for his opinion, he wanted to be firm that he was against showing Lou drunk. The meeting ended with no decision.

Three days later, the scene was cut.

"And the funny thing now is," he wrote Eleanor, "that everybody seems to be saying they didn't think it should have been in at all. Ain't Hollywood cute?"

Pride plays Lou's call-up to the Yankees for humor—and for a long tirade by Mom Gehrig. Because he allowed her to believe that he was at Harvard, Lou's summons to the Bronx was a surprise to Mom. Her neighbors read all about it and congratulated her, but she was having nothing of it. She was still hanging on to the Uncle Otto myth; Pop, who held no lofty ambitions for himself, tried to shush the proceedings, to no avail. Janssen, a German-born actress who was barely old enough to be Cooper's mother, had a talent for screwing her face into what in Yiddish is called a *farbissina*, or sullen expression. Now she is not only disappointed as Cooper bursts happily into the house with his good news. She realizes she's been fooled by her son and her husband (who told her he had a $25-a-week political job). Cooper tries to soothe her, once again calling her his "best girl," but she resists, mildly in the final script, but more so in the film.

Cooper's nuanced expressions waver between confidence that he can make her see things his way to concern about her anti-baseball ardor to certainty that she will change her mind. But her words suggest outrage that he had usurped her plans.

Explaining that he signed with the Yankees for the money to pay her medical bills, Cooper says, "The doctors said you might die."

"I wish I had died rather than see you give up everything we planned," Janssen says, pouty and outraged, like a disappointed mother, like a scorned lover. "For what? To play ball. A disgrace."

"It's not a disgrace to play for the Yankees," Cooper says.

The script gave Janssen a mouthful of patriotic, American Dream dialogue that culminates in her belief that being an engineer like Uncle Otto was a proper goal for the son of immigrants, not being a ballplayer.

"Uncle Otto's dead," Cooper says.

"Yes, and he'd turn over in his grave if he knew what happened in the family," she says as Cooper pulls her bulky frame onto his lap.

"That's what we came to America for?" Janssen says. "A wonderful country where everybody has an equal chance? That's why you studied, why you went to Columbia, so that you could play baseball—after all my plans for you to follow after your uncle Otto."

Whoever wrote her next words must have sensed a need for silly humor to undermine her anger. Those words distilled all her animosity toward baseball and anything that would take her boy away from her, the immigrant's suspicion of frivolity.

"All baseballers are good for nothing," she says. "Loafers in short pants."

In an early incarnation of the scene, Gallico still had Mom speaking like a new immigrant and her words sounded even more peculiar.

"Und dot what you do to your old mudder behind her back when she is sick?" she asks. "You leave the college to be a baseball bummer! He's a bad boy!"

Her choler over Lou's decision to play gives her the strength in the film to break from his grasp and hide in what appears to be the bathroom. Cooper talks through the door, hoping she is listening to his plea to give baseball a chance and attend a game. In their codependent relationship, what else could happen? He needed her to watch him play, if only to prove that he could be an honorable ballplayer. She was fated to evolve, accept Lou's chosen profession, attend games at Yankee Stadium, and bicker with Pop over manager Joe McCarthy's strategy.

Enter Wright, a tiny woman, just twenty-three, who projected a freshness and winsomeness that eluded the somewhat dowdy, thirty-six-year-old Eleanor. Wright's Eleanor is at Comiskey Park with her father, Frank, when Lou replaces Wally Pipp and begins his streak of playing in 2,130 consecutive games. The first game of his streak was actually against Washington on June 1, 1925, at Yankee Stadium. But that is sort of an inconvenient fact: Lou and Eleanor did not actually meet for several years.

Instead, the writers brought Lou and Eleanor together in Chicago, her hometown. By moving the date of their first encounter seven years earlier, Pride accelerated their romance: She and her father are ensconced in box seats when Cooper falls spectacularly over the bats arrayed in front of the Yankees dugout, a common practice in that era, as he rushes to pinch-hit for Pipp.

It takes a split second for the Yankees to react in the dugout, where the laughter is led by Babe Ruth, who, in one of several scenes in Pride, shows that he can act effectively in a supporting role without seeking center stage.

Wright rises, smiles, and cries out, "Tanglefoot!" She seems good-natured about the gibe and even gives the tense and befuddled Lou a knowing, flirtatious smile. Shouts of "Tanglefoot!" echo and follow him as he walks disconsolately to the plate.

When Gallico interviewed Eleanor, she described attending Yankees–White Sox games before meeting Lou and screaming at him to "break a leg or strike out" when he came up. In his notes, Gallico suggested a shot of Eleanor when she becomes "particularly loud and abusive," which would prompt Lou to look her way and "grin and wink at her."

In one of his scripts, she screams, "Fall down, Tanglefoot!" when Lou singles. In others, she uses a real nickname for him—"Biscuit Pants"—and claps her hands and chants, "Tanglefoot!" to distract Lou into striking out.

Mankiewicz and Swerling's script had fans taking Eleanor's lead and shouting, "Go sit on a bat, Tanglefoot!" and "Got lots of padding, Tanglefoot?" She suggests to her father that she has tagged him with an unfortunate nickname.

The "Tanglefoot" epithet was not entirely fictional—even if its genesis had nothing to do with Gehrig falling over two dozen Louisville Sluggers. Westbrook Pegler, the vituperative, anti-Franklin Roosevelt columnist and one-time sportswriter, slapped the nickname on Gehrig as early as 1927 for his cross-footed way of playing first base as a young Yankee. After Lou's death, Pegler wrote that while visiting Gehrig at his home in Larchmont, "he remembered the name of 'Tanglefoot,' and soothed my conscience by saying that he had been, for a fact, a clumsy number at the time and went on to explain how he learned his lessons from Miller Huggins."

Among Gehrig's lasting nicknames—from the "Iron Horse" to the "Dutchman" and "Biscuit Pants"—Tanglefoot never caught on.

In the film, Cooper singles to left field despite the razzing. Wright smiles, already smitten by him. After rounding first, he glances at Wright, and they exchange a playful look that is the opening act of their romance. As the White Sox try to turn a 6-4-3 double play, Cooper is conked unconscious when the relay throw nails him in the head; Cooper made an easy target by running with his head down, taboo in baseball but necessary for the little drama that it causes.

The only real-life connection to that fictional play was Gehrig being thrown out in a rundown during his first start in the lineup the next day, where he had three hits in the Yankees' 8–5 win over the Senators. That did not, however, provide the foreshadowing to the end of his life that the fictionalized throw to Lou's head did.

When he awakens, Cooper resists Adams's command that he leave the field.

"What do we have to do," Adams, as Huggins, says, "kill you to get you out of the lineup?"

The immediate reaction by Wright was less as a White Sox fan than as a worried future girlfriend. "We see, cutting to Eleanor, that she is standing, too, but with a look of concern on her face," the script says. "She is sorry for Lou and perhaps little ashamed of herself for having kidded him so."

Wright and her father (Pierre Watkins) head for a postgame meal at the local Rathskeller, where they meet up with the Yankees, who had lost that afternoon to the White Sox. Watkins plays Twitchell as a prosperous, friendly, and graceful businessman in an expensive-looking three-piece suit.

"Hello, losers," he says to a tableful of Yankees.

"Hey, how's Tanglefoot?" Eleanor asks. "Has he come to, or can't you tell?"

The confidence Wright shows in *Pride* suggests Eleanor's comfort in speakeasy society during Prohibition. She did poorly in public high school "so I pursued my love of philosophy and psychology not in the school, but in the park," she wrote. "To reform me, my parents sent me to St. Xavier's convent day school. I took up horseback riding, fast motor cars, regular attendance at the race track and in still another kind of park: the White Sox ballpark where the Yankees beat us regularly. The nuns rarely saw me."

Pride's portrayal of her father, a prominent food concessionaire in Chicago parks, as an upstanding citizen is a screenwriter's fable. By 1919, Frank Twitchell had been exposed in a public adultery scandal that prompted Eleanor's mother, Nell, to tail Frank in their car only to find that he was still cheating. He went broke shortly before the 1929 crash and fled to New Orleans with his girlfriend. It was a false characterization of Twitchell in 1925, when the film implies his daughter and Lou met, or in 1932, when they met at a party and fell for each other. Her father's moral and financial downfall forced Eleanor out of her lighthearted 1920s existence and into a more serious life, with jobs at Saks and the Chicago World's Fair.

Curiously, Eleanor's mother, Nell, is omitted from the movie, as if Eleanor had been raised by a single father. Eleanor's list of script corrections does not mention Nell, who moved to New York to help care for Lou in his dying days.

Gallico noted Nell's absence in a memo to Goldwyn, reminding him that she is "not mentioned at any time, is a living person who is still living with Mrs. Eleanor Gehrig. I suggest that this omission be called to the attention of the screenwriters now on the job." Whether he could not fit her into his story line or whether the truth of the fractured family led him to eliminate her is unknown. In the end, he created a fictional, debonair Frank Twitchell, who, in all likelihood, would not have accompanied Eleanor to Comiskey Park at that time in their lives.

If *Pride* wanted its moviegoers to accept that Lou and Eleanor met in 1925, then Eleanor was wise to remind Goldwyn that, contrary to an early Gallico script, the Yankees didn't wear uniform numbers (that practice began four seasons later) and that

Wally Pipp had been incorrectly assigned Lou's famous number four—"which became immortal, and which baseball will never allot to another Yankee player in memory of Lou."

The Gehrig legend lived deep inside the Ruthian myth. Lou's selflessness could not improve upon Ruth's earthy extravagance. Ruth's home runs were magnificent moon shots. Gehrig's were meaty line drives that offered fans less time to admire their flight. Ruth was a satyr, Gehrig a straight arrow.

How, then, to give Gehrig the advantage when the two are together in *Pride*?

The writers found their solution in a hospital room where the press gathers to watch Ruth visit sick children. Cooper is there, too, but the focus of the reporters and photographers is on the Babe with a little boy named Billy (Gene Collins) afflicted with polio. The boy does not seem thrilled with the attention or Ruth's unbidden vow to hit a home run for him that afternoon in the World Series game against the St. Louis Cardinals. Ruth tops off one promise with another that Collins is still unmoved by. "What's more, you can pick your own field," Ruth coos, playing himself with the same boisterous confidence he presented to the world. "Left? Center? Right? What did you say? Center field? Okay."

Cooper watches the shamelessness with a flicker of disdain and is about to leave, saying no more than "Keep your chin up, Billy," when the boy invites him to sign the ball that the Babe already autographed. Cooper animates Collins, telling him that "there isn't anything you can't do if you try hard enough," which the boy turns on Cooper when he tops his request for one home run with an appeal for a second one.

"I'll hit two homers for you if you hit one for me," Cooper says, his apprehension at satisfying the boy's requests slowly turning to confidence that they are bonding, perhaps in a way that Lou could not with his parents. Cooper, not a histrionic actor, had an arsenal full of facial flickers, small changes that register so well onscreen. When he smiles at Collins, it is in a natural way that overwhelms the Babe's staged promise.

"Me?" the wide-eyed Collins asks.

"You have to promise me that one of these days you're going to get up out of this bed and go home on your own power," Cooper says, his words potent.

"But how?" Collins asks.

"If you want to do something hard enough, you can do it," Cooper says. "Hey, we could both do it, can't we?"

Billy nods.

The movie paints Billy as a solitary boy, without parents at his bedside to witness the arrival of Gehrig and Ruth. In earlier drafts of the script, Billy was someone's child. He was, most interestingly, the child of Jim Van Allen, an early name for Lou's snooty fraternity nemesis, Van Tuyl, and Myra, the vampy young woman Lou fell for at the frat dance but who has also become Eleanor's friend. Lou visits Billy at the Van Allens' Chicago-area mansion, where Lou teaches the boy how to throw his teammate Red Ruffing's "dipsy doodle" pitch and volunteers to hit a second home run.

In another iteration, a down-on-his-luck Chicagoan named Jim Roberts comes to Lou at Comiskey Park to ask that Lou visit his son, Billy, at a local hospital. "Billy is just a pair of eyes, and they are dull and listless eyes that show a little sparkle when the great Ruth is brought to see him," Gallico writes, "but we see that the visit is not really having the desired effect in spite of the fact that the Great Man is gracious and kind, tells the kid he's going to get well, and, as the flashlights wink and glare, hands him an autographed baseball and even promises to hit a home run for him in the World Series the next day."

The scene is fiction even beyond the fable of Ruth and Gehrig vowing to hit home runs for a sick boy. The film seems to place the World Series game in 1933, when the New York Giants won in five games over the Washington Senators. The Yankees and Cardinals last played in the World Series in 1928. And while it is true that Lou hit two home runs in World Series games in 1928 and 1932, he could not have done it in 1933 or at the request of a boy struck by polio. Had *Pride* stuck to the truth and dramatized the 1932 World Series between the Yankees and Cubs, it could have shown Babe allegedly point to the spot in the bleachers where he would hit a home run off pitcher Charlie Root.

Back in New York, Eleanor was vetting the scripts. She wrote letters to Goldwyn and to Walsh conveying her concern over the errors. She understood that film biographies are semi-fictional, but she wanted *Pride* to hew to the facts of baseball and to Lou's career.

She spotted a slip regarding a World Series game that described not Ruth's called shot but Lou hitting four home runs. She wrote to Gallico:

I can just hear the critics yelp—"Gehrig's great records aren't enough for Hollywood. Goldwyn, with lawless disregard for millions of baseball fans, saw fit to change the record books," etc. etc. etc. In other words, Paul, they depicted Sergeant York as routing 26 Germans out of the trench, which everyone know is historically correct. What if Warners showed him marching along, prodding a few hundred guys. Get it?

Eleanor also noticed that St. Louis had erroneously replaced Chicago as the Yankees' rival. Reacting to a version of a mid-January script, she wrote:

This is one where you will really get in trouble. It says here that we come into the World's Series games at St. Louis in 1932. It so happens that one of the most brilliant performances put on by Lou and Babe happened at this series and it most surely made baseball history, but the Series was vs. the Chicago Cubs.

Then, showing some concern over factual errors, she added: "Please, boys, I think you need me out there. Can I come?"

Despite the errors and time-shifting, there is a kind of goofy, simple drama to the scene with Billy, which is more about the hero, Lou, defying baseball logic (who would guarantee *anyone* he would hit two home runs in a World Series game?) to come through for the kid with polio, whose condition foreshadows Lou's disease. It makes him more humble and heroic than Ruth and gave Cooper the sort of tender moment that we could have envisioned if Gehrig had had children. The sequence is also worth remembering for some of the film's oddest moments.

First there was the presence of Bill Stern, one of the era's most popular sports announcers. Stern was the perfect choice for these made-up scenes, since he was known as a fabulist, willing to embellish or concoct details if it suited the moment. His rat-a-tat, overly dramatic style and vulpine look suited the occasionally purplish script direction, like those that preceded the second Gehrig home run: "His face is haggard with desperation as he listens to the clamor of the crowd. But his mind is on a hospital cot. His lips move and we get the feeling he may be praying. He gets ready to slug one." With Cooper circling the bases on that homer, Stern says, "What do you think of that one? Two home runs in one World Series game. He's really a man!"

The sequence included scenes showing the film's Greek chorus of two, Blake and Hank Hanneman, Blake's pro-Ruth newspaper rival (Dan Duryea). This is one of their several scenes together in which they invariably argue the merits of Gehrig versus Ruth. Here, they extend their ghostwriting rivalry by bringing notes to Stern in the radio booth that ratchet up the competition to hit home runs for "the little crippled kid," in Stern's words. Blake and Hanneman, who type occasionally but seem never to take notes, are less reporters than they are partisan commentators for Gehrig and Ruth.

The scenes at the stadium alternate with those at the Gehrig home, where friends gather around the radio. Janssen has now fully morphed into a proud baseball mom, a makeover Eleanor may have attributed to the once-domineering mother realizing she might have lost her son if she hadn't reformed, as well as to Lou buying his parents a house and easing her physical burdens. Now she is a bit daffy. When Lou strikes out after hitting his first homer for Billy, she tells the group, "Oh, Louie didn't want Babe Ruth to feel too bad." When he fans again, she suggests, "Papa, maybe you'd better call Lou on the long distance and tell him to stop fooling."

The strangest scene in the movie occurs at Mom and Pop Gehrig's house as well. When Lou hits his promise-fulfilling second home run, the Gehrig house erupts into one of cinema's oddest celebrations: The group, led by a teenage neighbor, forms a conga line and chants, "Lou, Lou, Lou. Gehrig. Gehrig. Gehrig, Gehrig, Gehrig"—which they repeat over and over—as they circle the living room. Stossel leaves the line to turn a portrait of Uncle Otto to the wall.

At the hospital, ten-year-old Gene Collins has a look of satisfied glee. His delirious look—eyes wide and darting, his toothy smile—suggests that in the life of the polio-stricken kid, this was his happiest day. It's a bit over the top, but Collins is trying to channel what any Yankee fan might feel when their hero delivers on a personal promise.

Goldwyn must have been pleased at how the romance between Lou and Eleanor kept moving to the forefront of *Pride*. The love story is mature and sweet, teasing and humorous, a beautiful cinematic match-up of the tall, angular Cooper and the petite Wright. They banter lightly in a nightclub over whether Cooper has a girlfriend in every American League city—but he wants to short-circuit any talk of being a rogue by asking her to be his "best girl," a big deal for a man who refers to his mother that way.

The romance moves to a new and challenging level when Wright meets Janssen's obdurate Mom Gehrig. Crestfallen can barely describe Janssen's face when she spots the engagement ring on Wright's finger. More important, she looks scared that her power is dissipating. Janssen can't help but be crushed and overwhelmed with anxiety when Cooper says, "Mrs. Gehrig, meet Mrs. Gehrig."

In dialogue eliminated from *Pride's* final cut, Pop Gehrig's crush on Eleanor—young, pretty, and easy to be with—meets Mom's deep-seated jealousy.

"Isn't she beautiful, Mama?" he asks. "Isn't she sweet? Isn't she wonderful?"

"She's a nice girl, Papa," Mom says. "I never said she wasn't."

After pausing, Mom reveals her lack of self-awareness.

"But the way she looks at him," she says, "you'd think she *owned him*."

Mom Gehrig's attempt to reassert her control over Lou by dominating Eleanor—a clear attempt to break them up, said Lou's sportswriter friend Fred Lieb—hit its zenith with her countermanding Eleanor's furniture, wallpaper, and rug choices for her and Lou's new apartment. Janssen is at her best passive-aggressive here: smilingly presenting herself as the helpful mother-in-law with opinions about practical furnishings but steamrolling Eleanor by choosing a chifforobe, rug, and wallpaper pattern that offend Eleanor.

"You are so sweet, Ellie, to admit you were wrong," Janssen tells Wright after winning the battle of the chifforobes without recognizing Wright's dismay and suspicion that her love for Lou might be wrecked by Mom's love for him.

Cooper shows a quiet panic; his eyes register with confusion and anger as he recognizes that he has to confront Janssen in order to keep his future wife. In Wright's glistening eyes, you see how much Eleanor adores him and how much she appreciates the difficulty Lou had in rebelling against his mother's tyranny. When Cooper approaches the overwhelmed Wright as she scrubs the stove, he tells her how he reversed his mother's interior decorating flats in favor of his fiancée's. As she turns around, her smile broad, her eyes shining with tears, he tells her there can only be one boss in the house, and that he has asked the mayor of New Rochelle to marry them that day.

"Lou Gehrig," she says ecstatically, "I think I can learn to like you."

The crisis between Lou and Eleanor was actually more serious than *Pride* let on. Mom's heavy-handedness toward Eleanor, an interloper into the Gehrig family, was building. By Eleanor's account, they loathed each other. Eleanor had found an apartment in New Rochelle near the Gehrigs' house, and the time she spent with Mom persuaded her that life would be intolerable for her if she wed Lou.

"I broke our engagement," she wrote. "He cried. I cried; everybody cried."

Gallico dramatized the breakup in several ways that didn't make the film.

He invented a friend to whom Eleanor confides, "He isn't the kind of guy who ought to get married. He will be much happier and much better off living at home with his mother to look after him." He also had Lou confess to a weeping Eleanor, "I'm not the kind of guy for you. You'll be better off without me." With that, he heads to see his mother, where he tells her of the breakup, that he doesn't blame her (but wants to) yet must leave their house for a life on his own.

"You go away from your mama?" she asks pathetically. He returns to the apartment, where Eleanor is still packing to return to Chicago, he takes her in his arms, and they renew their commitment to marry.

"There'll never be anyone but you," he says in an early version of the screenplay.

As a symbol of his independence, Lou tosses away the portrait of Uncle Otto that his mother had brought stealthily to Lou and Eleanor's apartment.

"And that's the end of Uncle Otto and Mom!" Lou exclaims.

Wood moves *Pride* to the wedding in the young Gehrigs' apartment, amid a group of noisy, clueless workers and deliverymen, with Mom and Pop Gehrig among the guests. Janssen is conciliatory and cheerful—having been dressed down by Lou—at the service that was performed by New Rochelle mayor Walter Otto (George Lessey). While it is true that the Westchester city's mayor wed the younger Gehrigs, Mom and Pop weren't there.

Eleanor brought the error to Goldwyn's attention through a memo delivered by Walsh: "Reference made to Mom and Pop Gehrig attending wedding of Lou and Eleanor. Mrs. Gehrig does not object to this but points out that it is not accurate."

Further details showed how much more troubled the romance truly was—facts that would have extended the story and turned Mom Gehrig into even more of a harridan. Lou asked Lieb, who got along well with Mom, to persuade her to attend the wedding reception on Long Island the day after the quickie ceremony, but she emphatically rejected his request.

"I won't go!" she told Lieb. "I have no intention of going."

"Now, Mom, that's no way to talk," Lieb recalled telling her, adding, "Your son is marrying another woman and that other woman is coming between him and his mother, and you now have that choice, whether he's to be married under good circumstances or bad. This could lead to a complete break, which it does sometimes."

Mom responded, first with unprintable words about Eleanor, then said, "If I went there I would only raise hell."

Still, he offered to pick her up and deliver her to the reception—and, objections aside, she was there at the appointed time.

And, Lieb wrote, "Everything went off all right."

Pride proceeds as if indeed everything will be all right. Cooper and Wright head to Yankee Stadium, with Brennan driving, and a police escort leads them, to avoid missing the day's game. Cooper shows his happiness, hitting a wedding day home run and shouting his thanks for marrying him as he rounds the bases. (Gehrig, in reality, went hitless that day but drove in two runs with a walk and sacrifice fly.) After the game, Cooper and Wright smooch for the press, and, in his ecstasy, Cooper says he doesn't care if the photographers have film in their cameras.

Wright recalled one kiss in the scene from Cooper lasting so long that she broke away and said, "A girl's got to breathe!" She said it was an ad lib that was so well received by Wood and the crew that Cooper insisted it be used in the film. The line, however, is in the shooting script—just as she improvised it.

The depth of their screen love—an affirming and frisky one—continues to evolve. As an elaborate ruse, Wright persuades Brennan that Cooper is cheating on her, only to drive him to a sandlot where Cooper is umpiring a kids' baseball game on a field reminiscent of the one that his younger self plays on to open *Pride*.

"Don't talk to me, you Borgia," the duped Brennan tells the giggling Wright.

By now, Cooper and Wright's portrayal of the Gehrigs' marriage has become the romantic ideal envisioned by Goldwyn—a moving depiction of a couple's deep love that would have been different if Goldwyn had chosen Barbara Stanwyck, an early favorite, as Eleanor, or had Eddie Albert played Lou. Wright's maturity three pictures into her career dissolves the age difference with Cooper, who is nearly two decades into his career. They make a credible onscreen couple that radiates joy and an ineffable ease in each other's company.

—————

Outside the Gehrig home in early 1938, snow is falling and spring training is approaching. Cooper suggests that Wright has had enough baseball and she should not join him in St. Petersburg. Cooper hopes she will not take his bait, and they fall into each other's arms, as if to say, *What a stupid idea that was, Lou.* Wright's feet rest on Cooper's—he is about a foot taller than she—and they dance with the joyful passion of newlyweds. After their subsequent beach-wrestling scene, he reminds her, with a bit of regret, that they've never had a honeymoon. She presses her cheek into his right arm and says, "We've never had anything but."

Their love defines bliss—before the deluge.

At breakfast before the two thousandth game, Wright suggests that Cooper miss the game, that the news would be if he stops at number 1,999, not continue building on what critics thought was a stunt—and still hold the record by nearly 700 games. The idea of Lou missing a game, let alone the two thousandth, briefly outrages Mom (now a well-dressed, well-behaved matron); Janssen urges Cooper "to get a wiggle on" lest he miss receiving a car (or a yacht, says Pop) from his appreciative fans. Wright argues that he will receive nothing more than a horseshoe of roses—the gift, in reality—which Cooper totes home around his neck after striking out three times (he actually had one hit, no strikeouts, and one RBI in four at-bats).

What follows is at the romantic and emotional core of the movie:

In one of the loveliest scenes, Cooper and Wright toss roses at each other. She accompanies each toss by noting all the moments in their lives together when he made her worry (for playing even after getting beaned, with broken toes, with a 103-degree fever, with the flu) and he responds with sweet ripostes (for having brown eyes, for being the greatest fan a man ever had, for putting up with him all these years). They giggle wildly and wrestle until her rambunctiousness sends him tumbling backward in his cushioned chair. They are all but making love, fully clothed, in the fearful era when the prudish censors at the Hays Office oversaw onscreen behavior.

With Wright on top, she declares, "I won, I won, fair and square." Her victory is short-lived when a look of concern overtakes Cooper's face: His eyebrows scrunch, his eyes widen—it is the look of a man fearing the end of something. Or, given what Gallico and the writers knew, this was a sensitive way to demonstrate the early onset of ALS, rather than show him stumbling over curbs. Gallico was more graphic when he first conceived the scene. When Eleanor pins Lou, he says, "Hey, what's going on here? You getting stronger?"

"You bet I am," she says.

"I'm not kidding," he says seriously. "You put me down too easily."

"When I'm ferocious, I don't know my own strength," she says, still not recognizing the gravity of what has happened. "Say 'Uncle'!"

In another version, she calls him a "sissy" for losing so easily. In the end, Mankiewicz and Swerling minimized Eleanor's post-match gloating and moved her quickly to show her worry.

"What is it, Lou?" Wright asks.

Clutching his right shoulder, Cooper says, "I must have sprained my shoulder. It felt kind of stiff at the game. Maybe that was why I struck out."

"I'll get the liniment," she says, rushing to help him.

Cooper flexes his arms, stands and picks up a bat, swings, and grimaces.

The screen directions suggest the gravity of the moment:

He keeps feeling his arms. They have failed him. He realizes that his strength had suddenly ebbed away so that he couldn't even make the flip that usually won him the wrestling match. Near the trophy cabinet is an inscribed bat. He reaches for it and swings it back and forth. The puzzled look in his eyes deepens.

The scene ends with that bewilderment and sense of doom, but without any words. Gallico thought the scene should continue a bit longer, with speculation about what the Gehrigs thought Lou was suffering from (a charley horse or nerve pressure) and with Lou's question to Eleanor: "Gee, wouldn't it be awful if anything happened that I couldn't swing the old bread-and-butter club anymore?"

13

"Lou Seems to Have Become More Gary Cooper Than Lou Gehrig"

The alarm shown by Cooper after his wrestling match with Wright is exacerbated when spring training begins. Cooper's Gehrig runs slowly and can barely hit, as if his age had doubled since the previous spring. The fear is apparent in Wright's eyes as she sits in the bleacher seats at La Cienega Park in Beverly Hills, the location used to stand in for the Yankees' spring training site in St. Petersburg, Florida. The scenes were shot at dusk so that once Cooper has run around the field to loosen his balky joints and meets Wright, they speak in a sepulchral darkness. When he lightheartedly suggests to her that he is slowing down, she jauntily responds with a line that would have jolted audiences.

"Oh, sure," Wright says. "I'll get a wheelchair and push you around."

Writer Paul Gallico's original intent was for the film to show dissension over Gehrig's failure to play as he once did. Fickle fans can be the quickest to turn on a player, however great, when his skills and performance erode. So, as Cooper is thrown out at first base on a single to short right field, two "crackers" in the stands carp, one shouting, "Oh, what a bum! He got throwd out from right field"; the other saying, "Hey, Gehrig, whyn't you-all git the lead outn' your pants?"

Lou's protector, Chuck Frawley—the coach Gallico created to follow Gehrig from the minor leagues to the Yankees and named for his friend William Frawley, the future Fred Mertz of *I Love Lucy*—good-naturedly tells him that he is working too hard and should take the rest of the day off (words that in the film are spoken by McCarthy's character). Lou insists that he must work even harder and begins taking laps around the field. With Lou out of sight, Gallico writes, a "lanky, unpleasant looking pitcher" named Joe Gribble—also fictional—angers Frawley by saying, "If he don't stop having off days, it's gonna be good-bye pennant this year. When a guy gets that bad, he ought to retire." Frawley "lets him have it with 'Lissen, wise guy, you'd better win yourself some games before you go making cracks about a guy like Lou. He'll be okay when the season gets going.' "

Frawley is only protecting the player he has followed from Hartford. He knew Lou could not play further; as the scene ends in twilight, Eleanor and Frawley sit together in the empty stands waiting for Lou to return.

"I don't get it, Eleanor," he says to her. "Ballplayers slow up gradually. This guy's falling apart all in one piece."

Eleanor says nothing but casts a "frightened look" Frawley's way.

While these scenes did not end up in the film, it was clear that Gallico couldn't help presenting the starkness of Lou's decline.

In a montage that parallels Lou's ascent from minor-league Hartford to the Yankees, he paints one of his failures: "We see him striking out and his batting average diminishing. We see a box score with zeroes in the hit column; we see a flash of tough faces of fans in various ballparks as they razz Lou. We see a flash of Lou making an error at first base and then a newspaper headline: 'YANKS LOSE AGAIN.'"

This negative approach could not survive, not with Goldwyn determined to elevate Gehrig as a hero, or with Eleanor reading every word of every script and alert to the nuances of her husband's portrayal.

So grammar-challenged crackers would not hoot at Lou.

He would not strike out meekly.

His dying batting average would not mock him.

And only those closest to him would get to convey what was wrong.

When a left-hander's high, inside pitch sends Cooper reeling toward the backstop, he is caught in the strong arms of Bill Dickey, Gehrig's closest friend and the star catcher of the Yankees. Cooper's face is, yet again, a mask of bewilderment, but Dickey, playing himself, offers solace, however false.

"Those kids don't know what to do with their speed," Dickey says with a smile while cradling Cooper. "Lucky you got out of the way so quick."

"Yeah," Cooper says, but his expression cannot hide that his character knows his reflexes and balance are flatlining and that he wasn't deftly avoiding a fireballer's brushback pitch. Dickey's wife, Violet, a former showgirl also playing herself, asks him, "Bill, what's the matter with Lou?" He can only shake his head.

Dickey's intervention is appropriate. Eleanor told Walsh that they had been inseparable on road trips, and she suggested a "cute shot" that showed Lou being "motherly such as finishing Bill's packing such as toothbrushes, handkerchiefs, shirts, etc., in the last minute's rush." Once Lou got ill, the roles reversed and Dickey became "the subtle nurse," and "as Lou became unsteady, Bill always lingered so that he would be able to help him."

Even before Dickey catches Cooper, Wright looks concerned. The camera tracks past other fans quickly to zoom in on her as she squeezes a glove or a handkerchief, concerned about what will happen next. Cooper's near-fall prompts her to rise from her seat—not to inspire Lou, as Iris Gaines (Glenn Close) did for Roy Hobbs (Robert Redford) in *The Natural*—but in fear for her now-vulnerable husband. A brief smile when he hits a grounder disappears quickly when he is thrown out easily at first.

Gehrig's failures are further shielded when the season begins in *Pride*. He is not contributing to a team that is no longer his: Joe DiMaggio is the team's biggest star, although he is not depicted in *Pride* nor does anyone wear his number five. When the film shifts from spring training to Yankee Stadium, frustrated players stream into the clubhouse, led by a pitcher, known only as Hammond, who fulminates that Gehrig's fielding cost him, and the team, the game. No errors are shown.

"That game was just booted away," he says. "I can't pitch and play first base, too. The old man at first base ought to have some crutches to get around with." His sacrilege gets him decked with a right by Dickey but, more important, after Cooper sits on a stool and tries to untie the laces of his cleats, he falls over, as if he has lost control of his body. Dickey holds up a hand, gesturing that no one should help him, if nothing else, to preserve his dignity.

Cooper takes twenty seconds to get off the floor. When he rights himself and none of his teammates look toward him, he deftly communicates the panic and desolation that Gehrig must have felt in his final days as a player.

Eleanor, who spent weeks in San Francisco working with Gallico on his outline and screenplay, apparently poured out her heart to him. Some of it survives, some of it does not. In one instance recorded by Gallico, she told him that "toward the end, he was no longer the warrior. His step was faltering by then. He fell several times and the boys pretended that they had not noticed it." In her autobiography, *My Luke and I*, she wrote that McCarthy "chose to look the other way" from Gehrig's spring training troubles and headed into the season with Lou at first base.

She wrote that after Lou went hitless in a loss to Washington in the eighth game of the season—his finale, it turns out—a teammate griped, "Why doesn't he quit? He's through. We can't win with him in there." Then, she added, "He hesitated a moment outside, got his composure back, then came into view inside the clubhouse. Then everybody stopped talking at once and he dressed in absolute silence." He took the train home on an off day before the Yankees headed west to Detroit, and "when I met him at the door, he was a changed man: troubled, shaken, even shocked." He told her: "They don't think I can do it anymore. Maybe I can, maybe I can't. But they're talking about it now, they're even writing about it. And when they're not talking, I can almost feel what they're thinking."

Gallico wanted to escalate the drama even further by playing up the team dissension. Gribble, the villain, is willing to challenge and deride Lou. As the players grumble about losing a game, Gehrig offers some "we'll get 'em next time" sentiment that Gribble is too angry to accept.

"Ah, quit the Boy Scout stuff," he says. "I could have won that game today if you hadn't made two errors on chances a kid could handle."

When Dickey intervenes, reminding Gribble of the home run ball he threw late in the game, Gribble biliously retorts: "We ain't going to win a pennant with a cripple on the team! And a lot of the guys feel the same way about it." The two sides keep muttering, and Gallico writes: "Lou sits there in a great agony of the soul all through these speeches. *Tears start streaming down his face.*" (Italics mine.)

Had Sam Wood filmed the scene, it would have seemed realistic—how could some teammates not resent Gehrig for jeopardizing their victories or McCarthy for leaving him in the lineup for sentimental reasons? But it would have contravened Goldwyn's intent that *his* Gehrig sport a pinstriped halo; that he was a baseball soldier mortally wounded, and that no one, not even teammates riled that Lou's illness was making the team suffer, would call him a cripple. (That acceptable epithet of the time was reserved for young Billy in the hospital.) In addition, having him weep at the unfairness of being criticized for playing through a disabling disease would have robbed *Pride* of the wallop of the tears Gehrig sheds at the end of the picture when he says farewell—while declaring with gratitude that seemed far too generous to the fates that he was the "luckiest man on the face of the earth."

Gallico tried to manufacture tear-jerking drama out of Lou's illness—creating scenes that depict Gehrig as having lost nearly all his ability to hit a ball.

In his outline, he returns to Billy, following a game against the

White Sox at Comiskey Park in 1939. Lou and coach Frawley meet the boy, who has recovered enough from polio to be wearing only braces, and Jim, his down-on-his-luck father.

Billy asks for another favor, to visit his school camp the next morning. When Lou arrives, the kids mob him. Lou steps to the plate to face Billy's pitching.

"The key to this scene," Gallico writes, "is that, try as Lou will, he cannot hit. He is slow, swinging awkwardly and missing easy pitches from Billy. Billy is just lobbing pitches. We see the strain on Lou's face as he redoubles his efforts, sweat standing on his face. For the first time he knows how bad he is."

The best Lou can do, Gallico writes, "is to foul some off."

The kids think he is kidding, whiffing on pitches to make Billy feel good, but they start asking him to hit a home run.

"Lou misses a pitch by so much it's laughable," Gallico writes.

That failure, Gallico writes, is the impetus for Lou to ask McCarthy, before that afternoon's game against the White Sox, to take him out of the lineup, ending his streak of playing in 2,130 consecutive games. That Lou actually made the request of McCarthy in a hotel lobby in Detroit on May 2, 1939, appears to have been an inconvenient fact to Gallico, who must have known the story quite well.

Never mind that Lou himself said that he decided to sit out, and perhaps return after a rest, after being unable to make an unassisted out on a grounder to first base against Washington on April 30, when he had to flip the ball to reliever Johnny Murphy. "When I returned to the bench, the boys said, 'Great play Lou.' I said to myself, 'Heavens, has it reached that stage?'"

In his subsequent scripts, Gallico posited that Lou leaves spring training after a terrible game and gives a kid a few dollars to pitch to him in a vacant lot behind some billboards, echoing the raucous sandlot scene at the start of *Pride*. The result, Gallico wrote, was pitiful: Lou swings on the pitches, mostly in vain, "too late most of the time, falling down, and when he does hit them, they are just weak grounders that barely reach the boy, or pop flies that just drop over his head."

In a third go-round, Lou leaves the Comiskey Park clubhouse during his brief regular season to join Billy, who, in this alternative version, is the son of his one-time fraternity tormentor, Van Tuyl, and coquettish Myra, who danced with virginal Lou at Columbia. They have a large country house where, six years after Lou hit those homers for the boy, Billy is wearing braces on his legs and wants to show Lou that he can play ball. Billy pitches but Lou is so debilitated that he can only hit a dribbler and a pop-up, and finally whiffs so badly he stumbles.

"Come on, Lou," Billy says, unaware that Lou is not pretending. "Let's see you hit a real home run this time. I won't try to strike you out."

Gallico and Baldwin end the scene with these directions:

Close-up on Lou's face: He is desperate and drenched with sweat. His face is lined, haggard. He looks years older. He grits his teeth. The ball comes at him and he swings. A terribly desperate look comes to his face as he realizes he has missed it.

Pride shifts to Detroit, where Gehrig ends his career. Telling McCarthy to sit him hours before the game is not dramatic, so the film tells it another way: It is the sixth inning of a Yankees-Tigers game. The Yankees lead, 4–2. Cooper awaits his at-bat in the dugout, flexing his stiff fingers, looking at them as if he cannot believe their betrayal of him, and then tucking them in his belt, as if ashamed of their failure. As he moves to the on-deck circle, he stops at an array of bats in foul territory, a reminder of when he met Eleanor by stumbling over the lineup of bats that led Eleanor and other White Sox fans to dub him "Tanglefoot." Now there is something ominous as he approaches his second or third plate appearance of the game. As he lifts two bats to his shoulder, he looks concerned, as if he knows he cannot hold two for long, let alone swing one as he once did. When the third out is made, leaving Lou on deck, he trudges back to the dugout, passing Wright in a box seat, then Dickey, who looks back at him unaware of his best friend's plan.

"Joe," he tells Harry Harvey, who plays McCarthy, "you better send someone in for me. I can't make it anymore."

Harvey, his head down, asks, "Sure you want it that way?"

"Yup," says Cooper with the terseness of the Western star he was.

Harvey turns his neck and calls on Lou's replacement.

"Dahlgren, get in there at first," he says.

As Cooper and Dahlgren (Rip Russell) pass on the dugout steps, Cooper says, "Good luck."

Cooper then passes a gantlet of his teammates, none of whom by their numbers is a star, save for Dickey. He walks slowly, haltingly. He doesn't look at them. They each lower their glances to the dugout floor, avoiding eye contact with Cooper. He settles on a seat a fair distance from any of his teammates when we hear the announcement: "Dahlgren now playing first base for New York. Replacing Gehrig." The camera zooms in on Lou, who stares out at the field, his eyes glistening before lowering his head until we only see the top of his cap.

The change in the story line to have Gehrig leave in the sixth works dramatically, but squelches what really happened that day. Gehrig and Dahlgren posed for photographers before the first pitch. Gehrig played catch with Dickey. Dahlgren even pleaded with Gehrig to change his mind. "You've put me in a terrible spot," Dahlgren said, but Gehrig slapped him on the back and told him, "Go on out there and knock in some runs." When Lou brought the lineup card out to the umpires, fans cheered him, prompted by Tigers radio voice Ty Tyson. As for the game itself, the Yankees were not in a close 4–2 game; after six innings they were leading 13–2, en route to a 22–2 victory. Dahlgren homered and drove in two runs.

Cooper was creating a new Gehrig. By this point in *Pride*, Cooper has fully occupied and absorbed the Gehrig character. Fans knew as much about sports stars as radio, newsreels, and papers allowed, and rarely did a full picture emerge. Sportswriters willing to ask hard and rude questions and reveal what troubles players got into off the field were decades away.

The chaste intimacies of the Gehrigs' marriage, Lou's relationship with his mother, and his marriage to Eleanor were private matters the public probably learned more about from *Pride* than from any other source. They were left to accept the "truths" created by *Pride*, which did not stick to many of the facts.

Cooper became a more fully realized version of Gehrig than the public knew, much as he did in his Academy Award–winning portrayal of Sergeant York. Gallico recognized this metamorphosis when he later read Mankiewicz and Swerling's shooting script. Moviegoers have understood it since.

"Lou seems to have become more Gary Cooper than Lou Gehrig but I suppose they had to do that," he told Eleanor in a letter about halfway through filming of *Pride*. "I think he still comes out a very lovely character."

Cooper's ability to evoke empathy was a hallmark of his career. You followed Cooper where he took you, as his friend James Stewart did in *It's a Wonderful Life*, or *The Stratton Story*, a baseball film also directed by Sam Wood about a Chicago White Sox pitcher who accidentally shoots his leg in a hunting accident, requiring its amputation, and makes a brief comeback to the minor leagues.

So when Cooper's Gehrig is diagnosed with amyotrophic lateral sclerosis, you feel his relief that there is an explanation for his decline—even if his dialogue could have been salvaged from its clichés.

"Go ahead, Doc, I'm a man who likes to know his batting average," Cooper says as the doctor rifles through X-rays.

"Give it to me straight, Doc, am I through with baseball?" Cooper asks.

"I'm afraid so," the doctor says, unable to look him in the eye.

"Any worse than that?" he asks. "Is it three strikes, Doc?"

"You want it straight?" the doctor responds.

"Sure, I do. Straight," Cooper says, in an exchange that could easily pass for one between a sheriff and an outlaw.

"It's three strikes," the doctor says, finally able to look directly at Lou.

With a forced smile, Cooper says, "Doc, I've learned one thing. All the arguing in the world can't change the decision of the umpire. How much time have I got?"

Before the doctor answers, Wright enters, and the prognosis is never given.

In real life, Lou went alone to the Mayo Clinic to be diagnosed, flying directly from Chicago, where he had accompanied the Yankees. Eleanor, who stayed at home in Larchmont, New York, had arranged through a friend to have Lou examined at Mayo, in Rochester, Minnesota. She waited six days for the diagnosis.

She said she heard from Drs. Paul O'Leary and Charles Mayo that Lou had, at most, two and a half years to live, and got them to promise that they wouldn't tell Lou.

In the film, Wright's Eleanor is present (at the fictional Scripps Clinic), as is Blake, giving Cooper gum as he awaits the diagnosis; allaying his anxieties (the doctor, he said, "never ran up against a better physical specimen"); helping to hide the truth from Wright; and agreeing to Cooper's request that he concoct a cover story for the press.

Pride does not divulge that Lou has ALS (only that he can't pronounce what he has, and the doctor demurs saying it aloud when Eleanor asks him) or his outlook. Wright guesses how dire his health is when Cooper and the doctor leave the office. She knows she is being lied to, by her husband, by the doctor, and by Blake. She wants to know the truth. Wright looks up at Brennan.

"When is Lou going to die?" she asks, her eyes slowly looking downward. Her question surprises Brennan.

Brennan hesitates, kneads the brim of his fedora, and asks, "Who told you?"

"I could read it in your eyes," she says. "All of you." Then, rising, she looks directly at Brennan as if director Sam Wood had told her that now she had to show strength; now Lou needed her more than ever. "It's all right, Sam," she says, "I'll never let him know I know. Oh, he's so young and so strong."

For once, she needs the sidekick's services and weeps in Brennan's arms.

Gallico offers two bolder variations on the story. First, he has the doctor (at the fictional Graham Foundation Clinic) tell Lou he has ALS and only a year or two to live. Second, when the doctor describes ALS as a "sort of paralysis bug," the words give Lou some hope. "Like infantile?," he asks, recalling all the incarnations of Billy, who has polio, or infantile paralysis. The doctor tells him he has something quite different from polio. When Lou heads to the door, he gestures with his fist and turns his thumb downward. The doctor nods slightly.

"Will my mind go, too?" Lou asks, a direction that *Pride* never headed in, but one that Eleanor provided Gallico in their interviews, using almost the same words.

"No," the doctor says, confirming the irony of a fatal, fast-moving neuromuscular disease that viciously paralyzes the body but leaves the mind intact.

Gallico also wrote a scene with Eleanor visiting a Dr. Jensen, a family physician, skeptical of the clinic's finding that Lou has a fifty-fifty chance of recovery.

"Why aren't you satisfied with what is stated here?" Jensen asks. "Sometimes, you know, it's better to—"

"Because he's my husband," she says loudly, rising to her feet. "And I love him and want to help him and protect him. But I've got to know the truth to do it."

"You make it very difficult, Eleanor," he says, patronizing her. "But I agree with you—you should know the truth."

Gallico writes: "Eleanor, her eyes bug-eyed, her face terrified, barely whispers, 'You mean—he hasn't got a fifty-fifty chance?'"

Jensen shakes his head and says the clinic was "merciful" with its odds.

Gallico's inexperience as a screenplay writer made him bolder and willing to add more—true or not—than the veterans Mankiewicz and Swerling felt necessary or Goldwyn or Wood felt suitable for the film. Goldwyn and Gallico kept up a correspondence well after his work ended. Days before shooting began, Goldwyn confided to Gallico: "I am still having my troubles trying to get the Gehrig script in shape but I feel that I am making some progress now. I have Jo Swerling and Herman Mankiewicz working on it." Six weeks later, Goldwyn told Gallico: "It has been a tough job so far because of the baseball and other things that had to be put up with." Gallico occasionally sent in fixes through the shooting and suggested the scene where Eleanor pretends to Blake that Lou is cheating on her, only to take him to a sandlot where her happy husband is umpiring a kids' ballgame.

Gallico took an adventurous, if wrong-headed, detour when he advised in his lengthy outline (for what was to be called *Lou Gehrig: All American*) that "it might strengthen the story if perhaps we don't know Lou ever actually finds out the real truth of his sickness and instead he always plays the fifty-fifty chance to recover in Eleanor's presence." Gallico then created a lengthy scene in Lou's parole commission office where one Mary Misnicki, a teenaged dope fiend and prostitute with a bad attitude, seeks parole from Lou, who did not start his post-Yankees job as a New York City parole commissioner until October 1939. Gallico jumbled the calendar, placing the parolee scene before Lou spoke on Lou Gehrig Appreciation Day. Gallico's intent was to show that Gehrig knew all along how dire his illness was, though the encounter might have been a scene from a bad gangster movie.

Lou is faced with a young, hardened criminal who is unimpressed with him.

"You're sorry," she says. "You're so smug sitting there. I gotta tell ya I gotta get out. What's it to you? You don't know what two years means? Didn't I answer all yer questions? I didn't lie, did I?"

Lou's foot searches for the button beneath his desk to summon his secretary but stops short of pressing it. "Why do I have to let you go?" he asks icily.

She brings her face to Lou's and half whispers, "Because I'm gonna die. I got a cancer here. I been told I won't be here any more when the two years is up."

Gehrig stares into Mary's face with "horror, sympathy and understanding," and in a barely audible voice says, "Going to die. I'm . . . I'm sorry. I didn't know."

Had the scene been filmed, his empathy would clearly be the trigger for a confession of his own imminent death.

Seeing that Lou is a softie, Mary tells him that she'll "live like I wanna live" if she gets out and "I'll get drunk if I wanna get drunk."

Lou, shocked as much by her cancer as her desire to continue her criminal activities, nods at a pack of cigarettes on his desk and asks her to light one for him.

"Whyn't you light it yourself?" she asks brutally.

Lou says, "I would if I could. But I can't. And . . . I need one."

Mary comes closer to his desk, takes one of his hands in hers, and lets it fall. "It drops with a relaxed and helpless thud," Gallico writes. She regards him with pity and confusion. They say nothing, but she taps the cigarette pack, takes one out, places it between his lips, and lights it.

"Lou puffs deeply so that the end glows," Gallico writes.

Mary hovers over him maternally and removes the cigarette when the ashes are nearly falling off. She puts the cigarette in an ashtray.

After he thanks her, she asks what is wrong with him.

"Isn't it funny," he says softly. "You and me? I'm going to die, too."

"Tell me about it," she says.

"There isn't much to tell," he says. "It's a disease that can't be cured. In two years, I won't be here, either. That's why I know what you're talking about."

"I gets ya," Mary says. "Ya just wanna go out and do everything at once like if there's a minute when yer not doing something ya can never get it back."

Now she is gently stroking Lou's head as she recognizes his torment.

"So what's the answer when a guy does what he thinks is right all his life and then has to get out of it when he's happy for the first time in his life?" he asks Mary.

Lou asks his secretary to mark Mary's file "parole recommended," and tells her he will see her again when she reports to him in the future.

Gallico probably realized that this scene was a long shot to survive; after all, if it were filmed, Lou would have had to deliver his speech from a wheelchair. It is doubtful that among the liberties that *Pride* takes with the truth, it would show Lou being wheeled to the galaxy of microphones to deliver his speech, rather than standing, as he did in reality, somewhat unsteadily for his nearly three-minute address.

A scene at Lou's parole commissioner office was written with a craps-playing kid holding a handful of pictures for Lou to sign, who tells him, "Yeah, all the kids want to get arrested to come to talk to you." Blake soon enters to tell Lou about the upcoming day in his honor on July 4—another out-of-order scene that had Lou working for the city before he had even made his farewell address.

Lou: What do you think of that?
Blake: You'll get back in uniform again.
Lou: They'll probably want me to do some pinch-hitting.

Blake: The trouble with the kind of hits you make is that you have to run so far.

Lou: But did you ever stop to think that the kind of hits I make let me run slower? Why, if I can sock one hard enough, I can get you to push me around the diamond in a wheelchair!

The notion that Gehrig's hits were the sort that allowed him to run slowly is an ignorant one. He hit a lot of home runs, of course, but he hit a lot of doubles and triples, the sort of hits that force batters to expend a lot of effort.

Pride shifts from the clinic to the Gehrigs' home, where they are preparing for the day in his honor, on July 4. The scene is the most heartbreaking of the film: Cooper has trouble tying his bow tie. Wright watches him through the slight crack between the bathroom door and its hinges; he struggles with his lost dexterity as he whistles "Always." In a film that avoids graphically showing Gehrig's physical decline, seeing Cooper demonstrate his failure to fashion a bow tie is a significant but subtle sign of his deterioration. Seeing his problem, Wright appears pained, then looks to cheer him up: She finds thread that she turns into a mustache; a small lampshade that becomes a megaphone; a pen that turns into a cigar and a beret; and recasts herself as a bellowing vendor at Yankee Stadium. Then, dropping the act, she ties his tie, an act that Cooper shows silent gratitude for, and suggests they go on their long-delayed honeymoon. One after another, they say, *"We've got all the time in the world,"* and the words stop them cold.

Gallico and Baldwin had them playfully rehearse the farewell ceremony in a scene that did not survive to the next draft of the script.

Eleanor hands him a dozen roses, and Lou asks, "What do I do now?"

Eleanor: You make a speech. Give 'em Number 12A.
Lou [rises slowly]: Ladies and gentlemen, unprepared as I am today—and furthermore, if I am elected.
Eleanor: Louder! [and looking at her wrist] Oh, Lou, aren't we terrible? We ought to be dressing right now for the stadium. Mom and Pop will be coming by for us any minute.
Lou: I wish I didn't have to go, El. I don't deserve all that fuss.
Eleanor: Yes, you do. You deserve twice as much.

Wright and Cooper are at their best as a couple in love coping with the imminent tragedy that is only hinted at. With baseball gone for Lou, Eleanor is his world; he will grow increasingly needy and dependent on her. While we never see Cooper any more dependent than when she ties his tie, her difficult future is easily envisioned. In her memoir, Eleanor writes that Lou was "shaken to tears" when they saw *Tristan and Isolde*. What struck him, she wrote, was the story of the lovers "who found their way together too late in the world and maybe only in death." Watching that unfold several times at the Metropolitan Opera destroyed him emotionally—"and that was long before he lay dying on his own couch."

Rather than delve too deeply into the Gehrigs' marriage or even stage a bit of *Tristan and Isolde*, *Pride*'s makers used a piece of jewelry as a symbol of their love. Wright feels a bulge inside Cooper's sport jacket and opens a box to reveal his gift to her: a charm bracelet, made from medals and awards he received in his career that is similar to the one Lou gave Eleanor in 1937. Wright regards it immediately as her greatest treasure.

"Oh, Lou, I adore it," she says. "I remember when you got every one of these medals."

"This is the one I get the most kick out of," Cooper says as he kisses her on the top of her head. "The batting championship I won the year we got married." (Which is not accurate, since their wedding at the end of the 1933 season predated his 1934 Triple Crown for leading the American League in batting, home runs, and runs batted in.)

Wright was adept at crying, and as she reacted to the gift from Lou, she began to sob. Her left hand hung on to one of Lou's jacket lapels.

"I've got a right to cry a little," she says with her face buried in Cooper's chest. "It's such a beautiful thing." As Cooper's eyes fill with tears, he tells her, "I wanted you to have it, Ellie, because you've given me so much."

Wright quickly transforms from weeping to cheerful wife as she pulls from their tight embrace and asks, "Are you making love to me, you big ape?"

"You bet I am, you big dope," Cooper says.

If there was any doubt by now, *Pride* is officially a weeper—*Stella Dallas* in a baseball setting, precisely what Goldwyn desired.

Jim Mulvey had already assured Eleanor late in the filming that the emotion of her and Lou's story was being felt at the top rung of the studio.

"I saw some of the scenes this morning with Mr. Goldwyn and honestly, when we got through and the lights went up both of us were actually crying like children," he wrote her. "I have never seen more beautifully or more heart appealing scenes in my life."

In nearly every version of the script, the bracelet scene precedes the ceremony at Yankee Stadium that culminates in Cooper's delivery of Gehrig's "luckiest man" speech. But Wood or Goldwyn apparently believed something else was needed, and they found it in a scene delivered on May 7, 1942, by unknown writers—perhaps Mankiewicz and Swerling, Gallico, or other contributors who moved in and out of the film's orbit, like the tart-tongued Dorothy Parker or Richard Maibaum, who was best known decades later for writing scripts for the James Bond films. With so many writers around—Walsh said that at one point, he was also part of the team—it was sometimes hard to tell who wrote what. Mankiewicz, an alcoholic and gambler whose wit and facility at screenwriting were balanced with immense self-doubt, found himself at odds with Goldwyn, not surprising given the strong wills of the two men. Goldwyn had hired Maibaum to write a competing script, according to Richard Meryman's biography of Mankiewicz.

Mankiewicz had another battle on his hands, a reminder of his bruising fight for credit with Orson Welles over *Citizen Kane*. Now, here was Goldwyn taunting him with Maibaum's own script at the Cock 'n' Bull restaurant.

"This is what I mean by screenwriting!" Goldwyn announced. Mankiewicz leafed through the script.

"He should drink," he said.

In the scene that was delivered on May 7, Billy returns to Gehrig's life as a healthy teenager in a suit and tie, without braces on his legs. An older actor, David Holt, has by now replaced Gene Collins. He stands at the entrance to the Yankee offices in advance of the tribute to Gehrig, hoping to speak to him. It is a resonant use of Billy, one that alludes to a role reversal between the once-crippled little boy and the newly disabled Gehrig.

Holt was about fourteen when he got the job. He was already a veteran child actor, once billed by Paramount as the male equivalent of Shirley Temple, and initially cast in *David Copperfield*, only to be replaced by the British actor Freddie Bartholomew. He was only acting to support his family and actually hated it, his daughter said, finding creative contentment later in life as a composer and jazz musician. According to studio publicity, Goldwyn tested him personally and briefed the young actor on the role, his character's suffering, and his gratitude to Lou for raising his spirits in the hospital room. At one point, the studio publicity file claims, after Goldwyn explained to Holt that Billy has polio, Holt looked breathlessly at the producer with tears in his eyes.

"I know, Mr. Goldwyn," he said, "I—I had infantile paralysis."

It was a surprising revelation to Goldwyn—and Holt was hired.

When Cooper and Wright pull up in a taxicab at the stadium, Holt steps out from the group of fans and police.

"Mr. Gehrig," Holt says, trying to stop Cooper before he walks into the stadium. "Oh, Mr. Gehrig, please."

Cooper turns around but says nothing.

"Don't you remember me?" Holt asks.

Cooper's blank face suggests that he does not.

"You knocked out two home runs for me one afternoon," Holt says.

"Sure, sure, I remember you," Cooper says, shaking Holt's hand and acting genuinely happy to see him. "How are you?"

"Just great," Holt says as tears fill his eyes.

"I had to tell you something," he continues. "I just got into town today and I had to tell you. I did what you said. I tried hard. And I made it. Look. I can walk."

Billy walks back and forth amid a group of admiring fans, and Cooper reacts as we imagine Lou would have. He gulps and smiles.

"Gee that's great work, kid, that's wonderful," Cooper says. He hesitates, almost unable to say more, Cooper's way of communicating without saying much.

All he can think of saying is to ask, "Have you got a ticket for the game?"

"Yes, sir, you bet," Holt says.

"So long," Cooper says, smiling broadly.

Tears fill Holt's eyes as he turns away.

Cooper enters the stadium.

14

Words for All Time

L ou Gehrig could not have looked any lonelier.

It was July 4, 1939, the day of his baseball funeral.

Nearly every image of Gehrig that day conveyed his desolation. When he was not standing alone—his arms in front of him or his hands grasping his blue Yankee cap—he was being helped by Joe McCarthy or Ed Barrow. His body was wasting from ALS. When well-wishers shook his hand, they stepped toward Lou's isolated form, then stepped back, leaving him alone again. On this sunny and hot Tuesday, Lou had waited on the dugout bench during the Yankees' loss to the Washington Senators in the first game of a doubleheader, then stood for the entire length of a ceremony he sought to avoid.

McCarthy was worried, fearful that Lou would wilt—or worse. Lou's baggy flannel uniform was hanging on him as if it were a size too large for the once-muscular frame of the Iron Horse. His gait had become a shuffle. He limped.

So the fretful McCarthy, who doted on Lou, told his new first baseman, Babe Dahlgren: "If Lou starts to fall, catch him."

Gehrig's weakness contrasted with the physically hale men surrounding him in the infield: the current Yankees—already 51-17 and in first place in the American League by eleven and a half games—and the Senators, as well as a dozen teammates from the 1927 Murderers' Row team, from Babe Ruth and Waite Hoyt to Wally Pipp and Bob Meusel. All of the retirees were dressed in somber suits and ties, except for the Babe, who arrived snazzily dressed in a midsummer white suit and open-collared shirt as if he were headed to a polo match in Southampton. Each man would outlive Lou, by as few as five years (Tony Lazzeri) and as many as fifty-two (Mark Koenig).

There was no prototype for this kind of event. Players did not part from baseball as dramatically or tragically as Gehrig did. Careers ended, and athletes left the stage. They became managers and coaches or deliverymen and bartenders. They grew old and paunchy in and out of their uniforms. Today, retiring stars speak at press conferences, or, more elaborately, on arena floors and stadium fields. The Yankees have mastered the art of the farewell, with stars delivering speeches. Elite players have their numbers retired and receive bronze plaques that are screwed to the walls of the cemetery-like Monument Park. The tribute eventually extended to an owner, the blustery George Steinbrenner, whose five-by-seven-foot plaque, with its enormous image of the Boss, is far larger than anyone else's who actually played the game.

None of that was standard in 1939.

"In my eight-year-old head, I thought this was just a retirement ceremony," said Larry Merchant, who in later years became one of America's greatest sports columnists, but on this day was at the game with his parents, one of many games he attended. "I was aware that there was a certain solemnity, but I had no clue that the adults knew that Gehrig was, apparently, sick, or had a fatal disease."

There was no plan for Lou to speak. His day of appreciation might have ended with the giving of gifts and the delivery of dignitaries' remarks.

Lou, however, was quite prepared to speak. He had arrived that afternoon with something to say, if not the absolute will to do it. The dynamic of their six-year-old marriage suggests that a speech was Eleanor's idea. Through her scrapbooks, she had already become his legacy keeper. She knew that he had played in the shadow of Ruth and would not have wanted him to leave his stage without saying something.

Eleanor described their plans in various ways over more than thirty years. After being consulted, if not always followed, from the day she signed her contract with Samuel Goldwyn, she had every reason to guard the sanctity of Lou's words. From reading Gallico and Finkel's outline and various scripts by other writers, she knew the speech had been shortened and altered into something significantly different. It was a rewrite. They moved words around. They thanked fewer people. But she wanted nothing changed from the text she provided Goldwyn, reminding him that Gary Cooper had to recite it exactly as it was written.

The challenge in meeting her demand, though, was whether there actually was a written version of the speech. In her letter to Goldwyn, she wrote, "A few days ago, I sent Christy a copy of Lou's speech."

From her memory of…a written version she had suddenly found?

From her memory of…remarks that Lou ad-libbed?

If anything had been written, where had it gone? After all, Lou spoke extemporaneously. Had he left the written speech in his locker? Did he forget it at home?

As the guardian of her husband's legacy, it was Eleanor's job to uphold the speech's authenticity—as she defined it. It had to be galling to have entrusted Goldwyn with Lou's story but to see what Lou said that day, the screenwriters relied, perhaps, on the newsreel's account, which may never have been complete, and the myriad newspaper accounts of what he had said.

Eleanor insisted to Goldwyn that she had the only version that mattered.

"You can count on the wording being perfect," she wrote, "because *Lou and I worked on it the night before* it was delivered, and naturally my memory could not fail me in this instance." (Italics are mine.)

Where did Gehrig's magnificent speech arise from? In Eleanor's telling, the speech's authorship remained murky. Which Gehrig had thought of it? Had they collaborated? Jotted down notes that Lou expanded into a speech on the spot?

Lou and Eleanor were literate enough to be its creators. The composition was so poignant. But the effort was so skillful, especially for first-timers, that it suggested professional help from sportswriter friends like Fred Lieb or John Kieran, of the *Times*.

A different version of the speech's genesis is found in sportswriter Frank Graham's 1942 book, *Lou Gehrig: A Quiet Hero*. Here, Eleanor said Lou worked on the speech on his own. "He was composing it at home last night," she said, "and he kept crossing out sentences and rewriting them and finally I said to him, 'Let me see if I can help you.' And he said, 'No thanks, Eleanor. Not this time. This must be my speech and I must say these things my way.'"

　Words for All Time | 199

Was this an attempt at hagiography—a speech written on his own, her husband struggling to find a way to turn his emotions into a small masterpiece?

If, in her account, there was a written speech, where had it gone?

Why hadn't she saved it in her scrapbook, where she preserved so many important articles and documents?

Graham flatly wrote that Gehrig had discarded the speech by the time he spoke.

Thirty-four years later in her memoir, *My Luke and I*, Eleanor expanded on the Great Man theme. "He had written it down but hadn't rehearsed it," she wrote, "probably because it was simple enough and agonizing enough and he was still shy enough, groping for some way to phrase the emotions that usually were kept securely locked up." Saying he had not rehearsed strains credulity; he was a shy man, dying as he stood at home plate, and had never been involved in an agonizing scene that begged for rehearsal time. Short as it was, it was not a simple speech, or a simple stage, and certainly not unworthy of rehearsal. Eleanor's protective impulses suggest she was making him braver by saying he did not need to practice.

As Gehrig stepped nervously and unsteadily to the microphones, his oratorical skills were unknown. Lou's personality was ill suited to public speaking. He did not need to say much as a Yankee superstar, let alone make speeches. On a team dominated by Ruth's Brobdingnagian personality, Lou had no reason to raise his voice. Ruth had no filters: He spoke to anyone, anytime, about almost anything. He was a man-child as unshackled from societal restraints as the introverted Gehrig was understated.

A scene captured by newsreel cameras on June 1, 1925, illustrated the interplay of their divergent personalities. It was the day

Ruth returned to the Yankees from a season-long illness known as the "bellyache heard round the world"—which might have been an intestinal abscess or a venereal disease—and also the day Gehrig played in the first of 2,130 consecutive games. As Ruth stood on the steps of the dugout yapping to the cameraman, Gehrig sat silently on the bench, a timid young player who preferred shrinking into the background. Much later, Gehrig found his voice—though never a loud one—when he became the Yankees' captain in 1935 after the Yankees released Ruth, making Lou the team's undisputed center of power.

Gehrig did not have to be as skilled an orator as Franklin Delano Roosevelt to be effective. The same characteristics that made him unprepared for public oratory—his shyness and thick Manhattan accent—were ideal for a selfless speech that defined a tragically shortened life. It was a perfect model for Cooper to remake in his dignified, reserved Westerner's image that he had fused with other decent characters for more than a decade.

On that hot Fourth of July, the wind was whipping the 1927 World Series championship flag on a pole beyond the bleachers, and Gehrig looked vulnerable as never before. Not only could he not play, he could barely lift the trophies he was handed. He looked thin, his flannel pinstripes bagging on his once muscular body. Still, he shook hands with white-clad groundskeepers. He endured presentations from Harry M. Stevens, the concessionaire who sold hot dogs at the stadium, and the Old Timers' Association of Colorado.

Gehrig listened to speeches by Mayor Fiorello LaGuardia ("Hello, Lou!" the city's pint-sized leader shouted jauntily) and Postmaster General James Farley. Choked up and "almost incoherent," according to the New York Post, McCarthy told Lou, and the crowd: "When you came to my room you told me you thought that you were hindering the chances of the ball club by staying in the ball game. That was a day that I never thought that this time would come."

Lou was led onto the field by Barrow, but broke away to walk on his own, pleasing Eleanor, who knew that he was faltering a little more each day. Once Lou was stationed on the field, McCarthy took over, keeping watch on him, fearing that his swaying might result in a fall. Eleanor was sitting in a box with McCarthy's and Barrow's wives, as well as her mother and brother, and Lou's mother. Lou said later on that he had been "scared silly" and would rather have "struck out in the ninth with the score tied, two down and the bases loaded" than walk onto the field to give his speech. No one could fault him for being self-conscious.

He was no longer the Iron Horse, a once-indestructible force for most of fourteen seasons. He had changed physically in just the two months since he removed himself from the Yankees lineup when he was hitting .143 with no home runs and only one run batted in.

He was, by various accounts, too moved to speak after the tributes were spoken and the gifts (silver candlesticks, pitcher, fruit bowl, and platters; a smoking stand, and a loving cup; a fishing rod and tackle, and scrolls from Senators' fans and the Old Timers' Association) presented. Gallico, who adapted his work for Goldwyn into a Gehrig biography of the same name, wrote in his book: "The objects were a mockery, because he could no longer possess them. But the warmth of the feeling that prompted their purchase and presentation melted the iron reserve in him and broke him down."

Lou was weakening, shaky, and sweaty. Barrow took his arm to steady his wavering body. "He gulped and fought to keep back the tears as he kept his eyes fastened on the ground," the *New York*

Times wrote. "His face twitched," the *Daily News* reported. "The muscles of his jaw contracted." He was close to breaking down, the *New York Post* insisted.

He could not speak. He waved off Sid Mercer, the emcee and a local sportswriter, who told the crowd: "Ladies and gentlemen, Lou has asked me to thank you all for him. He is too moved to speak." According to the *Washington Post*, he also said: "I shall not ask Lou Gehrig to make a speech. I do not believe that I should."

Gehrig's reticence prompted the crowd to chant, "We want Lou!," but it also led workers to start hauling away the microphone cables to end the ceremony and begin the second game of the doubleheader. McCarthy intervened, though, whispering some sort of encouragement in Lou's ear. Lou nodded and moved slowly, with his manager's help, toward the microphone in a "peculiar, shuffling, flat-footed gait as he hobbled out to face his public." One can only imagine what McCarthy said to prod Lou forward, but sportswriter Rud Rennie assumed it carried the force of a strong-willed manager. "Gehrig, who has always obeyed orders, obeyed this one," Rennie wrote, "with the same courage that brought him back smiling from the Mayo Clinic with the shocking report that he was an invalid." In her memoir thirty-seven years later, Eleanor wrote that Lou "glanced briefly at the 70,000 or so people, who were all standing now and he replied to it all with the mixed feelings of the class valedictorian, trying to sum up things in words before moving into whatever waited 'beyond.'"

It is not a perfect speech but it is a great one, notable for its power, structure, generosity, and modesty. He opened with two stunning sentences that set its tone, the first underplaying the seriousness of his disease as "a bad break" and the second asserting that for all the reasons he would enumerate, he was "the luckiest man on the face of the earth," not the unfortunate victim of a fatal disease. Those sentiments became anchors of the Gehrig legend: that a man found great fortune in a terrible diagnosis delivered barely two weeks earlier remains extraordinary. He said nothing about the details of his career, preferring to thank the fans, the leaders of the Yankees, the rival Giants across the Harlem River, the groundskeepers, and the concessionaires. Thanking his parents and wife would have been expected in any farewell message, but when he declared his gratitude to his mother-in-law, Nell Twitchell, an easier-to-love maternal figure than Mom Gehrig, he had no idea that Nell would move in to his Bronx house to help care for him until the day he died.

Without any full audio or video recordings, the speech went something like this:

Fans, for the past two weeks, you have been reading about a bad break.

Yet today, I consider myself the luckiest man on the face of the earth.

I have been in ballparks for seventeen years, and I have never received anything but kindness and encouragement from you fans.

Look at these grand men. Which of you wouldn't consider it the highlight of his career just to associate with them for even one day? Sure, I'm lucky.

Who wouldn't consider it an honor to have known Jacob Ruppert? Also the builder of baseball's greatest empire, Ed Barrow. To have spent six years with that wonderful little fellow, Miller Huggins.

Then to have spent the next nine years with that outstanding leader, that smart student of psychology, the best manager in baseball today, Joe McCarthy? Sure, I'm lucky.

When the New York Giants, a team you would give your right arm to beat, and vice versa, sends you a gift—that's something. When everybody down to the ground-skeepers and those boys in white coats remembers you with trophies—that's something.

When you have a wonderful mother-in-law who takes sides with you in squabbles with her own daughter—that's something.

When you have a father and mother who work all their lives so that you can have an education and build your body—it's a blessing.

When you have a wife who has been a tower of strength and shown more courage than you dreamed existed—that's the finest I know.

So I close in saying that I may have had a tough break, but I have an awful lot to live for.

For young Larry Merchant, hearing Gehrig say that most famous of lines—that he was "the luckiest man on the face of the earth"—"gripped people in a way that I didn't quite understand."

A New York Post headline read, "A TEAR FOR ALL TO SEE" to describe a picture of Lou wiping tears from his eyes with his right hand. "Lou Gehrig came close to breaking down during the ceremony," the caption said, "but pulled himself together in typical

Gehrig fashion and delivered a soul-stirring valedictory." Eleanor resisted weeping as she watched from a box seat.

Rosaleen Doherty, a thirty-five-year-old reporter for the New York *Daily News*, sat with Eleanor and, in the style of a women's page account, wrote that Eleanor "didn't cry although all around us women, and quite a few men, were openly sobbing. I had a lump in my throat—and I'm supposed to be a hard-boiled reporter." Eleanor trembled from "head to foot" as the crowd demanded that Lou speak but relaxed once the speech was over.

"I'm glad Lou was able to walk out there and make his little talk over the microphone," Eleanor said. "I knew he wouldn't let the fans down."

Asked if the day for Lou had made a difference in her life, Eleanor said, "Of course it's changed our life, but maybe not in the way you think I mean. The game is over for us but there is a lot left. Don't waste any sympathy on us. We're going to get along and Lou—who is a good soldier—is going to do what the doctors told him and get well. I had a bad moment when I first heard that he was through—I won't deny that—but it is over with."

Eleanor's reaction was not re-enacted in *Pride*. Instead, Teresa Wright was still in the dugout tunnel sobbing inconsolably while glancing adoringly at the charm bracelet made of some of the trinkets Lou had been awarded.

Silenced by Gehrig's words, the crowd erupted in cheers when the speech ended. Ruth took the stage and took over the show. He delivered a bit of a speech himself, declaring the 1927 team better than the current one, saying that "while Lazzeri pointed out to me that there are only about thirteen or fourteen of us here, my answer is shucks, we only need nine to beat 'em." With that, he moved toward Lou and embraced him—number three and number four together again, unifying on Lou's saddest day and putting aside old enmities, at least for the cameras.

Whatever the Babe said quietly to Lou brought a smile to the dying man's face and inspired sportswriter Jack Miley to tap out a paean to Ruth: "But leave it to big, fat jovial Babe—it did the work! Gehrig's face brightened, those famous dimples flashed and he burst out laughing for Ruth slapped him on the back, he clasped baseball's most famous invalid in a bear hug and Lou's ceremonial was a success. A great fellow that Ruth and always the life of the party!"

Gehrig's retirement speech remains unmatched as a piece of athletic oratory nearly eight decades later and remains a significant element of his soulful legacy. Athletes routinely say farewell on fields, on courts, and at press conferences. When Magic Johnson announced that he had HIV at the peak of the AIDS epidemic, he made global news but did not speak of good fortune despite a prescience that he would somehow survive. In *Brian's Song*, one of sports cinema's finest speeches was made not by the dying athlete, but by his friend Gale Sayers, played by Billy Dee Williams. "I love Brian Piccolo," he said through tears, "and I'd like all of you to love him, too. And so tonight, when you hit your knees, please ask God to love him." Farewells by elite athletes are often elaborate events, like those for Kareem Abdul-Jabbar and Larry Bird, but their speeches did not produce oratorical memories.

The Gehrig ceremony, with its gathering of former players, became the template for the Yankees' Old-Timers' Day, and for the retirement rites of greats like Mickey Mantle and Mariano Rivera. The natural end of their careers, though, lacked the poignant urgency of a forced end due to illness. They had long careers, and now it was time to go. Mantle was shrewd enough, at a ceremony in 1969 to celebrate his career, to invoke Gehrig. "I often wondered how a man who knew he was dying could get up here and say he's the luckiest man in the world," he said. "Now I think I know how Lou Gehrig felt." Rivera and Derek Jeter had year-long retirement tours, but their pleasant valedictories failed to resonate beyond the end of the days. Willie Mays, playing past his prime for the New York Mets, announced in September 1973 that he would retire after the season. With underrated eloquence, he said that "as you know, there always comes a time for someone to get out. And I look at these kids over there, the way they are playing and the way they are fighting for themselves and it tells me one thing: 'Willie, say good-bye to America.'"

Gehrig needed fewer than three hundred words to transform how the public viewed him. No longer a magnificent ballplayer, he became a thirty-six-year-old man near death who somehow found gratitude in his limited future. He gave his audience the Gehrig that Eleanor wanted the public to see: a decent, articulate man faced with dramatically altered circumstances. He lacked a baritone like Cooper or any known skill as a public speaker. His Manhattan accent—so rare to hear in those pre-television days—made his words even more effective as they reverberated from the public address system, through millions of radios, and into our collective memory. He sounded like a nervous, native, preternaturally grateful New Yorker, like almost anyone in the stadium. Gehrig, with a strong assist from Cooper, became a symbol of courage and the soul of the Yankees' cold-as-steel empire.

The speech has been dubbed, with some exaggeration, "baseball's Gettysburg address." The connection to Lincoln is strained, but the speech has so many lovely touches—could it really have been written, polished, and not rehearsed the night before?—and nothing is hackneyed. It praised "that wonderful fellow" and "that smart student of psychology." Three sentences began with "When you have," emphasizing the theme through parallel structure. Notice the short phrases that followed the dash in five sentences: "that's something," "it's a blessing," and "that's the finest I know." By breaking up each thought, he let his gratitude linger, as if he were punctuating those thoughts with a "Wow!" In the last sentence, he returned to his misfortune, likening his disease to a "bad break" that minimized its severity.

Irv Welzer, then eleven, watched the speech from the bleachers, happy for the doubleheader ("Two games for the price of one? Of course I was going!") and recalled that "the bleachers were so packed that you couldn't imagine one more person squeezing in. But somehow more did. You kept sliding over an inch."

By the end of the first game, "the bleachers were so full of cigar and cigarette smoke so that we really couldn't see the infield well. But we could hear because we were right under the speakers."

What stuck with him was not the "luckiest man" line, but rather when Gehrig said he had a "bad break." "We didn't really know what his injury was; it hadn't been fully explained or at least I didn't understand it. I knew he was retiring but I didn't know how sick he was until he said the 'bad break' thing." Welzer, who became a Tony Award–winning producer, said the "luckiest man" line began to resonate as it was heard on newsreels in theaters over the next few weeks.

Greater distance has further distinguished the speech. Jonathan Eig, who wrote *Luckiest Man*, a Gehrig biography, in 2005, said, "The speech resonates, because it speaks to everyone who has suffered illness or lost a loved one. Gehrig says we shouldn't think about ourselves and whatever troubles we might have. Instead, we should think about all the good fortunes we've had in life. To die is to lose everything, everyone we've loved, but he looks at it from another angle and says death helps him see all he has been blessed with—his family, his friends, his teammates, his career. He chooses life. He chooses optimism."

Gehrig's rhetorical decision to emphasize his good fortune continues to inspire and surprise people. But questions still linger: How could he have been so positive? Months later, he offered a further explanation. In a newspaper article, "Why I Am Thankful," he wrote that when he was seven or eight, "I thought I would be the luckiest kid on earth if I could ever play football on the high school team," and when he was in high school, he thought he would be the "luckiest boy on earth if I could only go to college," and when he was in college, he thought he would be the luckiest fellow on earth "if I could just break into big league baseball."

And so on, until he wrapped up the sequel to his speech by saying, "This summer, I got a bad break. The doctors said I couldn't play baseball any more. All right, I'm still the luckiest man on earth, when you add things up. I've got a long season of life to play out and my team—America—is absolutely the best in the league. That's what counts."

Newspaper reporters did not make it easy to accurately reconstruct what Lou said. Their accounts differed, sometimes wildly, from each other, from Eleanor's version of the original text, or the four lines that exist on newsreel. The *New York Herald Tribune* confusingly placed the "luckiest man" line at the end of the speech, foreshadowing its placement in *Pride* by its screenwriters. The *New York Times* combined elements of the first and last paragraphs and gave it a tepid rewrite: "You've been reading about my bad break for weeks now. But today I think I'm the luckiest man alive. I now feel more than ever that I have much to live for."

A notably peculiar version came from Leslie Avery of the United Press: "For weeks I have been reading in the newspapers that I am a fellow who got a tough break. I don't believe it. I have been a lucky guy. For eighteen years into every ballpark in which I have ever walked, I received nothing but kindness and encouragement. Mine has been a full life."

Lou's speech was unanticipated, and even if it had been, newspapers were unlikely to have sent anyone to transcribe it. He was not a president or a king. The gravity of his illness was not known. The absence of a complete text, film, or audio copy means that it might have faded without the existence of *Pride*.

Cooper's rendition has become the de facto version of record, replacing Gehrig's original. Those who recall Gehrig's words echoing on the Yankee Stadium public address system—"*Today . . . today . . . today . . . I consider myself . . . myself . . .*"—are thinking of Cooper reading a rewrite of Gehrig's speech on a Goldwyn soundstage nearly three years after the original was spoken.

Has any other rendering of a historic speech ever become so closely identified with the actor? It has not happened to actors playing Franklin D. Roosevelt, John F. Kennedy, Winston Churchill, or Martin Luther King (whose estate would not let David Oyelowo use King's "I have a dream" speech in the film *Selma*). Perhaps the best comparison is represented by *The King's Speech*, where Colin Firth portrayed the reluctant King George VI overcoming his severe stammer to deliver Great Britain's declaration of war against Germany in 1939. But that speech was remembered less for its rhetorical brilliance than for the challenge it posed to a new monarch thrust into a major crisis caused by the abdication of his brother, Edward VIII.

Had Goldwyn chosen a lesser actor, one not as beloved as Cooper, the speech's power might have diminished long ago, and *Pride* might not have remained a staple on local stations, the TCM cable channel, and the MLB Network. The repeated showings keep the speech alive and remind people that there is more to *Pride* than the speech.

"If not for the movie, the speech might well have been forgotten, especially considering the absence of a complete newsreel version," Eig, the biographer, said. "Throughout history, great speeches have been handed down, using whatever medium was available at the time. The retelling is always important. Without the retelling, many of the greatest oratories would have been lost."

Cooper understood that Gehrig was a familiar type of character in his canon: a dignified man of honor, like Sergeant Alvin C. York; Long John Willoughby in *Meet John Doe*; and, in a future film, Marshal Will Kane in *High Noon*, who, as he is to retire as sheriff of the fictional Hadleyville, must decide to face down murderous outlaws gunning for him or abandon the small town he had made safe.

Gehrig, though, presented Cooper with a new challenge—a real person far more contemporary and recognizable than York or two other flesh-and-blood characters, Marco Polo (whom he played in *The Adventures of Marco Polo*) or Wild Bill Hickok (his role in *The Plainsman*). When the filming of *Pride* began in February 1942, Gehrig had been dead for eight months. Memories of him were clear and strong. Some fans were probably still grieving. Cooper knew that he would be compared to Gehrig, for whether they looked alike (not much), whether Cooper understood Gehrig's character, and whether he could credibly play baseball.

His ultimate test would take place in uniform, but without a bat or ball.

It would only require words and emotion.

"Gehrig, that's no cinch," he wrote in a career retrospective in the *Saturday Evening Post* in 1956. "Quite a responsibility, in fact, when you think of all those millions of people who knew him, watched him, knew just how he handled himself. You can't trick up a character like that with mannerisms, bits of business. I honestly didn't want to take the part, but Mrs. Gehrig came out and she told me that's the way she wanted it." There is no evidence that Eleanor persuaded Cooper to take the part—although she favored him more than any other actor—so it is likelier that she helped Cooper understand her late husband, especially if she was aware of how little he knew about baseball.

Three voices are heard in the final minutes of *Pride*: Bill Stern's, Gary Cooper's, and the umpire's who shouts "Play ball!" to end the film.

Between the 1930s and 1950s, Stern was known to millions for his polished radio play-by-play but also for the Colgate Sports Newsreel that let him indulge his instinct as a myth-making fabulist, telling elaborate tales of sports legends larded with fictional details—like Abraham Lincoln summoning General Abner Doubleday, the putative inventor of baseball, to his deathbed to tell him, "Keep baseball alive. In the trying days ahead, this country will need it." Stern's earlier appearance in *Pride*, when he described the home runs hit by Gehrig and Ruth for polio-stricken Billy, captured him delivering a scripted yarn with all the panache of his long-running Colgate show. He sounds almost too delighted to be in *Pride*, perhaps because he had replaced his main rival, Ted Husing, in the role.

Stern set up the Gehrig farewell ceremony from a press box created on a Goldwyn soundstage as if he were at Yankee

Stadium. Over newsreel images of Lieutenant Francis Sutherland's 7th Regiment Band—playing "It's a Long Way to Tipperary"—white-uniformed concessionaires and a packed Yankee Stadium, Stern brought the scene to life in his rapid, clear, brassy, town crier's voice:

Never in the history of baseball has there been such a spontaneous demonstration of love and affection for one man. Perhaps you know him as Larrupin' Lou, perhaps as the Iron Horse, but no matter how you knew him, he'll never be forgotten, nor will his great records. They'll never forget his greatest record of all, his amazing feat of playing 2,130 consecutive ballgames over a period of 16 years. Though everyone is here today to show Lou Gehrig just what they feel in their hearts, to say hail and farewell to the pride of the Yankees.

The scene cuts to the far end of the tunnel that leads to the Yankee dugout. Wright and Cooper enter arm-in-arm, then walk slowly down a small flight of five steps into semi-darkness. They are indulging in a romantic fantasy—a wife in an area of a ballpark that was prohibited to all but authorized personnel—that was as real to Goldwyn as Heathcliff and Cathy on the moors in his 1939 film, *Wuthering Heights*, where Cathy's romantic words might have echoed Eleanor's passion for her dying Lou: "Forgive me, Heathcliff. Forgive me. Heathcliff. Make the world stop right here. Make everything stop and stand still and never move again. Make the moors never change, and you and I never change."

The infield is filled with Lou's teammates, former teammates, executives, and dignitaries, but the Gehrigs stand alone in the tunnel that is lit like a mausoleum. Stern's voice is muted as they gaze at each other before reluctantly parting, their fingers slowly disentangling from each other's. Imagining the dread Lou must have felt that day, Cooper walks slowly into the light, his face revealing to fans a grim, bewildered expression. The camera cuts quickly to a medium close-up of Wright, her smile vanished, never to be seen again in *Pride* with Cooper. She begins to weep while bringing her new bracelet to her face, caressing it as if it were a widow's greatest inheritance.

In their screenplay, Mankiewicz and Swerling prepared Cooper, somewhat hyperbolically, with a sense of what Gehrig faced as he began to speak that day.

The roar of the crowd is like a sustained note from a mighty organ. Lou waits for it to subside but it doesn't. For him this is crucifixion as well as triumph, because he knows he'll have to die twice and perhaps the worst ordeal for him is that little death known as Goodbye. It's just like that guy said—the last half of the last inning. Why don't they stop cheering? Why don't they let him speak? This is the dream he had when he was a kid, but he didn't know it would be so hard. He loves Ellie—she's been a wonderful pal, but most of all he loves this thing he's got to leave—baseball. Why isn't Blake here to tell him what to say—how to say it? What can he say? There's a game to be played and he mustn't hold it up. Without lifting his head, he raises his hand, and as if by magic, the great roar subsides and the ensuing silence is frightening. When Lou speaks, his voice echoes over the stilled stadium.

Their scene-setting—a crucifixion! magic!—had its roots in the outline in which Gallico and Finkel described an emcee asking the crowd to hush. But it did not. They wrote:

Instead of quiet, it appears that the cheers redouble. Hats are being thrown into the air, handkerchiefs waved, torn paper is flying. He speaks into the microphone, but the half-hysterical crowd still cheering for Gehrig drowns out even the loudspeakers. Then, seeing that it is impossible to quell the crowd, he goes over to Lou, takes him by the arm gently and leads him over to the microphone and then walks away, leaving him standing there alone. Tears are falling from his eyes.

He dries them and suddenly raises his head and faces the huge throng. The storm of sound is cut off instantaneously as though by magic. For a few seconds, there is such absolute silence that it sounds almost louder than the cheers. Then slowly, his voice sounding cracked and brassy through the public address system, and echoing, Gehrig begins to speak. His speech is slow and halting because of his deep emotion, and is frequently interrupted by bursts of cheering and applause.

When Lou spoke, he kept his hands on his hips, pausing to run his hand through his hair or cover his tear-streaked face, movements Cooper copied. In the seconds before he started the speech, Cooper took a big breath and hesitated three times. His eyes moistened and his eyes fluttered. He looked around the stadium as he spoke of receiving "nothing but kindness and encouragement from you fans" and smiled as he introduced the Murderers' Row team of 1927.

He gazed at the press box and thanked reporters for the "fame and undeserved praise" they bestowed on him and tilted his head toward McCarthy when he said that he has played for the "two greatest managers of all time" (McCarthy and Miller Huggins). As he thanked his parents he looked down, saying they "fought to give me health" (and we see Elsa Janssen's fully rehabilitated, sympathetic Mom Gehrig dabbing at her tears with a handkerchief). Now he slowed his pace, producing more of his tears as he praised Eleanor for showing him "more courage than I've ever known" (as the camera cut to Wright, sobbing, as "Auld Lang Syne" is heard).

Gallico's instructions were for Cooper to feel that when Lou looks "out and over the fields or the stands, it is like a man saying farewell to something he will never see again." And by the time Cooper came to the end, Gallico wanted him to feel overwhelmed, unable for his character to say more, even if he wanted to: "He is close to exhaustion now, physically as well as emotionally," he wrote in his screenplay. "He sways a little but holds himself erect. There is a long pause and once more his glance sweeps over the entire stadium and again the hush falls over the crowd. With a little motion of one crooked finger, he brushes another tear from his eye, takes a deep breath and speaks. His voice is quite clear now."

Cooper played the coda a bit differently. If he did not appear to be gaining strength as he headed to his last words, he was not on the verge of a collapse. It was Gehrig who was exhausted from the physical and emotional toll of an oration delivered on a hot day between games of a holiday doubleheader. His undershirt, he said later, was wringing wet.

Cooper did not sway and did not falter as he got to his finale: "People all say that I've had a bad break," he said, looking around, then steadying his eyes as if he were staring at one person. "But today...today...I consider myself the luckiest man on the face of the earth."

Finally done, Cooper licked his lips, put his hand over his mouth—perhaps contemplating saying more, as Gehrig seemed to—then walked off, passing slowly between McCarthy and Ruth on a direct path to the dugout.

What Cooper said differed significantly from what Gehrig said. He thanked fewer people in the shorter version, mostly against Eleanor's wishes.

"You see," she wrote to Goldwyn, "the whole charm of the closing scene seems to me to be the fact that Lou thanked everyone even remotely connected with his career for making him the 'luckiest man on earth.'" Arguing unsuccessfully that Cooper should thank Barrow in the film, she added, "It never occurred to him to give himself credit for being what he was. In other words, complete humility, which is true greatness."

The screenplay cut Gehrig's gratitude to his mother-in-law and to the rival Giants and pared from seventeen to sixteen years the length of his career.

Shifting the "luckiest man" line to the end, where it would have the most impact, was approved by Eleanor, according to Gallico. And the new version of the speech, one that is notably different from Lou's, was delivered by Cooper:

I have been walking on ball fields for sixteen years, and I have never received anything but kindness and encouragement from you fans. I have had the great honor to have played with these great veteran ballplayers on my left— Murderers' Row, our championship team of 1927. I have had the further honor of living with and playing with these men on my right—the Bronx Bombers, the Yankees of today.

"I have been given fame and undeserved praise by the boys up there behind the wire in the press box—my friends, the sportswriters. I have worked under the two greatest managers of all time—Miller Huggins and Joe McCarthy.

"I have a mother and father who fought to give me health and a solid background in my youth. I have a wife, a companion for life, who has shown me more courage than I ever knew.

"People all say that I've had a bad break. But today… today, I consider myself the luckiest man on the face of the earth."

Although Wood wanted the audience to believe the speech was filmed at Wrigley Field, it was shot on a soundstage on Goldwyn's lot. And Eleanor was there, according to studio publicity records. Surely, it was a bittersweet prospect: watching Cooper re-create Lou's public death. On Stage 4, Eleanor took a seat, trying to be unobtrusive. The stage was dark except for spotlights illuminating Cooper.

"Quiet," an assistant director shouted.

Cooper gave the speech with hesitations and moistened eyes, speaking of his good fortune in the face of tragedy. It was all very familiar to Eleanor; all too real, all too difficult to watch. Her sobbing interrupted a take. Cooper started again, but Eleanor rose to leave, a young widow in a black dress, unable to stay, as she did when Lou delivered his speech. Now she didn't have to stay.

The filming of the "luckiest man" speech accounts for some subtle shifts in the final scene. After Cooper is led to the microphones by Harry Harvey (as McCarthy), the backdrop is still clearly that of Wrigley Field, with extras filling the portions of the ballpark that had to look full for the scene to be credible. Cooper was filmed from a low angle on the field to enhance his stature, and Ruth stood behind him and to his left, finally in Gehrig's shadow. After a cut to wildly cheering fans, the camera angle changed to a slightly higher, direct one that exposed a small glitch: Cooper's haircut changes slightly, because in one shot he is at Wrigley Field and in the second he is on the soundstage. Behind him, the backdrop for the soundstage shoot shifts to the newsreel shot on the day of the farewell at Yankee Stadium.

When the speech ends, *Pride* is once again at Wrigley Field. Cooper steps back from the microphones, then walks away, taking forty-nine painstaking steps to the dugout, where he puts his hand on its roof for support. He descends the few steps, one by one, and heads back into darkness.

An umpire shouts, "Play ball!" and *Pride* is over.

That was the ending as it has been seen for seventy-five years and, seemingly, nothing else would seem right. Does a doomed man who fades into the pitch-blackness of certain death need a final scene? By now, Cooper has achieved what Eleanor and Goldwyn desired: He had made Gehrig his own, allowing fans to see in his portrayal the dignity, decency, and heroism that Gehrig had shown.

But Mankiewicz and Swerling had envisioned a little more, perhaps an attempt to satisfy Goldwyn with one more injection of romance to appeal to the women the producer believed would make *Pride* a hit.

The script picks up from Lou's disappearance into the dugout with his emergence from the dugout tunnel "like a man walking in a dream." He "stops and looks off-scene," where he spots Eleanor, where we had left her earlier, sobbing.

"He tries very hard to smile and succeeds a little," they write. "Eleanor comes into the shot. She has been waiting for him. Neither one speaks. She looks at him for a moment, then takes his arm and they start away together. She is wearing his bracelet." The camera then moves to a long shot from outside Yankee Stadium to show them "arm in arm" as they "walk away from camera. We stay on them until they're almost out of range of camera. The music swells, as we FADE OUT."

15

A Screening

It was late May and Teresa Wright had every reason to be confident and happy. The production had all but wrapped. Her Hollywood career was off to a rousing start—she would receive Academy Award nominations for her first three films, *The Little Foxes, Mrs. Miniver,* and, in 1943, *The Pride of the Yankees.* She was marrying writer Niven Busch, who introduced Goldwyn to the newsreels that made him want to produce the movie. She was anxious, though, over what Eleanor would think of her portrayal.

Eleanor was on her way back to Hollywood to see a rough cut of *Pride.* Alexandra Giddens and Carol Beldon, the fictional characters Wright played in *Foxes* and *Miniver,* couldn't squawk about her work. But Eleanor—not one to restrain her opinions about Lou and a film she was so deeply involved in—could.

"I find myself pacing the floor at night and I haven't slept well in weeks," Wright said in a release from the studio that might have amplified her own worries to help sell the film. "I've never experienced anything like it before in my life. I keep thinking, 'Suppose she doesn't like me? Suppose she doesn't like the way I laugh or cry or smile or walk—or anything about me?' I'll die a thousand deaths while Mrs. Gehrig is seeing the picture—just as she probably will—but then I have to think of the horrible experience of seeing her after the screening."

Goldwyn's publicity chief, William Hebert, used Eleanor's imminent arrival in Hollywood to screen the film as an event worthy of promoting. Here was a studio wringing as much ink as it could out of the Gehrig story—continuing the effort that began with the Scarlett O'Hara–like search for the actor to play Lou.

"Mrs. Gehrig, a handsome young woman who looked as if she should be in pictures herself, arrived in Hollywood a few days ago to see the shooting of the final scenes of the picture and then see the first rough cut of the film," Hebert's press release read. It quoted Eleanor saying, "Mr. Goldwyn promised when we started shooting that I'd be the first to see the picture, because I wouldn't want anyone else to see it before I did."

When the day to watch *Pride* arrived, Eleanor entered the screening room alone. As she sat down, she feared looking at the screen, knowing so many memories of her life, wonderful and terrible, would overwhelm her. She had to watch, if only to cast a critical eye and to fix whatever was grievously wrong.

When it ended, she said, she felt like she had lived her married life all over again—even if many details had been altered—as she watched Cooper, so like Lou in her mind, playing her husband with sympathy and simplicity. She needed time in the darkness to gather her thoughts. Goldwyn said that it was as long as twenty minutes before she emerged. She confided afterward to Hedda

Hopper that she was too upset to let anyone see her until she had gotten hold of herself.

"Then I saw Sam Goldwyn who was waiting for me," she said. "I thanked him for the truthful and wholly satisfactory manner in which he handled the story."

She sought no changes—unlike the fixes she asked for as she read one script after another—and accepted Goldwyn's treatment of the Gehrigs' lives.

She quickly sent a telegram to Gallico. "All she said was," he wrote to Goldwyn. "'It is unbelievably beautiful.' It made me happy because I am so fond of her that I did hope that she would be pleased with the result."

As for the anxious Teresa Wright? She need not have worried. At first Eleanor believed Wright too young to play her and would have preferred a more experienced actress like Barbara Stanwyck or Jean Arthur, but, she said, "I know no one could do better, or even as well, as little Teresa."

Decades later, Wright recalled how pleased Eleanor was with the film.

"I think it meant a lot to her," she said. "With the sadness of Lou's early death, I think in a way, it gave him back to her for a while."

Goldwyn wasn't only courting Eleanor's approval by showing her a rough cut; he was also screening parts of *Pride* to members of the press, including the influential gossip columnist and radio personality Walter Winchell.

"Winchell saw a few reels of it last week and without my asking him, gave me a line to use in our advertising which sums up his reaction to it," he told Gallico. "He said, 'Sam Goldwyn couldn't have given the youth of America a finer gift, nor to the sweethearts of America a finer love story.'"

It had only been a year since Lou's death, and now *Pride* was set to open at the Astor Theatre in New York on July 15, and in Hollywood a month later.

The main players were moving on. Cooper was off to film *For Whom the Bell Tolls* in the Sierra Nevada with Ingrid Bergman, fulfilling Ernest Hemingway's wish to have his friend star in the adaptation of his novel of the Spanish Civil War. Hemingway had modeled the main character, Robert Jordan, a tall, lean Montanan, after Cooper. Wright was preparing to shoot *Shadow of a Doubt* for Alfred Hitchcock. Sam Wood was working in back-to-back pictures with Cooper, directing him and Ingrid Bergman in *For Whom the Bell Tolls.* Goldwyn's next project was *They Got Me Covered,* a comedy starring Bob Hope, on loan from Paramount.

The Yankees, meanwhile, were halfway through another pennant-winning season without Lou. Although these Yankees would not win the World Series, they were largely intact eight months into World War II. Bill Dickey was still behind the plate but was winding down his career. Joe DiMaggio, Tommy Henrich, and Charlie Keller remained in the outfield. Little, superstitious Phil Rizzuto—"The Scooter," who would become a beloved character—was at shortstop. McCarthy, so emotional when fans and the baseball world said good-bye to Lou, was in his twelfth consecutive winning season as the manager.

On the afternoon of *Pride's* premiere, the Yankees shut out the Cleveland Indians, 4–0, at Yankee Stadium behind a four-hitter by Atley Donald, a right-hander from Louisiana whose back problems forced him to wear a corset while pitching. The Yankees were in first place with a 56-28 record, but DiMaggio, their star, was having a subpar 1942, compared with his sensational '41; Joe Gordon, the power-hitting second baseman, was leading the team with a .342 batting average.

The day game over, the Astor Theatre in Times Square beckoned the Yankees for the premiere of *Pride*. Three years earlier, *Gone with the Wind* had made its New York debut there, starting the epic Civil War melodrama on a path to a global gross of $3.8 billion (in adjusted dollars). At Broadway and 45th Street, the Astor was part of Times Square's neon jungle, a one-time home to a legitimate theater that had become a go-to house for major movie openings, especially for MGM's Technicolor musicals. Its neighbor up the block, with its huge billboard, was known as the Gaiety Theatre, Minsky's Burlesque and Victoria Theater.

Pride was opening that day in another forty theaters in the New York City area, as part of Goldwyn's promotional blitz. At four of those theaters in Westchester, stilt-walkers in top hats, white ties, and tails wore signs that read, "The biggest attraction to play any theater." A guest of honor at the premiere in Manhattan was former New Rochelle mayor Walter Otto, who had been hastily summoned by Lou to officiate at his marriage to Eleanor in 1933.

Newspaper ads that emphasized the romantic story of Eleanor and Lou—and said nothing about baseball—shouted to their readers:

See! Gary Cooper in the greatest role of his career—LOU GEHRIG

Marvel! At the outstanding performance of TERESA WRIGHT, sweetheart in "Mrs. Miniver" as Mrs. Lou Gehrig

Thrill! as VELOZ AND YOLANDA dance to the music of RAY NOBLE & HIS ORCHESTRA

Enjoy! "THE PRIDE OF THE YANKEES," Samuel Goldwyn's finest production

Another showed Cooper and Wright in a gentle embrace (although a close look appears to show the pictures were merged in those pre-Photoshop days). He nuzzled her, wearing a bow tie. She looked up at him adoringly.

"It's the Great American Story!" the ad declared. "The Private Life of the Man Millions Cheered! In her heart he found a love such as few men have ever known…and few women ever give!"

Goldwyn's intentions had never been clearer: This was not produced as a baseball movie and it would not be promoted as one.

DiMaggio and Dickey and their wives—the former, Dorothy Arnold, an actress, the latter, showgirl Violet Arnold (no relation), who played herself in *Pride*—took their stardom to the Astor. Reliever Johnny Murphy, third baseman Red Rolfe, and Charlie Keller brought their wives, as did McCarthy and Barrow.

Mom Gehrig, now living off Lou's bequest, was there as well. Babe Ruth stepped into the Astor lobby, accompanied by his wife, Claire, in a white suit and open shirt reminiscent of—or precisely like—his ensemble on Lou Gehrig Appreciation Day. He had resumed golfing as frequently as possible, for fun and charity, including a match in New Jersey with Bob Hope. He was made aware that Japanese soldiers were shouting, "The hell with Babe Ruth" when they were attacked by Allied soldiers. But the Babe, once a friend of the Japanese, responded, "I hope every Jap that mentions my name gets shot."

He would return to the Astor six years later for the opening of *The Babe Ruth Story*, starring William Bendix. But there was no cause for celebration, although it was a major event, with 1,400 guests. Ruth was three weeks from death, perspiring heavily, requiring support at both arms; he would return afterward to Memorial Hospital. Unlike *Pride*, his movie was a failure.

Eleanor was now near the end of the cinematic odyssey she had begun with Christy Walsh as her Hollywood guide and Samuel Goldwyn winning her hand. She had been a widow for a year, and would be one for forty-two more, ever mindful to protect and burnish Lou's name. Nothing, save for his baseball statistics and memories of his decency, preserved him better than *The Pride of the Yankees*.

She arrived that midsummer's night in a dark dress and dark hat and was photographed between Goldwyn and Wendell Willkie, who lost the 1940 presidential election to Franklin D. Roosevelt by a landslide. Months earlier, Willkie had defended Hollywood producers against a Senate subcommittee's charges of war propaganda before the U.S. entered World War II.

At shortly after eleven p.m., at the Astor and all around New York, *Pride* was ending its first run. At just over two hours, it is not a short film, but one can imagine that the audiences, there to see a picture about a man so familiar as a ballplayer and as a dying hero, cheered as the credits rolled under another refrain of "Always."

The reviews were nearly all positive, praising *Pride* for Cooper's courageous portrayal of Gehrig, as well as Wright's performance, and the American spirit the film portrayed at a time of war. *Variety* called it a "stirring epitaph." The *Hollywood Reporter* described it as a "spine-tingling, heart-tugging, human document" that is "24K Goldwyn." Bosley Crowther of the *New York Times* wrote that "it reaches the height of true nobility in its final ironic fate. How could it have been any other, with Gary Cooper playing the leading role in his diffident, taciturn manner and with Sam Wood directing an excellent cast?"

The *New York Herald Tribune* wrote: "Mr. Cooper is as splendid as one might have expected him to be as Gehrig but Teresa Wright is not far behind him in her radiant and sympathetic characterization of Mrs. Gehrig." Their scenes together, the *Herald Tribune* reviewer Howard Barnes added, "have a real burden of sentiment and genuine feeling." The New York *Daily News* went further, placing *Pride* in a different cinematic context for its millions of mostly blue-collar readers.

The tabloid praised it in a review but made a stronger case in an editorial:

The picture is a new thing in its way, so far as we know. We don't remember that the movies ever before tried seriously to portray the life, character, hopes and tragedies of a ball player. Such former baseball pictures as we remember were comedies, or far-fetched melodramas, or intricately worked-out stories of how somebody managed to murder somebody else while a baseball game was going on. *The Pride of the Yankees* is different. It is a fine and moving story of a fine and very human man whose life happened to be bound up with the national game of the United States.

Some critics wrote, accurately, that *Pride* faced, then overcame, a major flaw: The Gehrig story lacked inherent drama. The "luckiest man" speech is an emotional two minutes but not the culmination of a clash between personalities or philosophies. Goldwyn had ordained no ninth-inning heroics, no victory celebration as climax. *New York Post* critic Archer Winsten grasped the problem but saw that death had ennobled a bland main character and raised him to a level of significance that would not have been possible without his fatal disease.

"Unquestionably," he wrote, "if Gehrig had not died of a rare and spectacular paralysis he would not now be the subject of a movie biography." But his paralysis "gave him the opportunity of becoming a symbol of quiet courage in the face of certain, slow death. And today, with many young men facing equally tragic death, his example becomes a shining beacon. For he was essentially an ordinary American who proved he could die, without a whimper."

Reviewers did not focus much on the authenticity of the baseball in *Pride*. Dan Daniel, who began covering baseball in 1910, did complain in the *New York World Telegram and Sun* that Gallico was handicapped in writing the original story by not knowing Gehrig as a daily Yankee beat reporter and that screenwriters Herman Mankiewicz and Jo Swerling did not know Gehrig at all—gripes suggesting that Daniel might have felt like Goldwyn should have hired him to proffer his knowledge of Gehrig the ballplayer.

He suggested that Elsa Janssen's portrayal of Mom Gehrig was the most accurate but disliked the unflattering way that Mom and Pop were depicted—perhaps unaware of how much Eleanor's animosity colored their portrayals. For someone so steeped in covering baseball, it was curious that Daniel wrote that *Pride* showed "baseball as it is," without raising any doubts about Cooper's modest skills as a ballplayer or the errors that Eleanor had pointed out to Goldwyn.

Pride's release, so soon after Gehrig's death, was likely to rouse some resentment by sportswriters about the accuracy of the film. *Pride* took its fair share of liberties, as an early example of the "based on a true story" genre, fabricating scenes to enhance the story; changing the time frame in the Gehrigs' lives; and asserting that Lou benched himself during a ballgame instead of before it. Daniel did not take that route, but a wire-service editor named Harry Grayson said there were "too many inexcusable errors" to call *Pride* a good film for baseball fans, and lamented that Cooper played Gehrig "as a clumsy rube. He was a bashful young man but never a naïve hick." Cooper, he said, "was almost totally miscast."

Those who came to see *Pride* were spared certain indignities thanks to the industry's censors enforcing the Production Code. A preliminary report from what was known as the Hays Office ordained that no "razzberry" sounds would be heard and that "no undue exposure of the persons of the ball players in the locker room" would be seen. It ruled that the drinking in scenes between sportswriters Blake and Hanneman would be "held to a minimum" and that one of the gamins playing with young Lou in the sandlot would not say, "Hit or get off the bucket" because of its "vulgar connotation." It said that "no comedy interruptions" would be made during the actual reading of the mayor's words during Lou and Eleanor's wedding.

Never mind that the scene was being played for laughs—the wedding ceremony was sacrosanct to the Puritans judging such tame material.

"It is acceptable if the comedy comes before or after the ceremony itself," the report said. That mandate was violated in the mayor's short service, first by workmen delivering a bathtub, then by a carpenter inadvertently turning on a drill.

In the eighth month of America's involvement in World War II, the war's impact was being felt in Hollywood, and not only in the increasing number of war films in production, the drafting of actors to serve, or the limiting of nighttime shooting.

As the premiere of *Pride* at the Pantages Hollywood Theatre neared, it became clear that the opening would usher in another change in the movie capital: It would be the last major film pre-miere until the war was over, although a few movies, like *Yankee Doodle Dandy*, had already opened with subdued fanfare.

Nighttime dim-outs were coming to Hollywood, where brightly lit marquees, photographers' flashes capturing stars entering the-aters, and klieg lights crisscrossing the sky heralding the openings of new pictures were being banned, lest the illumination give the enemy help in targeting coastal southern California. The prohibi-tion was scheduled to start on August 20—two days after *Pride's* opening.

There were no spotlights for *Pride*, but "one of the really vocal premiere crowds, on hand to cheer the dimming out of the Hol-lywood tradition," the *Los Angeles Times* reported. "They shrieked for the platform to be brought closer to the curb in the manner in which a football crowd clamors for its favorite player."

Inside the theater, Fred Astaire, Jack Benny, Elsa Maxwell, Dorothy Lamour, Hedy Lamarr, Ginger Rogers, Mary Pickford, Lana Turner, Edward G. Robinson, Ronald Reagan and Jane Wyman, and Ava Gardner and Mickey Rooney awaited the start of the film. A navy band played military fighting songs. Irene

Manning, the lyric soprano in *Yankee Doodle Dandy*, sang the national anthem.

Programs were handed out by a group of actresses like Betty Grable, Gene Tierney, Linda Darnell, and Virginia Gilmore, *Pride*'s vixenish Myra.

Bob Hope arrived having seen the movie, thanks to a sneak preview from Goldwyn. A press release prepared in Hope's name for Hollywood columnist Sidney Skolsky called *Pride* "the kind of a picture that makes a fellow feel good."

Skolsky did not seem to write it. Maybe Hope didn't say it.

The reviews remained positive, if not effusive.

Edwin Schallert of the *Los Angeles Times* called it a "splendid and moving picture," with a "heartwarming narrative, which encompasses so much of romance, comedy and humanness." Cooper, he said, bears no resemblance to Gehrig, and "remains as always Cooper on the screen," but created a "kinship between his forthrightness as an actor and the sincerity of the man whom he depicts." Virginia Wright of the *Los Angeles Daily News* said *Pride* was "simple and unpretentious" and "as respectful a biography as the screen has ever produced." She also suggested that the lack of additional baseball action "will be disappointing to every fan who has looked forward to the film" and that the significance of Lou's consecutive-game streak was underplayed. Still, she added, "You aren't likely to emerge dry-eyed from this touching portrait of a national hero."

In the days after Goldwyn announced his deal to make *Pride*, some fellow Hollywood executives wagered how well it would do at the box office.

"I bet you $1,000 that the picture would gross $3,000,000 in the entire world," Mervyn LeRoy at MGM wrote Buddy DeSylva at Paramount. "I also bet you $500 that the picture would gross $2,000,000 domestic, making a total bet of $1,500." A day later, DeSylva responded: "I really thought you had had that extra cocktail and were not responsible. I was willing to forget the whole matter. But here you go out on a limb and there is no way I can let you off the hook."

A month later, LeRoy confided to Goldwyn: "You have half of those bets." He signed it, "Love and kisses, Mervyn."

Pride was Goldwyn's highest-grossing film to date, a hit from the day it opened. *Variety* called it the "sensation of the week," grossing $30,000 in its first seven days at the Astor in New York, a new high at the theater. Another $90,000 in receipts were collected at the forty other New York–area theaters where *Pride* was shown. In Los Angeles, the first night's take at the Pantages was $5,005, all of it donated to the Naval Aid Auxiliary; the total first week's gross at the Pantages and another Los Angeles theater came to $38,000. Soon after, at the Golden Gate Theater in San Francisco, *Pride* ran up a record opening-week gross of $31,000.

Months later, Goldwyn read *Variety*'s list of the top-grossing films of 1942.

When he saw *Pride* listed at just over $2.4 million—below others like *Mrs. Miniver, Road to Morocco, Holiday Inn,* and *Wake Island*—he dictated a letter to Abel Green, the show business trade paper's editor, wondering sarcastically if the figure was based on "hearsay or intuition." And, he noted, "if it was intuition, I wouldn't want to strike a woman." He didn't deny the box office for *Pride* but predicted much more business as it opened to even wider release.

It was obvious to Goldwyn that "the reporter who totaled up the above gross for you must have been running out of space on his cuff." And it was just as obvious that Goldwyn was not going to say how much more he expected to make on *Pride*, but did not like being on *Variety*'s list of films that had done business like *Pride*, including *Once Upon a Honeymoon*, *Kings Row*, and *My Sister Eileen*.

Bullish as Goldwyn was, he probably knew *Pride* was not going to match the grosses of *Mrs. Miniver*, which had sold $6 million in tickets and would beat *Pride* and nine other movies to win the Best Picture Oscar the following February.

He was relieved, too, that *Pride* would soon be in his past.

"It's been a tough picture to produce," he wrote to a friend, "as there are so many people throughout America who knew Gehrig that his biography had to be handled with the greatest of care. I also had to watch my baseball so that it didn't get the best of the personal story. As the picture now stands the baseball is purely background and the love story is the dominant factor."

Goldwyn fled baseball for good. But Cooper did not. Or, at least, he did not leave Lou Gehrig behind. The unanticipated chance to re-create the "luckiest man" speech took place 7,000 miles away in the South Pacific.

And the audience was not the women and families Goldwyn was seeking, but soldiers at war, looking to a ballplayer for inspiration.

16

"Luckiest Man" in the South Pacific

onsoonal rain did not deter 15,000 troops on Port Moresby from wanting to see Gary Cooper and the other entertainers on a long USO tour in November 1943. The cloudburst threatened to cancel the show, but heavy rains were commonplace in Papua New Guinea and other parts of Southwest Asia being visited by Cooper, actresses Una Merkel and Phyllis Brooks, and accordionist Andy Arcari. Soldiers held up canvas tarps with poles to allow the troupe to perform, dumping water when a tarp sagged.

The soldiers' need to see stars from home—especially women—impressed Cooper, who was too young to serve in World War I and too old for World War II.

"Those kids'll be sitting out on a muddy hillside for hours for the show to start," he said. "It can rain like all hell but they wouldn't think of moving an inch until it's over. Under those conditions, you rise above yourself and give it every bit you've got."

Cooper was not a vaudevillian, but he tried his best. He performed from his friend Jack Benny's scripts, sang "Pistol Packin' Mama" (a hit song earlier that year), and did a romantic act with Brooks, a B-movie actress. Reviewing the Cooper-Brooks shtick from newsreel footage, gossip columnist Dorothy Kilgallen wrote that their kissing "is warmer than anything the two ever did in pictures."

A different assessment came from Pfc. Randon Gahlbeck, who wrote home to Palatine, Illinois, saying, "Gary's a swell guy. The girls stressed the lack of white women over here and they felt sorry for us. Same old line, but it killed the evening."

The show in Port Moresby was half over when a clamor for something not in the act began. A soldier shouted a request.

"Hey, Coop!" he yelled out. "How about Lou Gehrig's farewell speech to the Yankees?" The soldiers had recently seen *The Pride of the Yankees* and were moved by the selfless speech of a dying man. The suggestion circulated among the troops. More and more demanded that Cooper slip anew into his Iron Horse role.

"The boys began to shout in unison for the farewell speech," he recalled, and told them: "Give me a minute to get it straight. I don't want to leave out anything."

It had been nearly eighteen months since he had delivered the speech at Samuel Goldwyn's soundstage. Memorable as it was, Cooper had not memorized it. He had, however, revisited it shortly before the trip for Cecil B. DeMille's radio show, *Lux Radio Theater*, where abridged film scripts were reenacted. Cooper was joined on October 4 by Edgar Buchanan, playing Blake, and Virginia Bruce as Eleanor, standing in for Teresa Wright. But the tinny sound of the radio studio prevented the audio reprise of *Pride* from mimicking the film's visual power.

Cooper retreated offstage while the storm continued, getting soaked as he wrote down the words that he could remember from the film.

Then he returned to the stage, giving the speech for thousands of men in need of inspiration. "It was a silent bunch that listened to it," he wrote.

"They were," he added, "the words of a brave American who had only a short time to live, and they mean something to those kids in the Pacific."

Cooper's account, written years later for the *Saturday Evening Post*, suggested that the speech was so successful that word got around on other stops in the 24,000-mile trip—in Dobodura, Milne Bay, Goodenough Island, Hollandia, Lae, and Darwin— and requests kept coming from the soldiers.

At the Theatre Royal in Sydney, Australia, a storied nineteenth-century relic, Cooper gave the speech—perhaps for the final time ever—before flying home.

Cooper was known as a star with a taciturn Westerner's style. It became an industry joke that all he really ever said was "Yep." But he was not always that terse. In *Meet John Doe* he gave a moving radio address that placed him in the forefront of a movement of "average guys . . . If anybody should ask you what the average John Doe is like you couldn't tell him because he's a million and one things. He's Mr. Big and Mr. Small. He's simple and he's wise. He's inherently honest but he's got a streak of larceny in his heart."

In *The Fountainhead*, Cooper gave a very long courtroom speech about man's natural urge to invent that expressed the objectivist philosophy of Ayn Rand, who wrote the screenplay for her novel.

Cooper was more characteristically reticent in *High Noon*, for which he won his second Oscar. Little that he said as Marshal Will Kane is remembered. Rather, it was the morality and bravery that Cooper demonstrated as Kane that still stand out.

Cooper's last words as Gehrig were clearly his most enduring, not only for their resonance over three generations but for their uniqueness. Athletes routinely give thanks for a career, but the circumstances that led Gehrig to his speech have not been repeated: A still-great athlete, dying of a rare disease that will kill him within two years, says farewell to more than 60,000 fans in one of the most famous stadiums on earth. And because Cooper's version of Gehrig's good-bye has persisted unabated, it continues to make us contemplate the impulse that made Gehrig, with his body withering, believe he was a lucky man.

Cooper worked with Sam Wood three more times, in *For Whom the Bell Tolls*, *Casanova Brown* (with Teresa Wright), and *Saratoga Trunk*. But they were also Hollywood conservatives—Wood was overtly right-wing—who played roles on Capitol Hill as Congress sought to root out Communists in Hollywood.

Wood was happy to cooperate.

Samuel Grosvenor Wood's directorial career was solid, perhaps even distinguished, with three Oscar nominations and a diverse list of films that included two Marx Brothers pictures (*A Night at the Opera* and *A Day at the Races*) and *Goodbye, Mr. Chips*, *Kitty Foyle*, *Our Town*, and *Kings Row*. He followed George Cukor as a director on *Gone with the Wind*, which was credited to Victor Fleming.

As a former athlete, he was comfortable with sports films, directing *One Minute to Play*, with the football star Red Grange; *Huddle*, another football picture; *Pride*; and *The Stratton Story*, in 1949, with James Stewart as Monty Stratton, who returns to pitching after shooting himself in the leg in a hunting accident. Wood followed the *Pride* model: A brave ballplayer and his supportive wife (June Allyson) face a crisis. The big difference, of course, is that Stratton lived for decades after and Gehrig died.

Wood's screen accomplishments, however, have been obscured by the extreme right-wing politics that led him to name five directors and several writers as Communists in testimony to the House Un-American Activities Committee (HUAC) in October 1947. Wood was a leading Hollywood conservative who, along with Walt Disney, had formed the Motion Picture Alliance for the Preservation of American Ideals in 1944. Its members included Cooper, John Wayne, and Clark Gable.

Wood's status as a friendly witness was amplified by his direct, colorful way of speaking. He was used to leadership on the set and offered the committee his confidence and certainty that Communism had to be eradicated in Hollywood.

"I think you have to awaken the public to the fact that they are here and what they are doing," he testified. "If you mention you are opposed to the Communist Party, then you are anti-labor, anti-Semitic or anti-Negro, and you will end up being called a fascist, but they never start that until they find out you are opposed to the Communist Party; but if you want to drop their rompers you would find the hammer and sickle on their rear ends, I think."

Under questioning by Robert Stripling, HUAC's chief investigator, Wood recalled that director John Cromwell had tried to steer the Screen Directors Guild "into the red river," with the help of Irving Pichel, Edward Dmytryk, and Frank Tuttle, and that the Motion Picture Alliance's goal was to prevent Communists from taking control of Hollywood's unions and guilds, and spreading their propaganda.

Stripling: Do you feel that the Communists have succeeded in putting in pictures scenes which—or leaving scenes out of pictures—which indirectly attack our system of government?

Wood: Well, unquestionably they are always trying. It is very difficult for the American people to understand what you mean by "Communist propaganda" in pictures. You might refer to some pictures, something is mentioned, and they say, "This is ridiculous, there is no propaganda there," because they are looking for some howl for Stalin or showing the Russian way of life. But they don't show that. They have nothing to sell. All they want to do is unsell America.

Stripling: That can be done just as effectively by leaving stuff out of pictures as by putting it in?

Wood: Yes. They don't want to show the American way of life.

Wood claimed to never encounter any trouble with Communists in his productions. "Because I don't have them," he said. "Don't want them."

While he said that no studio head would knowingly allow Communist propaganda in their films, he believed that "it is utterly impossible for the heads of the studios to read the number of scripts they would have to read. There is the danger. They are always trying. So you have to be a watchdog." Then, asked which group had to be watched most, he answered flatly: "The writers."

Later, when Richard M. Nixon, a first-term congressman, questioned Wood, he returned to an earlier theme: that the main success of Hollywood Communists was not what they got into pictures, but what they kept out.

Wood: I think they are both dangers, but I think what they keep out is doubly dangerous. You wouldn't notice that. If the script is accepted, you don't check back. I do. I generally go back over the book and try to check to see if anything important was left out. But if they don't check back, they leave things out that put this country and our way of living in a favorable light.

When his testimony ended, he had the full gratitude of the red-baiting committee. J. Parnell Thomas, a New Jersey Republican who was its chairman, told the director: "Mr. Wood, to use the slang expression, you really 'lay it on the line.' If the great majority of persons in industry, labor and education showed the same amount of courage that you show we would not have to worry about communism or fascism in this country. In other words, you've got guts."

And three movies left before he died in 1949, at age sixty-six.

Cooper testified at the HUAC hearings a few days after Wood and, as his biographer Jeffrey Meyers wrote, charmed the committee with his "'shitkicker' image—boyish, naïve and soft-spoken" and often quite vague. When asked if he'd turned down any scripts that smacked of Communist influence, he said he had rejected a few that were "tinged with Communist ideas." But when asked if he could name any of those scripts, he said he could not.

Thomas, the chairman, who was questioning Cooper, was incredulous, and their byplay reads like a scene from a comedy script about Washington politics.

Thomas: Just a minute, Mr. Cooper, you haven't got that bad a memory.

Cooper: I beg your pardon, sir?

Thomas: I say, you haven't got that bad a memory, have you? You must be able to remember some of those scripts you turned down because you thought they were Communist scripts.

Cooper: Well, I can't actually give you a title to any of them, no.

Thomas: Will you think it over, then, and supply the committee with a list of those scripts?

Cooper: I don't think I could, because most of the scripts I read at night, and if they don't look good to me, I don't finish them, or if I do finish them I send them back as soon as possible to their author.

Later, he said that he had heard people in Hollywood discuss Communism and its supposed benefits to actors and artists, but it never interested him.

"I could never take any of this pinko mouthing very seriously," he said, "because I didn't feel it was on the level."

In 1956, *The Lou Gehrig Story* debuted on a CBS anthology series called *Climax!* With Wendell Corey as Lou and Jean Hagen as Eleanor, the film follows their story from the moment Lou's physical frailties present themselves, and he is shown inelegantly flopping on his face and pouring coffee on his hand (but not feeling its scalding heat). Corey was a dour Gehrig and Hagen a terrified and fearful Eleanor, frantically calling Bill Dickey (Harry Carey, Jr.) in the hotel room he shared on the road with Lou to urge him to see a doctor.

There are similarities to *Pride:* One player, in this case Rusty (Russell Johnson, the future Professor in *Gilligan's Island*), gripes that Lou's fumbling at first base cost him a victory (but unlike a similar incident in *Pride*, the Dickey character is restrained from slugging him). Dr. Adams (Harry Townes), who diagnoses Lou, uses baseball language to convey the gravity of ALS. Whereas the doctor in *Pride* tells Lou it's "three strikes," the physician in *The Lou Gehrig Story* meanders, struggling mightily to find the proper words.

Lou: What's the final score?

Adams: Well, you might say you're at bat at the end of nine innings. We're all tied up.

Lou: After five days of tests?

Adams: Lou, let's see how I can put this to you.

Lou: You can put it to me straight, Doc.

Adams: Yes, Lou, I believe I can. Well, when I said we're tied at the end of nine that sounds like a poor analogy, but that's not too far from the truth. What I'm trying to say, Lou, a game that's tied can go on 10, 15, 20 innings. It depends on so many factors.

Anthology series like *Climax!* did not lavish money on their productions, although some, like *Playhouse 90*, consistently turned out quality programs. *The Lou Gehrig Story* looks cheaply produced, relying on interiors (Lou's apartment, the Yankee clubhouse) and newsreels of Gehrig and the day in his honor. The movie's worst moment occurs at its climax.

In the press box, an uncredited actor playing sportswriter Grantland Rice riffs about Lou: "This isn't the Rock of Gibraltar in baseball pants, just a very sick man," who "might not say any more than 'Thank you.'"

After a reporter spreads news that Lou might not speak at all, we never see Corey again. Instead, the film cuts to the newsreel of Lou with Corey performing an undistinguished voice-over of a speech that is a poorly rewritten hash of Eleanor's and *Pride*'s versions of the speech. The decision to muddle the speech was bad enough, but Corey's voice-over devalues the newsreel and cannot sync with its audio. His dour, affectless voice (amplified and echoing as if he were inside Yankee Stadium) is jarring when compared to the familiar sounds of Cooper's from *Pride* and Lou's from the few extant lines of his original speech.

In the era before videocassettes and DVDs, if you didn't see an old movie on the new channels on television, you wouldn't see it. Movie channels like HBO, Showtime, and TCM did not exist. MLB Network, the full-time baseball channel, where *Pride* found a natural home, did not exist until 2009.

So it is unsurprising that in 1964, a woman named Jean Klein wrote to Goldwyn asking him, "Can you tell me what has happened to the movie *The Pride of the Yankees*—starring Gary Cooper as Lou Gehrig? Will it ever be shown again in theaters? Has it been sold to television or what? I loved the picture myself as a child (I saw it three or four times) and now I would like very much to have my children see it." Or that Gary Johnson, apparently a child from his handwriting, wondered, "Can you give me some information about buying a film: *Pride of the Yankees*?" Before signing off, he wrote, "Ans. my letter."

Living alone in an apartment on East 53rd Street in Manhattan, Eleanor tried to watch *Pride* whenever it was on in those pre-cable days, most likely on WPIX, the station that was carrying Yankee games. "Whenever it aired, I would use it as a reason to check in on her and call her the next day," said Marty Appel, the Yankee historian who served the team as a publicist and executive producer of its broadcasts. "I'd say 'I saw your movie last night. You're looking good.' She'd laugh and actually explain to me that it wasn't her but it was Teresa Wright."

Nostalgia was not her only response to seeing *Pride* televised.

In April 1969, she wrote to Michael Burke, the president of the Yankees, wondering if the sale of television rights to *Pride* would generate additional income. But, as Burke learned, Goldwyn still owned the film, and television stations only licensed the right to televise *Pride*.

Nonetheless, George Pollack, Eleanor's lawyer, wrote to Goldwyn, reminding him that *Pride* "has achieved the status for many years of a classic motion picture which is shown on television at least once a year here in the East and I am sure is exhibited throughout the country on many occasions. All those showings, Pollack wrote, suggested that "the sale of the picture is on a level and volume that probably was not contemplated by the parties many years ago." He added that additional sales called for an evaluation of the situation that "would call for an adequate and equitable compensation for Mrs. Gehrig."

Goldwyn was, by now, almost ninety and incapacitated by a cerebral thrombosis. He did not answer Eleanor or Pollack, but one of his lawyers did, responding: "We are somewhat at a loss to understand upon which you base your belief that Mrs. Gehrig is entitled to receive compensation other than already paid to her pursuant to the provisions of Paragraph 6 of the agreement of July 14, 1941." The clause directed her to receive $30,000 in three installments but did not foresee the prospect of paying her if *Pride* ran on television, a medium that was barely a reality when the original agreement was made.

In response, Pollack wrote that Eleanor "informs me that she has mislaid the agreement of July 14, 1941," and would appreciate the lawyer sending him a copy of the contract. Doing so, he added, "may dispose of the entire problem."

My *Luke and I*, Eleanor's 1976 memoir about her life with Lou, offered a more complex version of the Gehrigs' lives than *Pride*. Eleanor emerged as the stronger, more worldly personality who fell for a sheltered man insulated by poverty, adored by his mother, and devoted single-mindedly to baseball. The message of Eleanor as the stronger person was conveyed, without reservation, a year later when she met with Blythe Danner, the thirty-four-year-old stage and film actress who was cast as Eleanor in *A Love Affair: The Eleanor and Lou Gehrig Story*, which NBC showed in 1978.

"She was quite a presence," Danner said nearly forty years later. "She scared me a little. She said, 'Listen, kid, I wasn't a sweet young thing so don't play me like Teresa Wright.' I took that to heart." As she promoted the film in the days before the original premiere date (it would be delayed from October 1977 to the next January), Danner told an interviewer, "When I read the book, I saw that Eleanor was a much different lady than she was portrayed in the movie." Eleanor, she added, "struck me as the kind of woman who wore the pants in the family."

It is framed as Eleanor's look back at her life. It cuts from Danner—as an older Eleanor, telling her story in an empty Yankee Stadium to her collaborator, Joe Durso (Richard Burr)—to scenes from her past, particularly Lou's illness.

Goldwyn would have enjoyed it. It has even less baseball action than *Pride* and focuses even more on the romance between the Gehrigs than Goldwyn did in *Pride*. They meet at a party in A *Love Affair*, not after Lou tumbles over bats after rushing onto the field at Comiskey Park. Eleanor is less the "sweet young thing" than a boozy card-playing broad smitten with Lou but confused by his timidity and insistence that he call her "Miss Twitchell." Mom Gehrig is seen much less than in *Pride* but, as played by Patricia Neal, is the hellish mother-in-law of Eleanor's book (and interviews with Gallico) without any of the redemption in *Pride.*

Edward Herrmann plays Lou, a year after playing Franklin D. Roosevelt in *Eleanor and Franklin,* the acclaimed TV miniseries. He, too, consulted with Eleanor. "I was trying to get hold of the quality, trying to get her to tell me the things she wanted brought out," he said in 1977. "His honesty and simplicity are difficult to define. There were no quirks, no cigarette holder, no hat."

Like Gary Cooper, Herrmann was tall and thin, and not thickly muscled like Gehrig—which made the decision by director Fielder Cook to limit baseball a wise one. Herrmann's Gehrig is a nice young man fully in love with Eleanor. Instead of wrestling on a St. Petersburg beach, as Cooper and Wright did in *Pride,* Herrmann and Danner snuggle by a fire. They celebrate their first anniversary on a boat heading to Japan on a Major Leaguers' tour of the country. Here they discuss having children, a subject never raised in *Pride.* Herrmann brings it up, but Eleanor tells him: "I don't want to share you with anybody yet."

Ramon Bieri, nearing fifty at the time, plays Babe Ruth and has the mug and physicality for the role. Ruth was restrained from being fully Ruthian in *Pride*—he was nearly statesmanlike, considering his renowned personal excesses. But Bieri drinks, chows down on hot dogs, and hints at philandering. It was not known if Eleanor objected to Bieri stealing scenes, as she did Ruth in *Pride.*

The first sign of Lou's illness is not a sudden jolt of pain in his shoulder, as it was in *Pride,* but Herrmann's slip and fall when he's teaching Danner to play baseball. "I just put my foot wrong," he says as Danner helps him to his feet. The story then moves through Gehrig's physical decline—he drops things and is too weak to open a bottle of ketchup—and his insistence that he bench himself.

The doctors (played by David Ogden Stiers and Michael Lerner) bluntly discuss their diagnosis of Lou, although the script incorrectly brings Eleanor to the Mayo Clinic as he undergoes days of tests. That factual liberty allows Danner to tell the doctors, who at first want to inform Lou, not her, that she, not Lou, is "the head of the family." They agree and tell her that ALS is terminal; that he will be paralyzed; that he will exhibit spasticity; that he has, at best, two years to live.

Rather than take *Pride*'s lead and cut to New York for Lou's speech, Herrmann and Danner head to a fishing cabin for a fictional romantic interlude. The truth was that Eleanor stayed at home while Lou was at the clinic; after his last day in Rochester, Minnesota, he visited a Boy Scout camp and returned to his hotel for dinner with his doctors. He flew home the next day.

The speech is far less the highlight in *A Love Affair* that it was in *Pride*. Herrmann recites the speech from a very low angle (and into a cloudy sky) in a less resonant voice than Cooper's, and without Cooper's palpable emotion and tears.

The film does not end there. *A Love Affair* takes the story to Gehrig's deathbed. Herrmann lay in his pajamas, immobile but for his breathing, his voice weakened. As he fades, Danner whispers, "Don't go away," as she watches him die.

As much as she contributed to *Pride*, through interviews with Gallico and letters to Goldwyn, *A Love Affair* is truly her story, told as close to her wishes as possible. She was not as sweet as Wright, but Danner showed some steel mixed with winsomeness and tears. Herrmann, who had shot his way to stardom as FDR, gave a sweeter interpretation of Gehrig than Cooper but was left to survive almost entirely as an off-the-field character, with almost no baseball action to balance his portrayal.

Eleanor died in 1984—on her eightieth birthday. She had spent a lonely forty-three years without Lou, much of it in an apartment on East 53rd Street in Manhattan. There were doilies on the sofa arms but little memorabilia of Lou's life, one visitor said. She had no children, but her mother lived with her until her death in 1968.

One day in 1971, the collector Barry Halper accompanied Eleanor to the apartment, hoping to make a deal for something valuable. "She told me she was thirsty and I said, 'Do you have any soda?'" said Halper, who was dogged after his death with allegations of fraud in his memorabilia business. "She said no, but she said she wanted some hooch, a term I'd only heard in black-and-white movies. 'That's what I could use, some hooch.' I assumed it was liquor. She said, 'When you come back, I have something special for you.'"

When Halper returned with six bottles of J&B scotch, she presented him with the uniform Lou wore on July 4, 1939. She signed a photograph of Lou that said, "I know Lou would want you to have this."

By then, she was no longer a public person, except for appearances at Yankee Stadium for Old-Timers' Days. She was known to drink too much. But in 1949, she testified to a Senate subcommittee about finding a cure for ALS, which became her defining cause.

"To watch someone close to you become a helpless, hopeless paralytic and to know that medical science is powerless to halt the progress of the disease," she said, "is something which no person should be called upon to endure."

A few weeks later, she appeared on Bill Stern's radio show, the same fabulist who called Lou's two home runs for polio-stricken Billy. After re-creating her testimony for him, Stern (who twice said that Lou had died of multiple sclerosis) closed the segment in a melodramatic whisper: "Mrs. Gehrig, you have the satisfaction of knowing that your husband can never be forgotten!"

But in death she was. Only two mourners attended her funeral: her lawyer, George Pollack, her usual companion at Old-Timers' Day, and his wife.

She was cremated and her ashes were mixed with Lou's.

In a note to Pollack written in 1974, she wrote, "It just occurred to me that you should know the key to the monument holding Lou's ashes is in my top dresser drawer. You will need it in order to intermingle my ashes in the bronze container therein. Also my mother's."

Devoted as she was to Lou's memory, it is almost certain that she would not have liked the way that *Pride*, and Lou, eventually became the subjects of parody.

Seinfeld took the first two stabs.

In a 1995 episode that rests partly on George Constanza's employment in the Yankee front office, a birthday card intended for George Steinbrenner—framed and signed by almost everyone in the Yankee organization—winds up with a sick boy in a hospital thanks to Kramer. The little boy and Kramer, the series' hipster doofus, wittily mocked the scene in *Pride* where Lou promises a boy that he will hit two home runs in a World Series game.

Bobby: I'd never part with this card for anything in the world.
Kramer: Well, Bobby, who's your favorite Yankee?
Bobby: Paul O'Neill.

Kramer: All right. What if I tell Paul O'Neill to hit a home run tomorrow, just for you?

Bobby: Would he? Paul O'Neill would do that?

Kramer: For you he would.

Bobby: Would he hit two home runs?

Kramer: Two? Sure, kid, yeah. But then you gotta promise you'll do something for me.

Bobby: I know. Get out of bed one day and walk again.

Kramer: Yeah, that would be nice. But I really just need this card.

Kramer joins Bobby in his hospital room as they listen to O'Neill hit one home run, then another that is called back as a triple and an error. Bobby, at first, refuses to give up the framed card, but a later scene reveals that Kramer has made another deal: "Tomorrow night, Paul O'Neill has to catch a fly ball in his hat."

Two years later, Costanza enters Steinbrenner's office and finds the owner (rendered degrees more eccentric and manic by the voice of Larry David, the co-creator of the series) wearing a pair of historic pants.

"Hey, check this out," he says. "Lou Gehrig's pants. Not a bad fit. Hey, you don't think that nerve disease of his was contagious, do you? Uh, I better take 'em off. I'm too important to the team." As he removes the pants, he says, with the ardor of a lunatic: "Big Stein can't be flopping and twitching."

Then, in 1999, *Saturday Night Live* went after the very core of *Pride*—Lou's speech—which raised an essential question: How could a dying man *really* describe himself as fortunate, knowing that he was mortally ill and had to retire? Playing Gehrig, Norm Macdonald stands at a microphone, surrounded by teammates, and recites the "luckiest man" line. Macdonald, whose voice almost always reeks of insincerity, then confesses to a cheering crowd that he was being sarcastic.

"I'm unlucky," he says. "I may be the *unluckiest* man on the face of the earth. I have a disease so rare they named it after me! Yeah, lucky me." He waves to the crowd, which is still cheering him. "You people," he adds, "are hopeless."

———

Baseball knowledge was not a requirement to make or star in *Pride.* Goldwyn knew nothing about it. Cooper and Wright were similarly lacking in knowledge about the sport. They were nominated by the motion picture academy for Best Actor and Best Actress, and although they didn't win, they didn't lose because they didn't know whose fielding play stopped Joe DiMaggio's fifty-six-game hitting streak (Ken Keltner of the Cleveland Indians).

As she entered her eighties, though, Wright became a Yankee fan. A *big* Yankee fan.

In 1998, a year past her final movie, Francis Ford Coppola's *The Rainmaker*, where she played Matt Damon's landlord, Miss Birdie, she discovered a new passion because of Rick Cerrone, the Yankees' publicity director.

A longtime fan of *Pride*, Cerrone was watching the Academy Awards show that March while in spring training in Tampa, Florida. He saw Wright sitting onstage with seventy past winners of the acting Oscars. They were introduced alphabetically, leaving Wright's name the last to be announced after Vincent Winter (who, as a six-year-old, got a tiny statue for his role in *The Little Kidnappers*) and Shelley Winters (*The Diary of Anne Frank* and *A Patch of Blue*).

"There was this elderly woman looking meek and happy to be there and I say, 'Holy crap, that's Teresa Wright,'" he said. "And

I'm thinking, 'Eleanor Gehrig, *Pride of the Yankees*,' and a light-bulb went off and I said we have to get her to Yankee Stadium to throw out the first pitch."

Any plan had to go through the mercurial Steinbrenner, who was not known to try on Gehrig's pants in real life.

"So up in New York," Cerrone said, "I went to Mr. Steinbrenner's suite. He went into a Seinfeldian riff about the movie. He said, 'It's my favorite movie, I loved her in the movie, she's great, it's a great, great idea, go to it. Go! Go! Go!'"

Wright's agent initially rejected Cerrone's idea, but he persisted, saying she didn't have to strike out anyone; she could simply hand the ball to the pitcher. "We just wanted to introduce her," he said, "and have fans give her a standing ovation."

The day of the game, July 4, she arrived with her grandson. She sat in the Yankee dugout talking to manager Joe Torre, pitcher David Cone, and coach Don Zimmer. Before she got to the mound for the first pitch, a video clip of her and Cooper dancing played on the scoreboard. Nervously, she wondered if fans would remember her, but before the video ended, fans were standing and cheering.

The next day, she wrote to Cerrone, telling him, "I'm sorry it's taken me some fifty-six years to get to a Yankee game but it was an occasion I'll never forget. Thank you for the beautiful huge bouquet of roses, lunch in the club, the great seats—everything! Please wish Mr. Steinbrenner a belated happy birthday."

Thus began her octogenarian's love of baseball. Her son-in-law said that it had become impossible to get her out of the house if the Yankees were on TV; her daughter told Cerrone that she often fell asleep listening to games on her transistor radio, like a kid from the 1950s or 1960s. Ray Robinson, a friend of Wright's and author of a Gehrig biography, *Iron Horse*, said that in the mornings after Yankee night games, she called him to help her understand the game. He told Cerrone: "She read about the Yankees in the *New York Times* and now they were 'her boys.'"

Later that year, she attended her second baseball game: Game 1 of the American League Championship Series between the Yankees and Cleveland Indians at Yankee Stadium. She was introduced by NBC's Bob Costas and described her odyssey to Keith Olbermann.

"I saw my first game on July Fourth and I've just been a great mad fan ever since," she said, wearing a Yankee cap. "I started watching and reading, and the more I watched the more I read and the more fascinated I got."

Then, in 2000, she sat on a dais at a dinner beside Derek Jeter, who was entering the fifth season of a career that would end with his becoming the franchise's greatest shortstop and one of its best players. Talking to reporters, she talked about what fed her baseball passion: "You see the skill, the professionalism, and when they win, you see the smile reflected all over Joe Torre's face and you live it all over again."

In a handwritten letter to Cerrone soon after attending the dinner, she wrote:

From the day you first invited me to throw out the first ball on Lou Gehrig's Day at Yankee Stadium, you opened the door to the great pleasure of learning about baseball and the New York Yankees and I've said before I cannot thank you enough. Now, once again I thank you for finding the N.Y. Times photo that Derek Jeter so kindly signed for me; I'm only sorry that I dislike the shot of me—not that it doesn't look like me—it does, but as I've grown old it is not easy to have my deformities photographed—so I may just have to paste something over my face and neck and just enjoy the photo of Derek.

Two months later, she was at the Baseball Hall of Fame in Cooperstown, New York, for a screening of *Pride* and a discussion. At one point she began to sound like James Earl Jones in *Field of Dreams* delivering his love-of-baseball speech.

"It is a very American game," she said. "Everything that is good about his country is in baseball."

She died in 2005, in rapturous love with Lou Gehrig's game.

Epilogue

Cooper Says Good-bye

For his last public appearance Gary Cooper was among the Hollywood elite of the day at a Friars Club roast in his honor on January 8, 1961, a warm winter's day in Southern California, twelve days before John F. Kennedy's inauguration as president.

In Cooper's pocket was a speech that linked him to Gehrig and *Pride*.

Cooper, his wife, Veronica, known widely as Rocky, and their twenty-three-year-old daughter, Maria, stepped into a limousine outside their Holmby Hills mansion for the short ride to the Beverly Hilton Hotel. Cooper looked older than fifty-nine, but still lean and handsome in a tuxedo, his hair slicked back, his bow tie a bit askew.

Cooper was dying of cancer that had infiltrated his bones. Rocky would not tell him of the fatal diagnosis until the end of February, much as Eleanor insisted that she never told Lou that amyotrophic lateral sclerosis was going to paralyze him first, then kill him in short order.

"My father allegedly didn't know," Maria Cooper Janis said. "I'm ninety-nine percent sure he came to his own summation of what was going on." But there was no doubt he would attend the roast. "He had committed to it, and he wanted to do it."

He sat for a few hours of love and insults from actors, comedians, studio bosses, and the white-haired, octogenarian poet, Carl Sandburg, who seemingly had no place in a room with Milton Berle, Dean Martin, and Jack Benny—or singer Tony Martin gently tweaking Cooper with a parody of Cole Porter's "I Love Paris."

"I love Cooper as a Sergeant (York)," he began, then continued:

I love him as a sheriff, too.
I love Cooper 'cause his style is so effectual.
And you know that I'm not nearly homosexual.

Audrey Hepburn had just wrapped *Breakfast at Tiffany's* and offered a besotted love note that conveyed some lingering affection from *Love in the Afternoon*, their May-December romantic film from a few years earlier. In her lilting, Belgian-bred voice, she said that when she was asked to speak about Cooper, "I went directly to my encyclopedia to learn exactly what a 'Gary Cooper' is." She described it as "the tallest, finest, thinnest, kindest, most patient, sportiest, quietest…the shootingest, ridingest, handsomest, unsnidiest." Also as: "bewitching, unaffected, enriching, and unexpected," "decent, daring, and beautiful," and "cheerful, charming, charitable, and disarming."

She did not share in the fixation by many of the speakers on

Cooper's cowboy terseness, specifically his reputation for saying, "Yep." They piled on, possibly because he gave them so little material, and they would not tread into his past philandering, not at a tribute whose proceeds were going to charity.

Benny: "When the talkies came in, he made the transition so smoothly. He was in talking pictures for five years before anyone realized it."

George Burns, on trying to find four minutes of material on Cooper: "This is not easy. In Gary Cooper's entire life he hasn't talked for four minutes."

Greer Garson, on the secret of his appeal: "Is it perhaps that you can be understood and enjoyed in all languages all over the world with less dubbing and translation than any other actor on the screen?"

Yet it was Sandburg whose remarks on "yep" had him sounding like an insult comic who had written a multivolume biography of Abe Lincoln. "I think this evening," he said, "it would be proper to call him 'America's most beloved illiterate.'"

Berle broke with the safe tenor of the roast with an unhinged stream-of-consciousness monologue that said, in part, "How can I make jokes about a man that doesn't drink, doesn't smoke, doesn't go out with girls? And confirms my first suspicion since I saw him in *Wings*: I knew he was a fairy." He then added, "Oh, that shy stuff. Look at him sitting there, so shy. He got his first Green Stamps from Polly Adler"—a Manhattan brothel owner of the 1920s and 1930s.

It is impossible to know if Cooper's delight at being celebrated for his full career alleviated the melancholy he had expressed that month to a writer from *McCall's* magazine. As he recovered from the past year's cancer surgeries, he revealed his displeasure with much of his output the previous eight years, from *Springfield Rifle* to *The Naked Edge*. It was an extraordinary admission for a star of his magnitude, suggesting that he had peaked in 1952 with *High Noon*.

"I've been coasting along," he said. "Some of the pictures I've made recently I'm genuinely sorry about."

When it was Cooper's turn to speak, he read from a speech written by his friend, director Billy Wilder, who collaborated on *Love in the Afternoon*. A witty cynic, Wilder found in Cooper an actor whose work needed to be seen onscreen to be appreciated. "When I shot a scene with Gary Cooper, it didn't look like anything," Wilder recalled. "But when you saw it on the screen in the rushes, there was an added something going on—some kind of love affair between the performer and the celluloid."

Wilder's words played to Cooper's image and the theme of the night.

"Well, before I got here, I heard that the betting in Las Vegas was ten to one that if I got up here I would say 'yep,'" Cooper said. "And that sort of leaves me without much of a speech left." He sniffled as he said he would not forget the night as long as he lived. At the end, he demonstrated an understanding of a star whose physical presence on film was indelible but whose verbal highlights were few. For the final words he said in public, Cooper merged his screen terseness with the farewell speech by Gehrig that concluded *Pride*. He did not quote directly from *Pride* but made a strong reference to the most memorable lines of his career.

"If anybody asks me, 'Am I the luckiest guy in the world?'" he said, choking up twice. "My answer is 'Yep.'"

Two months later, he was too sick to accept an honorary Oscar at the Academy Awards ceremony. His friend James Stewart accepted the statuette for him. Through tears, Stewart said,

"Coop, I want you to know this, that with this, goes all the warm friendship and the affection and the admiration and the deep respect of us all. We're very, very proud of you, Coop."

On May 13, Gary Cooper was gone.

But his Gehrig—the Gehrig he created in *Pride*—continues to live.

Acknowledgments

It is impossible for this litany of gratitude not to sound a little like a writer's version of Lou Gehrig's "luckiest man" speech.

I was blessed with the archivists at the Margaret Herrick Library in Beverly Hills, the research home of the Academy of Motion Picture Arts and Sciences. It was there, in the Katharine Hepburn reading room, that I pored through the Samuel Goldwyn archive. This book would not exist without the scripts, letters, memoranda, notes, and other documents that I examined in this wonderfully preserved archive.

With each file folder, the story of *The Pride of the Yankees* opened further to me.

Nearly everything that I needed was there, and thanks to archivists like Jenny Romero and Louise Hilton, my requests were not only fulfilled but I got more than I asked for because they know the archive so well. Faye Thompson and Kristine Krueger helped me with photos at the library that are important to this book.

As I was picking the photos I wanted, I came across the wonderful sketches that Gary Cooper drew of cast members like Teresa Wright and Babe Ruth—they were a revelation. Coop could have been a commercial artist if he hadn't been so good at acting.

Rorri Feinstein of the Samuel Goldwyn Foundation and the Samuel Goldwyn Jr. Family Trust was my gatekeeper to the archive, and once I produced a book contract, she opened the door. I am ever thankful for her help, enthusiasm, and interest.

This was the second time I had tried to get into the archive. A decade or so ago, when I first wrote a proposal for a book about *Pride*, I asked Samuel Goldwyn, Jr., for permission. I had no contract. He said no.

I knew, at that point, that there would be no book without access to primary information. It could not stand simply on my analysis of *Pride* or newspaper clips. I needed, at the very least, an original script that would be the foundation of any research. I found my script and other materials from a baseball memorabilia dealer named Daniel Lovegrove, who has generously let me hang on to his documents for so long. Seeing that first script for the first time was an inspiration—and it has continued to be. Many thanks, Daniel.

I have received encouragement from friends like James Andrew Miller, Michael D'Antonio, Ken Belson, Joe Drape, Tom Schieber, Rick Wolff, and Marty Appel. Marty guided me to a wonderful website, newspapers.com, which had enlivened his new biography of Casey Stengel. It provided me with access to articles from around the country that covered the short time period that I've focused on. For a modest price it proved to be an invaluable resource.

What a treat it has been to get to know Maria Cooper Janis, Gary's only child. She encouraged me with her good cheer and willingness to help me understand her adored father in many ways.

I have been the happy recipient of counsel from Jonathan Eig, the author of *Luckiest Man*, a 2005 biography of Lou Gehrig, and A. Scott Berg, the author of *Goldwyn: A Biography*. Jonathan was generous in providing me with early documents (especially the invaluable, gossipy letters between Eleanor Gehrig and her agent,

Christy Walsh) and he offered his biographer's wisdom for several years. This book might not have happened without the anecdote in Scott's book about Niven Busch persuading Goldwyn to make *Pride* by showing him the newsreel of Gehrig delivering the "luckiest man" speech.

I knew for many years about Eleanor Gehrig's lawyer, George Pollack, and talked to him once. He had died by the time I started writing this book, but I was fortunate that one of his daughters, Ruth Pollack Pappas, let me rummage through her father's files and take home some excellent documents and keep them until I was done with them. Thank you, Ruth.

I feel myself extremely fortunate to have found Andrew Blauner, my agent, who helped me resurrect a failed proposal for this book, but made it so much better. He is a calm, sagacious, encouraging friend who is as responsible as anyone for making this project happen. Andrew's selling skills brought me to Hachette to work with Mauro DiPreta, who embraced my proposal and has performed the necessary magic (along with his deputy, David Lamb) to turn my research and writing into the finest work of my career.

My mother, Shirley Winikoff, has always encouraged my work and has waited patiently for this book to become a reality. She predicted big things for it when she read the proposal and wept a bit as she read the first chapter. Thanks, Mom.

And, of course, there is my wife, Griffin Miller. She has always encouraged me in my work and has stood by me in the years since I first felt the need to write a book about *The Pride of the Yankees*. She understood the hours that I needed to put into this book, especially at nights and on weekends, and kept our cats, Cosmo and Reggie, from demanding food when my iMac was demanding my words. She is my great love and my best friend. I couldn't have done this without her.

Bibliography

The letters to and from Eleanor Gehrig that are cited throughout these notes provide an insider's view of the making of *The Pride of the Yankees*. She was at the center of the story, especially as she helped Paul Gallico with the outline and first script and corresponded with her agent, Christy Walsh, who was also working as a publicist for Samuel Goldwyn. Much of the documentation was provided by the National Baseball Hall of Fame, to which she donated many things, not just letters, and by the Samuel Goldwyn Foundation and Samuel Goldwyn Jr. Family Trust. Ruth Pollack Pappas, whose father, George, served as Eleanor's lawyer, provided access to still more material. This book benefited mightily from all their generosity.

Appel, Marty. *Pinstripe Empire: The New York Yankees from the Babe to After the Boss.* New York: Bloomsbury, 2012.

Berg, A. Scott. *Goldwyn: A Biography.* New York: Alfred A. Knopf, 1989.

Breslin, Jimmy. *Damon Runyon: A Life.* New York: Dell Publishing, 1991.

Easton, Carol. *The Search for Samuel Goldwyn.* Jackson, Miss.: University Press of Mississippi, 1975.

Eig, Jonathan. *Luckiest Man: The Life and Death of Lou Gehrig.* New York: Simon & Schuster, 2005.

Gallico, Paul. *Farewell to Sport.* Lincoln, Neb.: University of Nebraska Press, 2008.

Gallico, Paul. *Lou Gehrig: Pride of the "Yankees."* New York: Grosset & Dunlap, 1942.

Gehrig, Eleanor, and Joseph Durso. *My Luke and I: Mrs. Lou Gehrig's Joyous and Tragic Love for the "Iron Man of Baseball."* New York: Thomas Y. Crowell, 1976.

Graham, Frank. *Lou Gehrig.* New York: G. P. Putnam's Sons, 1942.

Holtzman, Jerome, editor. *No Cheering in the Press Box.* New York: Henry Holt and Company, 1995.

Koppes, Clayton R., and Gregory D. Black. *Hollywood Goes to War: How Politics, Profits and Propaganda Shaped World War II Movies.* Berkeley, Calif.: University of California Press, 1990.

Lerner, Barron H. *When Illness Goes Public: Celebrity Patients and How We Look at Medicine.* Baltimore: The Johns Hopkins University Press, 2006.

Lieb, Fred. *Baseball As I Have Known It.* New York: Coward, McCann & Geoghegan, 1977.

McGilligan, Pat, editor. *Backstory: Interviews with Screenwriters of Hollywood's Golden Age.* Berkeley, Calif.: University of California Press, 1986.

Meryman, Richard. *Mank: The Wit, World and Life of Herman Mankiewicz.* New York: William Morrow and Company, 1978.

Meyers, Jeffrey. *Gary Cooper: American Hero.* London: Aurum Press, 2001.

Montville, Leigh. *The Big Bam: The Life and Times of Babe Ruth.* New York: Doubleday, 2006.

Ritter, Lawrence S. *The Glory of Their Times: The Story of the Early Days of Baseball Told by the Men Who Played It.* New York: Vintage Books, 1985.

Robinson, Ray. *Iron Horse: Lou Gehrig in His Time.* New York: W. W. Norton & Company, 1990.

Rollyson, Carl. *A Real American Character: The Life of Walter Brennan.* Jackson, Miss.: University Press of Mississippi, 2015.

Ruth, Babe, as told to Bob Considine. *The Babe Ruth Story.* New York: E. P. Dutton & Co., 1948.

Spoto, Donald. *A Girl's Got to Breathe: The Life of Teresa Wright.* Jackson, Miss.: University Press of Mississippi, 2016.

Thomson, David. *The Moment of Psycho: How Alfred Hitchcock Taught America to Love Murder.* New York: Basic Books, 2009.

Source Notes

Foreword

Facing Grover Cleveland Alexander. John Kieran, "Looking Around with Lou Gehrig," *New York Times*, March 16, 1941.

"He can't miss." Ibid.

"I was telling Lou about the new breast stroke." John Kieran, "With an Assist for Lou Gehrig," *New York Times*, March 12, 1941.

"Doc has told me all about him." Ibid.

"It's the last glove I used." Kieran, *New York Times*, March 16, 1941.

"There was Alex." Ibid.

1. A Brilliant Career, a Tragic Death

It was impossible not to notice. James P. Dawson, "Henrich in Game at Gehrig's Post," *New York Times*, March 23, 1939.

James Kahn of the Sun. Eleanor Gehrig and Joseph Durso, *My Luke and I*, p. 209.

"His throwing has been open to question." Dawson, *New York Times*, March 23, 1939.

"has slowed up dreadfully." Gayle Talbot, "Iron Horse Seen as Weakening By Talbot," *Bakersfield Californian* via Associated Press, April 15, 1939.

But Lou had enough goodwill in the press corps. John Kieran, "One Man on a Horse," *New York Times*, March 28, 1939.

Lou could get inexplicably drowsy. Gehrig and Durso, *My Luke and I,* p. 4; and Interview of Eleanor Gehrig by Paul Gallico, Goldwyn studio files.

"He didn't have a shred of his former power." Jonathan Eig, *Luckiest Man,* p. 266.

"McCarthy will keep him in there." Talbot, *Bakersfield Californian,* April 15, 1939.

McCarthy sidestepped reporters' questions. Frank Graham, *Lou Gehrig,* p. 149.

"He would go down for a ground ball." Ibid.

Times writer Arthur J. Daley dropped a disquieting note. Arthur J. Daley, "Ruffing Wins, 8–4, But Injures Elbow," *New York Times,* April 26, 1939.

Lou knew it was over. Gehrig and Durso, *My Luke and I,* p. 213.

"I told him the heartbreaking words." Ibid.

"I'll let him take a rest." Charles P. Ward, "Ward to the Wise," *Detroit Free Press,* May 3, 1939.

Taking himself out of the lineup, he wrote, "was inevitable." Letter from Lou Gehrig to Eleanor, from Book-Cadillac Hotel in Detroit, May 3, 1939.

Johnny Schulte, a journeyman catcher. "Gehrig Reported Ailing," *New York Times,* June 2, 1939.

But a few days later. Eig, *Luckiest Man,* p. 295.

As soon as Gehrig. Eig, *Luckiest Man,* p. 299.

"There was some wasting of the muscles." Ibid.

"We think it's serious." Gehrig and Durso, *My Luke and I,* p. 11.

"I waited and worried." Ibid.

Dr. Habein's early, informed guess. Eig, *Luckiest Man,* p. 302.

"There is a fifty-fifty chance." Letter from Gehrig to Eleanor, cited in *My Luke and I,* pp. 13–14.

Lou was back at Yankee Stadium. Arthur J. Daley, "Infantile Paralysis Terminates Gehrig's Playing Career," *New York Times,* June 22, 1939.

"You have to take the bitter with the sweet." Ibid.

In the dugout. Ibid.

"a death warrant in his pocket." George Moore, "Columbia Lou Gehrig Steps from Diamond to Hall of Fame Add 100 Per Cent," *Arizona Republic,* June 24, 1939.

"He'd see them all." Gehrig and Durso, My Luke and I, p. 20.

"I've been over your record." Ray Robinson, Iron Horse: Lou Gehrig in His Time, p. 267.

Eleanor had to help him sign his name and light a cigarette. Gehrig and Durso, My Luke and I, p. 20.

In the final months. Letter from Eleanor Gehrig to Paul Gallico; interview of Eleanor Gehrig by Gallico for script preparation. Goldwyn studio files.

Nell added more. Letter from Nell Twitchell to A. F. Lorenzen, a friend of Lou's parents who was trying to intervene for money for them with Eleanor.

"Maybe if, one day, he had pulled up a little." Ira Wolfert, "Mrs. Lou Gehrig Reveals Unflinching Fight Made by Famous Yankee 'Iron Man' in Battle for his Life," The Sporting News, Jan. 1, 1942, p. 5.

In his final weeks, Lou's breathing slowed. Gehrig and Durso, My Luke and I, p. 228.

Barrow kissed Lou. Jack Mahon, "Final Tribute Paid Memory of Gehrig at Riverdale Church," Kane Republican via International News Service, June 4, 1941.

"My three pals." Eig, Luckiest Man, p. 356.

"The most beatified expression." Gehrig and Durso, My Luke and I, p. 228.

"She told me that Lou Gehrig had died." Phone interview with Larry Merchant.

In his office that day Barrow told reporters. "Gehrig Wasted to 150 Pounds, Barrow Avers," Cincinnati Enquirer via AP, June 4, 1941.

Eleanor followed, with her brother, Frank Twitchell, Jr. Eig, Luckiest Man, p. 358.

2. Hollywood Beckons the Widow Gehrig

Walsh had shrewdly gauged. Leigh Montville, The Big Bam, p. 263.

"I shall never forget the expression on Babe Ruth's face." Christy Walsh, Adios to Ghosts, p. 25.

"I had never had Babe Ruth." Ibid., p. 14.

"I read where Sol Lesser." "Slugging New York First Baseman May Enter Motion Pictures," United Press, Oct. 20, 1936.

"This is not a joke." Ibid.

Walsh's publicity ploy. "Mr. Gehrig as Tarzan," Montana Butte Standard, Oct. 24, 1936.

"knotty knees." Frederick Othman, "Gehrig Puts on Pants; Now Ready to Kiss Film Blonde," United Press, Jan. 5, 1936.

watching Gehrig "poke around a ranch and get tossed." Herbert Cohn, "At the Local Strand," *Brooklyn Daily Eagle*, May 7, 1938.

"Anything, El, you know that I consider a pleasure and a privilege." Letter from Walsh to Eleanor Gehrig, June 24, 1941.

"Not knowing how you have been feeling now that the shock is over." Ibid.

"That night the phone rang in my apartment." Ibid.

Sheehan suggested that the rights to Lou's story. Ibid.

"And why the hell should I?" Jerome Holtzman, editor, *No Cheering in the Press Box*, p. 104.

"By self-admission," he wrote to Eleanor. Ibid.

She said Selznick "is okay but in the long run." Ibid.

He was still waiting for a "respectable" offer from MGM. Letter from Walsh to Eleanor Gehrig, July 2, 1941.

3. The Tears of a Mogul

Busch's hankering, Pat McGilligan, editor, interview by David Thomson. *Backstory*.

"has accidentally got himself." Niven Busch, "The Little Heinie," *The New Yorker*, Aug. 10, 1929.

"he was the sort of boy." Ibid.

"My mother makes a home comfortable enough for me." Ibid.

"Goldwyn was not very smart." McGilligan.

He invited Goldwyn. A. Scott Berg, *Goldwyn: A Biography*, p. 370.

Walsh had negotiated. Letter from Walsh to Eleanor Gehrig, July 9, 1941.

Walsh reminded her. Ibid.

"It seems like the whole world is interested." Letter from Louella Parsons to Samuel Goldwyn, Feb. 3, 1942.

4. In Search of Lou Gehrig

"I have four or five different stars in mind." John Chapman, "Bob Hope Says He Feels Like 'Hess in Scotland,'" *Harrisburg Telegraph*, July 19, 1941.

"The results of a Hollywood poll." Goldwyn studio files.

"WHO IS GOING TO PLAY THE ROLE OF LOU GEHRIG?" Press release issued by Christy Walsh, Oct. 2, 1941.

"That silly contest." Letter from Walsh to Eleanor Gehrig, Oct. 28, 1941.

"If Sam Goldwyn, the movie producer, is finding it difficult." "Who Should Play Gehrig?" The Sporting News, Aug. 14, 1941.

"You know, it isn't such a bad idea." Hedda Hopper, "Eddie Albert's the Favorite to Play Life of Lou Gehrig," Des Moines Register, Aug. 7, 1941.

Barrow, a shrewd judge of talent. Letters from Edward G. Barrow to Eddie Albert's agent and Eleanor Gehrig, Aug. 18–19, 1941.

Bernard Sherling of Brooklyn. "Who Should Play Gehrig?" The Sporting News, Aug. 21, 1941, and Goldwyn studio files.

"But now comes a proposal." "No Calls for Pats on the Back," editorial, The Sporting News, Nov. 20, 1941.

Based only on physical resemblance." J. G. Taylor Spink, "Who Will Fill Gehrig Role—Film or Diamond Player—On Screen?" The Sporting News, Dec. 4, 1941.

"Here's something." "Cooper to Play Part of Gehrig," Montana Standard, Dec. 25, 1941.

Howard Hawks, who directed both films, understood Cooper. Frank Nugent, "The All-American Man," The New York Times, July 15, 1942.

5. Babe on Film

"I don't want anything from him." Leigh Montville, The Big Bam, p. 343.

"Grin, sure I'll grin." Paul Mickelson, "Babe Given Ovation and Forgotten," Oakland Tribune via Associated Press, April 15, 1936.

"But yesterday, while rehearsing a home run blow." Montville, The Big Bam, p. 243.

"He looked to me exactly as he did the last year I saw him play." Letter from Paul Gallico to Samuel Goldwyn, undated.

But a few days later, shortly after midnight. "Babe Ruth Is Ill," New York Times, Jan. 3, 1942.

"My suspicion is that he went on a bender." Gallico letter to Goldwyn.

"Ruth has not been looking quite right for several weeks." "Babe Ruth Case Cleared by Doctor," *New York Times*, Jan. 4, 1942.

"I never felt better in my life." "Babe Ready for Films," *San Bernardino County Sun via Associated Press*, Jan. 31, 1942.

Walsh had spent a week trying to arrange the perfect greeting. Letter from Walsh to Eleanor Gehrig, Feb. 8, 1942.

a recent immigrant from Australia with "a gorgeous dialect." Ibid.

"A crowd gathered." Ibid.

No pants. Dick Hyland, "Behind the Line," *Los Angeles Times*, Feb. 11, 1942.

"To tell the life story of Lou Gehrig without some reference." Memo from Walsh to Eleanor Gehrig, Nov. 25, 1941.

"He should not appear in the flesh." Gallico's notes from Eleanor Gehrig interviews.

"Babe himself would be a menace." Ibid.

"There was nothing Lou could do about it." Ibid.

"In the beginning." Memo from Walsh to Eleanor Gehrig, Nov. 25, 1941.

6. *Not All Yankees Welcome*

Goldwyn blew up at the challenge. Memo from Walsh to Eleanor Gehrig, Nov. 25, 1941.

Dahlgren lost his fight. Interview with Matt Dahlgren.

"IMPORTANT THAT YOU PHONE ME TODAY." Telegram from Wally Pipp to Christy Walsh, Jan. 21, 1942.

"I'm cutting Ruth's part in two." Ibid.

"It seems illogical." Ibid.

"To put it briefly he absolutely refuses." Ibid.

Dahlgren was insulted. Letter from Babe Dahlgren to Walsh, Feb. 25, 1942.

Walsh spurned him. Letter from Walsh to Pipp, Jan. 21, 1942.

Ruth the highest paid at $1,500 a week. List of contracts. Goldwyn studio files.

"You ought to hear what the 'old woman' said to him." Letter from Walsh to Eleanor Gehrig, Feb. 14, 1942.

7. The Producer and the Star

"First of all." Nelson Bell, "Mr. Goldwyn Explains About That Gehrig Film," Washington Post, Feb. 3, 1942.

"Baseball on the screen is dull." Goldwyn studio files.

Delehanty asked: "What is there so repellent." Thornton Delehanty, New York Times, May 3, 1942.

The writer Alva Johnston profiled Goldwyn. A. Scott Berg, Goldwyn, p. 268.

"I never knew what the Goldwyn touch was." Carol Easton, The Search for Sam Goldwyn, pp. 207–208.

"Can't we do that, Mank?" Interviews with Sara Mankiewicz and Frank Mankiewicz by Richard Maibaum, for Mank: The Wit, World and Life of Herman Mankiewicz, courtesy of Nick Davis.

"And honest to goodness." Letter from Walsh to Eleanor Gehrig.

Goldwyn started life far from the American sandlots depicted in Pride. Credit for details of Goldwyn's life are owed mainly to A. Scott Berg, Goldwyn: A Biography.

Watching a scene with the inexperienced Cooper. Gary Cooper, as told to George Scullin, "Well It Was This Way," Saturday Evening Post, March 7, 1956, part 4.

The relationship between Cooper and Goldwyn. Goldwyn studio files include telegrams describing contractual terms and threat by Goldwyn. Also cited in Jeffrey Meyers, Gary Cooper: An American Hero.

Cooper admitted that the criticism made him feel "pretty small." Gary Cooper, as told to George Scullin, "Well It Was This Way," Saturday Evening Post, March 31, 1956, part 7.

"I bow to your threats." Goldwyn studio files and Gary Cooper: An American Hero.

"My part is such that it cannot help." Carl Rollyson, The Life of Walter Brennan: A Real American Character, p. 79.

8. Eleanor: Defender of Lou's Legacy

She promised Pollack a longer version with more details. "Baseball Bride," by Eleanor Gehrig, book proposal, Jan. 24, 1972. From the files of George Pollack, Eleanor's lawyer, courtesy of his daughter, Ruth Pollack Pappas.

They were thick and meticulously maintained. Eleanor donated her scrapbooks to the Baseball Hall of Fame, which allowed me to examine them as well as the prop scrapbook that Goldwyn donated to the Hall.

Auburn-haired, brown-eyed, vivacious, and urbane. Ray Robinson, *Iron Horse*, p. 177.

"It was I who was to inherit as a mother-in-law." Eleanor Gehrig, "Baseball Bride."

"I could hold my liquor." Gehrig and Durso, *My Luke and I*, p. 77.

She observed Gehrig. Gallico-Eleanor Gehrig interviews, Goldwyn studio files. But her Prohibition-era Lark was not made to last. Details drawn from *My Luke and I*, and Gallico-Gehrig interviews.

"Listen, Eleanor, I'm only married to Tony Lazzeri." Tara Krieger, "Eleanor Gehrig," Society for American Baseball Research website, undated.

She revealed that "he took a New Rochelle girl out a few times." Gallico-Gehrig interviews.

"Eleanor was raised." Ibid.

"I would not have traded." Durso and Gehrig, *My Luke and I*, p. 229.

9. *Teresa Wright Will Not Do Cheesecake!*

"WANT YOU TO BE THE FIRST." Telegram to Eleanor Gehrig from William Hebert, Jan. 19, 1942.

"I don't believe anyone is surprised." Louella Parsons, "Teresa Wright Cast in Gehrig Film," *Philadelphia Inquirer*, Jan. 22, 1942.

Her father, Arthur. Donald Spoto, *A Girl's Got to Breathe*. This chapter owes a great debt to Mr. Spoto's biographical work on Teresa Wright. He knew her, interviewed her, and captured her spirit and life in his book.

Wright started acting. Ibid.

she "plays a young lady." Brooks Atkinson, "Speak Up Father," *New York Times*, Nov. 19, 1939.

Soon after Life opened. Spoto, *A Girl's Got to Breathe.*

"I had discovered in her." Ibid.

During a break in filming. Donald Hough, "Failure?" *Los Angeles Times*, Sept. 27, 1942.

"And don't mind if she twists her fingers." Ibid.

He further assessed her state of mind. Ibid.

"Teresa," Goldwyn exhorted her. Berg, *Goldwyn*, p. 358.

"Wyler was the first one out there." Teresa Wright interview by Joan and Robert Franklin, Columbia Center for Oral History Archives, 1959.

"Miss Wright," the trade magazine wrote. Herb Golden, "Review: 'Mrs. Miniver,'" *Variety*, May 13, 1942.

"I never knew anything about baseball and never cared." Bill Francis, "The Wright Stuff," National Baseball Hall of Fame website, undated.

"If you queried Miss Wright carefully." Goldwyn studio files.

"She despises bananas." Sidney Skolsky, "Skolsky's Hollywood: Meet Teresa Wright," *Cincinnati Enquirer*, Aug. 19, 1942.

Hebert put out word. Goldwyn studio files.

In Cooper's assessment. Ibid.

And Hebert reminded reporters. Ibid.

In her original, anti-cheesecake language. Spoto, *A Girl's Got to Breathe.*

"It must be the contour of the Wright limb." Kyle Crichton, "No Glamour Gal," *Collier's Weekly*, May 23, 1942.

"She incarnated a domestic radiance." Scott Eyman, "More Than a Shadow of a Doubt," *Wall Street Journal*, March 18, 2016.

10. Becoming Lou: Cooper Learns to Play Baseball

On his first day at Wrigley. Goldwyn studio files, production schedule.

On a gloomy day. Ibid.

"Now, in the first scene, you walk." Ibid., studio files.

The quest for authenticity began the previous fall. Studio files, production schedule.

"On old South Field." "Goldwyn Films Campus," *Columbia Spectator*, Oct. 9–10, 1941.

Led by Robert Cobb. "Film Crowd Jumps at the Chance to Buy a Ball Club of Its Own," *Harrisburg Telegraph*, March 4, 1940. And Stephen M. Daniels, "Hollywood Stars," SABR website.

His daughter, Maria, recalled attending games with her parents. Interview, Maria Cooper Janis.

"Big League baseball and big business trimmings." Bill Henry, "New Diamond, Built by Gum, Is Perfect," Los Angeles Times, Sept. 30, 1925.

"When I got back to Montana." Gary Cooper to George Scullin, "Well It Was This Way," Saturday Evening Post, Feb. 25, 1956, part 2.

"York wasn't so bad." Ibid.

"Do it all the time from force of habit." Harry Evans, "Hollywood Diary," Family Circle, August 1942.

"When I was playing ball in the big leagues, my bats would be jumping." Lawrence Ritter, The Glory of Their Times, p. 274.

"I am now an outfielder." Ibid., p. 273.

"If that Cooper doesn't get in there and play ball like Gehrig." Frederick Othman, "Former Yankee Star Picks Up $25,000 as an Actor," United Press, Feb. 12, 1942.

"Presently up the walk of the Tyrone Power home." Goldwyn studio files.

"It might have been apocryphal." Interview with Maria Cooper Janis.

"I see where Lefty O'Doul is taking a lot of bows teaching Gary Cooper to hit." "Did O'Doul Teach Fernandez to Hit? Ask Stengel," Belvedere Daily Republican, May 2, 1942.

11. Did Cooper, a Right-Hander, Become Gehrig, a Left-Hander?

Cooper stopped to light a cigarette one day. "Gary Cooper Left-Handed at Mr. Babe Ruth's Behest," Brooklyn Daily Eagle, May 31, 1942.

"The machine would pitch out the ball and I'd whang at it." Othman, "Former Yankee Star Picks Up $25,000 As An Actor," Oakland Tribune, via United Press, Feb. 12, 1942.

During filming one day at Wrigley, Wood called for Ruth to step up. Sidney Skolsky, "Watching Them Make Pictures," Cincinnati Enquirer, March 16, 1942.

Years later, Cooper confirmed some of the flip-flop story. "Well It Was This Way," Saturday Evening Post, Feb. 25, 1956, part 2.

"I said, 'Well, put the letters on his shirt backwards.'" Carol Easton, The Search for Sam Goldwyn, p. 207.

Sara Mankiewicz told her husband's biographer, Richard Meryman. Interviews by Meryman for Mank: The Wit, World and Life of Herman Mankiewicz, courtesy of Nick Davis.

In 2013, Tom Shieber. Tom Shieber, Baseball Researcher, "The Pride of the Seeknay," Feb. 3, 2013.

12. *Mama's Boy*

This chapter is drawn largely from the original outline of the Gehrig story by Paul Gallico and Abem Finkel, various scripts, including the first by Gallico and Earl Baldwin, and the so-called final one by Herman Mankiewicz and Jo Swerling. All are in the Goldwyn studio files. The remaining sources are:

"Beezark of Kerblam." Damon Runyon, "Runyon, With Aid of Babe, Picks Yankees," *Minneapolis Morning Tribune,* Oct. 5, 1927.

"We have not yet come to view the Japs." Damon Runyon, "The Brighter Side," *The Town Call,* via King Features Syndicate, Jan. 3, 1942.

"I think Gallico is going to find things missing." Letter from Walsh to Eleanor Gehrig, Jan. 28, 1942.

"Huggins is seen seated." Letter from Eleanor Gehrig to Walsh, Feb. 14, 1942.

"I will tell you, Baby." Letter from Gallico to Eleanor Gehrig, April 8, 1942.

"We don't want the public to think Gehrig was a sissy." Letter from Walsh to Eleanor Gehrig, Feb. 14, 1942.

The Tanglefoot epithet. Westbrook Pegler, "Ty Cobb Becomes Spry, Sneaks Base on Combs," *Detroit Free Press,* April 14, 1927, and "Fair Enough," *The Pittsburgh Press,* June 4, 1941.

"I broke our engagement." Gehrig and Durso, *My Luke and I,* p. 150.

Eleanor brought the error to Goldwyn's attention through a memo. Memo from Christy Walsh to Samuel Goldwyn, listing errors in the script. March 23, 1942.

13. *"Lou Seems to Have Become More Gary Cooper Than Lou Gehrig"*

Much like the previous chapter, this one leans heavily on the original outline and scripts in the Goldwyn archive, and on the movie itself. The story and its characters evolved with its succeeding script, and even the "final script" by Mankiewicz and Swerling lacks some of the dialogue and scenes that are in the final cut of the film.

Dahlgren even pleaded with Gehrig to change his mind. Babe Dahlgren, "Gehrig's Last Day," *Sports Illustrated,* June 18, 1956.

Lou was "shaken to tears" when they saw Tristan and Isolde. Eleanor Gehrig and Durso, *My Luke and I,* p. 26.

"This is what I mean by screenwriting!" Maibaum, *Mank*, p. 279.

"I know, Mr. Goldwyn." Holt's polio confirmed by his daughter.

14. Words for All Time

This chapter is also largely the product of what was found in the scripts in the Goldwyn archive and what survived to the final cut, as well as details from the Fox Movietone newsreel taken that day, which, unfortunately, is not intact, containing only a few lines from Gehrig's speech.

"If Lou starts to fall, catch him." Joe Gergen, "Dahlgren Recalls Decline of Gehrig 50 Years Ago," *Los Angeles Times* via *Newsday*, July 9, 1989.

"In my eight-year-old head." Interview with Larry Merchant.

"A few days ago, I sent Christy a copy of Lou's speech." Letter from Eleanor Gehrig to Goldwyn, April 16, 1942.

"You can count on the wording being perfect." Ibid.

"Gehrig, who had always obeyed orders." Rud Rennie, "Selkirk's Second Homer of Day Speeds Sundra to Fifth Straight," *New York Herald Tribune*, July 5, 1939.

"But leave it to big, fat, jovial Babe." Jack Miley, "Fun-Loving Guy Brings a Smile to Lou's Face," *New York Post*, July 5, 1939.

Rosaleen Doherty, a thirty-five-year-old reporter. Rosaleen Doherty, "Wife Brave, Lou Shaken, as 61,000 Cheer Gehrig," *New York Daily News*, July 5, 1939.

Irv Welzer, then eleven, watched the speech from the bleachers. Interview transcript courtesy of Marty Appel.

Soon after the speech, he wrote an article. Lou Gehrig, "Why I Am Thankful," *Baltimore Sun*, Nov. 19, 1939.

"If not for the movie." Interview with Jonathan Eig.

15. A Screening

"I find myself pacing the floor at night." Goldwyn studio files.

"Then I saw Sam Goldwyn who was waiting for me." Louella O. Parsons, "Gary's Portrait of Gehrig Pleases Widow at Preview," *Cincinnati Enquirer* via International News Service, June 14, 1942.

"I think it meant a lot to her." Bill Francis, "The Wright Stuff," National Baseball Hall of Fame website, undated.

"Winchell saw a few reels." Letter from Goldwyn to Gallico, June 1, 1942.

Willkie reminded the Academy Awards audience. "Take War to Foe, Willkie Demands," New York Times, Feb. 27, 1942.

A preliminary report from what was known as the Hays Office. Production Code Administration report on The Pride of the Yankees script, March 16, 1942.

he dictated a letter to Abel Green. Letter from Goldwyn to Abel Green, Jan. 19, 1943. Goldwyn studio files.

"It's been a tough picture to produce." Letter from Samuel Goldwyn to Joseph Schenck, June 4, 1942. Ibid.

"I bet you $1,000." Letter from Mervyn LeRoy to Buddy DeSylva, July 30, 1941; letter from DeSylva to LeRoy, Aug. 1, 1941; letter from LeRoy to Goldwyn, Sept. 11, 1941. Ibid.

16. "Luckiest Man" in the South Pacific

"Those kids'll be sitting out on a muddy hillside." "Gary Cooper Moved Greatly on Pacific Tour," Los Angeles Times, Dec. 29, 1943.

A different assessment came from Pfc. Randon Gahlbeck. Daily Herald, Jan. 7, 1944.

The show in Port Moresby. Cooper as told to George Scullin, "Well, It Was This Way," Saturday Evening Post, April 8, 1956, part 8.

"Hey, Coop!" Ibid.

It had been eighteen months. Transcript of Lux Radio Theatre broadcast, Oct. 4, 1943.

At the Theatre Royal in Sydney. "Gary Cooper in Sydney," Sydney Morning Herald, Dec. 20, 1943.

Under questioning by Robert Stripling. "Hearings Regarding the Communist Infiltration of the Motion Picture Industry," Sam Wood's testimony, Oct. 20, 1947.

Cooper testified at the HUAC hearings a few days after Wood. Meyers, Cooper: American Hero, p. 225.

Thomas, the chairman, who was questioning Cooper. "Hearings Regarding the Communist Infiltration," Cooper's testimony, Oct. 23, 1947.

Living alone in an apartment on East 53rd Street. Interview with Marty Appel.

In April, 1969, she wrote to Michael Burke. Letter from Eleanor Gehrig to Michael Burke, April 17, 1969. Letter from George Pollack to Goldwyn, April 24, 1969.

"We are somewhat at a loss." Letter from Martin Gang to Pollack, May 12, 1969. Letter from Pollack to Gang, May 15, 1969.

"She was quite a presence." Interview with Blythe Danner.

"I was trying to get hold of the quality." Jerry Buck, "Actor Romances Another Eleanor," Albuquerque Journal, via Associated Press, Jan. 15, 1978.

One day in 1971. Richard Sandomir, "A Little Gehrig Fantasy for Really Big Dollars," New York Times, June 29, 1999.

"To watch someone close to you become a helpless, hopeless paralytic." "Gehrig's Widow Asks U.S. to Seek Sclerosis Remedy," San Bernardino County Sun, via Associated Press, May 11, 1949.

"A few weeks later." Transcript of "Bill Stern's Sports Newsreel," with Eleanor Gehrig, June 3, 1949.

Only two mourners attended her funeral. Tara Krieger, "Eleanor Gehrig," SABR.org. Also confirmed in interview with Pollack's daughter, Ruth Pollack Pappas.

"There was this elderly woman looking meek and happy to be here." The story of Teresa Wright's late-in-life conversion to baseball fandom was told through interviews with Rick Cerrone, a former Yankees publicity director, and correspondence he had with Wright and her family. Also, Ray Robinson, "Backtalk: Becoming a Yankee Fan by Way of Hollywood," New York Times, July 4, 1999.

Epilogue: Cooper Says Good-bye

The primary source in this chapter is a recording that was serendipitously made of the Friars Club roast of Cooper and is available online.

Cooper, his wife, Veronica, known widely as Rocky. Interview with Maria Cooper Janis, Cooper's daughter.

But Rocky had not told him of the fatal diagnosis. Jeffrey Meyers, Gary Cooper: American Hero, p. 321. Also, interview with Maria Cooper Janis.

"I've been coasting along." Gary Cooper, as told to Leonard Slater, "I Took a Good Look at Myself and This Is What I Saw," McCall's, Jan. 1961, p. 62.

Index